George Augustus Burgoyne

The wool marks directory of Australia

Containing an alphabetical classification of wool marks

George Augustus Burgoyne

The wool marks directory of Australia
Containing an alphabetical classification of wool marks

ISBN/EAN: 9783337268992

Printed in Europe, USA, Canada, Australia, Japan

Cover: Foto ©Andreas Hilbeck / pixelio.de

More available books at **www.hansebooks.com**

THE

WOOL MARKS DIRECTORY OF AUSTRALIA

CONTAINING

AN ALPHABETICAL CLASSIFICATION OF WOOL MARKS,

WITH THE NAME OF OWNER, STATION, POSTAL ADDRESS, AND PASTORAL DISTRICT

IN AUSTRALIA AND TASMANIA.

COMPILED BY GEO. AUG. BURGOYNE,

Upon a basis of from 1,000 to 2,000 sheep and upwards, from information derived
from the various Australian Wool Growers and other sources.

✿

The compiler is also much indebted for valuable assistance
rendered by the following Wool-Selling Brokers, viz. :—

Messrs. Dalgely & Co., Ltd., at Sydney, Melbourne, Geelong and Brisbane : The
New Zealand Loan and Mercantile Co., Ltd., at Melbourne and Sydney ; The Pastoral
Finance Association, Ltd., Sydney ; Messrs. Harrison, Jones and Devlin, and Hill,
Clark & Co., Sydney ; Messrs. Goldsbrough, Mort & Co , Ltd. ; The Australian Estates and
Mortgage Co., Ltd , Melbourne ; Messrs. Dennys, Lascelles, Austin & Co. ; Strachan,
Murray and Shannon Proprietary, Ltd., Geelong. ; Messrs. Fenwick & Co.: Morcheads. Ltd.,
and Muctaggart Bros., Brisbane ; and Messrs. Elder, Smith & Co., Ltd , and Strachan,
Cheadle & Co., Adelaide. S.A.

✿

Printed and Published by
JOHN SANDS, GEORGE STREET, SYDNEY. N.S.W.

PREFACE.

FOR the first time in the history of the Australian Wool Trade a work has been issued giving an Alphabetical Classification of Wool Marks, the Grower's Name and Address, and the Pastoral District in which his sheep station is situated. Little aid, in some quarters, has hitherto been given to the buyer desirous of further knowledge respecting the districts in which suitable wools were grown. Memorising thousands of marks is a task of exceptional difficulty, so the Publisher trusts that this work will lighten the labours of all interested in the Wool Trade during the strenuous period of the auction sales. The European manufacturer, ever desirous of improvement, can also at leisure study the advantages resulting from knowing the pastoral district in which his favourite wools are grown—some districts being celebrated for the uniform excellence of their wool. On the other hand, pastoralists, honoured for the excellence of their flocks, the careful production and honest packing of their wool, may meet with due reward in a wider field.

SECTION II. comprises Wool Brands which the Compiler could not trace to the Grower. Some are good station brands; but others include dealers' mixed lots, speculative lots, and scoured lots of unknown origin.

EXPLANATION. EXPLICATION. ERKLAUERUNG. SPIEGAZIONI.

WOOL MARK.	MARQUE DE LAINE	WOOLL MÄRK.	MARCHE DELLA LANA.
WOOL GROWER'S NAME AND ADDRESS.	ELEVEUR DES MOUTONS, NOM ET ADRESSE	SCHAFTZÜCHTER, NAMA AND ADRESSE.	PRODUTTORI DI LANA, NOME E IL ADRESSA.
PASTORAL DISTRICT.	DISTRICT POUR PATURAGE.	WEIDEDISTRIKT.	DISTRETTI PASTORALE.
STATE.	ETÂT	STAAT.	STATO.

ABBREVIATIONS. ABRÉVIATIONS. ABKÜRZUNGEN. ABBREVIAZIONI.

NEW SOUTH WALES	N.S.W.
VICTORIA ...	VIC.
QUEENSLAND ...	Q.
SOUTH AUSTRALIA...	S.A.
WESTERN AUSTRALIA ...	W.A.
TASMANIA	TAS.

WOOL MARKS DIRECTORY OF AUSTRALIA

A

WOOL MARKS.	WOOL GROWERS' NAMES AND ADDRESSES.	PASTORAL DISTRICT.	STATE.
A ᐳ	A. S. Arndell, Lilburne, Timor	Murrurundi	N.S.W.
AA A WOOLTON	J. R. Hutchinson, Woolton, Taroom ...	Banana...	Q.
A A ATTUNGA	J. G. Wiseman, Attunga	Tamworth	N.S.W.
A A B R	A. A. Burge, Redbank	Wimmera	VIC.
A A C DOUGLAS	A. A. Cusack, Douglas, Galong	Young ...	N.S.W.
A A C NANDAI	W. T. Cowley, Nandai, Berrima	Berrima	N.S.W.
AA & Co	Dalgety and Co., Milroy Station, Brewarrina ...	Bourke ...	N.S.W.
A ADELONG	I. Arragon, Springdale, Adelong	Gundagai	N.S.W.
A A MUTTAMA	Union Bank of Australia, Muttama, Muttama ...	Gundagai	N.S.W.
A A OXLEY	A. Anderson, Lerap, Oxley ...	Hay	N.S.W.
A A QUAMBONE	A. Ashnall (exors.), Quambone, Coonamble	Coonamble	N.S.W.

WOOL MARKS.	WOOL GROWERS' NAMES AND ADDRESSES.	PASTORAL DISTRICT.	STATE.
A B AVENIL	P. Hoskins, Avenil, Muckadilla	Roma	Q.
ABBADOAH T M	T. W. Dawson, Abbadoah, Cunnamulla	Cunnamulla	Q.
A B BROS NELGOURIE	W. C. & M. E. A'Beckett, Nelgourie, Coonamble	Coonamble	N S.W.
(A B C) COOBA	J. Bourke, Cooba, Junee	Gundagai	N.S.W.
ABEDOUR T M	B. Proctor, Abedour, Mungindi	Moree	N.S.W.
A BELELE	E. L. Steere, Belele, Abbots...	...	W.A.
A ◇ SCONE	A. H. and J. Bell, Bundarraga, Burrai	Murrurundi	N.S.W.
A BEMBRICK RYEWOOD PARK	A. Bembrick, Ryewood, Grenfell	Young ...	N.S.W.
ABERBALDIE	J. L. Fitzpatrick, Aberbaldie, Walcha	Armidale	N.S.W.
A B GLENFERN	McKenzie and Sons, Glenfern, Brown's Plains ...		VIC.
ABINGTON	J. R. Foster, Abington, Armidale	Armidale ...	N.S.W.
ABL	A. B. Lawson, Riversdale, East Wellington	Wellington	S.A.
A B M A WIRRABARRA	D. F. McKenzie, Wirrabarra	Wirrabarra ...	S.A.
A BRANGA	R. A. and A. Wauch, Branga Park, Glen Morrison	Armidale ...	N.S.W.
A BROS SWITZERLAND	A. N. Aitken, Switzerland, Yea	Yea ...	VIC.

WOOL MARKS.	WOOL GROWERS' NAMES AND ADDRESSES.	PASTORAL DISTRICT.	STATE.
A B T **B R B** **YASS**	A. B. Triggs, Black Range, Yass	Yass	N.S.W.
A B T **HUMEWOOD**	A. B. Triggs, Humewood, Yass	Yass	N.S.W.
A B **TOOYAL**	A. Booth (exors.), Tooyal, Wagga	Wagga ..	N.S.W.
A B T **OTTERBOURNE** **YASS**	A. B. Triggs, Black Range, Yass	Yass	N.S.W.
A B T **W** **GOULBURN**	A. B. Triggs, Black Range, Yass	Goulburn	N.S.W.
A B **TWIN PEAKS**	A. Boddington, Twin Peaks, Murgoo ...	Murgoo ...	W.A.
A B T **W P**	W. Ploma, Gundagai	Gundagai ..	N.S.W.
A B T **YASS**	A. B. Triggs, Black Range, Yass	Yass	N.S.W.
A. BUCHANAN **MILLIE**	A. Buchanan, Millie	Pilliga ...	N.S.W.
A B **YASS**	A. Bullman, Green Hill, Yass	Yass ...	N.S.W.
A C **ARARAT**	A. J. Caldwell, Ararat, Cooma	Cooma	N.S.W.
A C **ARGYLE**	Mrs M. Carmichael, Argyle, Casterton	... ...	VIC.
A C **BYRON**	A. Cruickshank (exors.), Byron, Inverell	Glen Innes ...	N.S.W.
A C **CAMERON DOWNS**	A. Crombie, Cameron Downs, Hughenden	Hughenden ...	Q.
A C **CHANTICLEER**	A. Chant, Chanticleer, Morundah	Narandera ...	N.S.W.

WOOL MARKS.	WOOL GROWERS' NAMES AND ADDRESSES.	PASTORAL DISTRICT.	STATE.
A C & Co **DARR**	Edkins, Campbell and Co., Darr Farms, Longreach	Longreach	Q.
A C **COOMA**	A. Cochran, Yaouk, Rosedale, Cooma...	Cooma ...	N.S.W.
A C & Co **WEEWONDILLA**	A. C. Cooper, Weewondilla, Muttaburra	Muttaburra	Q.
A C D **GAMBARRA**	A. C. Dempster, Gambarra, Grenfell ...	Forbes	N.S.W.
A C & F Co	Australian Chilling and Freezing Co., Ltd., St. Heliers, Aberdeen	Murrurundi	N.S.W.
A C **KANGAROO** **LAKE**	A. Cameron, Kangaroo Lake, Coleraine	Western District...	VIC.
A C **T C**	A. Chirnish, Wimmera	Wimmera	VIC.
A D **BILLABALONG**	A. Macpherson, Billabalong, Murgoo ...	Murgoo	W.A.
A D **BOWEN**	Bowen's Estate, Bowen's Park, Trangie	Dubbo ...	N.S.W.
A D **BURROWA HILLS**	Mrs. M. A. Dwyer, Burrowa Hills, Burrowa	Young ...	N.S.W.
ADELARGO	Bank of Australasia, Adelargo, Grenfell	Forbes ..	N.S.W.
A. DUNN **TEA TREE**	A. Dunn, Tea Tree, Rylstone	Mudgee	N.S.W.
A D W **MOURABIE**	A. D. Wiseman, Mourabie, Walgett ...	Walgett	N.S.W.
A E **ALPHA**	K. McKenzie, Alpha, Tambaroora	Mudgee	N.S.W.
A E H **WYOMING**	A. E. Hunt, Wyoming, Dandaloo	Canonbar	N.S.W.

A

WOOL MARKS.	WOOL GROWERS' NAMES AND ADDRESSES.	PASTORAL DISTRICT.	STATE.
A E J **B M**	J. N. Moffatt, Dubbo	Dubbo ...	N.S.W.
A.E.M **WAITARA**	A. E. Mackay, Waitara, Dandaloo	Dubbo ...	N.S.W.
A E **PARK**	A. Emery, Bute Park, Cootamundra	Wagga ..	N.S.W.
A F (red)	A. Frazer, Ensay	Ensay	VIC.
A F **BETHUNGRA**	Freeborn Bros., Bethungra. Ironbong	Gundagai	N.S.W.
A & F **EMBY**	Fisher and Co., Emby and Tooloon. Galargambone	Coonamble	N.S.W.
A F G **T**	A. F. Gibson, Trigalana. Forbes	Forbes ...	N.S.W.
A F **MAIDEN CREEK** **NEW ENGLAND**	A. Fraser, Maiden Creek, Armidale	Armidale	N.S.W.
A **F** **TILPA**	Mrs. A. Ferguson, Tilpa, Canowindra...	Molong...	N.S.W.
AFTON **ALBA**	C. N. Armitage, Afton Downs, Hughenden	Hughenden	Q.
A G	A. Greendale, Maitland, Y.P.		S.A.
A G D **MELTON**	A. G. Downer, Melton, Waukaringa ...		S.A.
A **G** **ELLENGERAH**	W. A. Gardiner. Ellengerah, Trangie...	Dubbo ...	N.S.W.
A G **PAREORA**	A. G. Gebhardt, Pareora, Port Wakefield	Port Wakefield	S.A.
A G S **L**	A. G. Stewart, Louth, McArthur	Western District...	VIC.

WOOL MARKS.	WOOL GROWERS' NAMES AND ADDRESSES.	PASTORAL DISTRICT.	STATE.
A HAY **THE GLEN**	A. Hay (exors.), The Glen, Harrogate	Harrogate	S.A.
A H P **NEW ENGLAND**	A. H. Perrott, Enmore, Uralla	Armidale ...	N.S.W.
A H **OHIO** **NEW ENGLAND**	J. A. Nivison, Ohio, Walcha ...	Armidale ...	N.S.W.
◁ **AH&S** ▷ **ETON VALE**	A. Hodgson and Sons, Eton Vale, Cambooya ...	Toowoomba ...	Q.
A H & S **PIAN CREEK**	Hamilton and Sons, Pian Creek, Wee Waa ...	Pilliga ...	N.S.W.
A I V **EUROBLA**	A. A. and F. Firth, Eurobla, Trangie...	Coonamblo ...	N.S.W.
A I A B	Beveridge Bros., Tenandra Park, Gundagai	Gundagai ...	N.S.W.
A I A B **DOLLAR VALE**	A. J. A. Beveridge, Dollar Vale, Eurongilly ...	Gundagai	N.S.W.
A I A **YARRA YARRA**	McLaurin Bros., Yarra Yarra, Germanton	Hume	N.S.W.
A I F	A. L. Faithfull, Springfield, Goulburn	Goulburn ..	N.S.W.
A J A **W V**	A. and J. Armour, Wattle Vale, Bookham ...	Young	N.S.W.
A J **CONDON** **OMEO**	A. J. Condon, Omeo, Gippsland ...	Gippsland ...	VIC.
A J D **BOLAC**	A. J. Dalgleish, Lake Bolac... ...	... ...	VIC.
A J **DERWENT PARK**	A. Jackson, Derwent Park, Mullaley	Tamworth ...	N.S.W.
A J H **C**	A. J. Howard, Coorawong, Coonamble	Coonamble ...	N.S.W.

A

WOOL MARKS.	WOOL GROWERS' NAMES AND ADDRESSES.	PASTORAL DISTRICT.	STATE.
A J L L WYVERN	A. J. L. Learmouth, Wyvern, Carrathool	Hay	N.S.W.
A & J L MT STURT	A. and J. Lang, Mount Sturt, Milparinka	Milparinka	N.S.W.
A J M C	A. J. Murray, Cartapo, Hallett	Hallett ...	S.A.
A J M MILTON VILLE	A. J. Morrison, Miltonville, Moree	Moree	N.S.W.
A. J. MURRAY MT CRAWFORD	A. J. Murray, Mount Crawford	Mount Crawford	S.A.
A J RAVENSWOOD	A. Johnston, Ravenswood, Mount Moriac	Mount Moriac	VIC.
A J S	A. J. Stewart, Allandale, Terrabela	Dubbo	N.S.W.
A J W BREDBO	J. Clifford, Bredbo, Cooma ...	Cooma ...	N.S.W.
A K & A	Anderson and King, Corowa	Corowa ...	N.S.W.
A K C ALMA	C. J. Kenny, Alma, Bulyeroi	Moree	N.S.W.
AK	A. Knight, Carbeen, Wee Waa	Pilliga ...	N.S.W.
A K C GOWRIE	A. K. Cameron, Gowrie, Tenterden	Armidale	N.S.W.
A K COOMBE BANK	A. Harvey, Coombe Bank, North Allerton, Evandale ...	Evandale	TAS.
ALBILBAH	J. D. McCaush (exors.), Albilbah, Isisford	Isisford...	Q.
A L C	J. Lloyd, Cooma ...	Cooma ...	N.S.W.

WOOL MARKS.	WOOL GROWERS' NAMES AND ADDRESSES.	PASTORAL DISTRICT.	STATE.
A L OOOMA	T. Larkin, Como Valley, Ben Bullen ...	Bathurst ...	N.S.W.
A L F	A. L. Faithful, Springfield, Goulburn...	Goulburn	N.S.W.
A L K	A. W. Lynch, Tumut	Gundagai	N.S.W.
ALLAN McFARLANE	A. McFarlane, Wellington Lodge, East Wellington		S.A.
ALLAN VALE	D. McKay, Manager, Allanvale, Great Western	Western District...	VIC.
ALLEN NORTH CUIRINDI MANILLA	R. D. Allen (trustees of the late), N. Cuirindi and Springfield, Manilla	Tamworth	N.S.W.
A L MULUERINDIE NEW ENGLAND	A. Lauri, Muluerindie, Walcha	Armidale	N.S.W.
A L TOURABLE	P. Landers, Tourable, Coonamble	Coonamble	N.S.W.
A L Z	A. Lumby, Tambar Springs, Tamworth	Tamworth	N.S.W.
A M	A. M. Isaac, Urangeline Creek, Urana	Urana ...	N.S.W.
(AM)	A. Moffatt, Aloeburn, Urana	Urana ...	N.S.W.
A M ALPHA	K. McKenzie, Alpha, Tambaroora	Mudgee ...	N.S.W.
AMBO	Winton, Newton and Co., Ambo, Longreach	Longreach	Q.
A M BURRAMUNDA	J. Garry, Mylora, Binalong ...	Young ...	N.S.W.
A McC ARMIDALE	A. McClenaghan, Greendale, Armidale	Armidale	N.S.W.

WOOL MARKS.	WOOL GROWERS' NAMES AND ADDRESSES.	PASTORAL DISTRICT.	STATE.
A McC **CHEPSTOWE**	A. McCook, Chepstowe	Western District	VIC.
A McD	A. McDonald, Timmering	Northern District	VIC.
A M C **EDDINGTON**	S. Reid, Eddington, Camperdown	Camperdown	VIC.
A McINTOSH	A. McIntosh, The Ranche, Tocumwall	Deniliquin	N.S.W.
A Mc **IVOR** **JUNEE**	A. McKinnon, Junee Reefs, Junee	Wagga ...	N.S.W.
A McI **WILLOW LEE**	A. McIntosh (exors.), Willow Lee, Moree	Moree	N.S.W.
A McM **INAVALE**	A. McMillan, Inavale, via Wagga	Wagga ...	N.S.W.
A M C **PALLERANG**	A. M. Corrigan, Pallerang, Boomi	Moree	N.S.W.
A McP **BALRANALD**	P. McPherson (exors.), Paika, Balranald	Balranald	N.S.W
AMc **W**	A. McWilliam, Kangaroobie, Goolagong	Bathurst	N.S.W.
A M **G**	J. Major, Giffard, via Sale	Gippsland	VIC.
A M **MORESTONE DOWNS**	D. E. Murray, Morestone Downs, Camooweal	Camooweal	Q.
AMOS **TULLOONA**	A. Amos, Tulloona, Moree	Moree	N.S.W.
A M R	A. McRae, Sutton Grange ...	Central District ...	VIC
A M **SNIZORT**	A. Munro, Snizort, Glendonald		VIC.

WOOL MARKS.	WOOL GROWERS' NAMES AND ADDRESSES.	PASTORAL DISTRICT.	STATE.
A M **WALLENDBEEN**	Mrs. A. Mackay, Wallendbeen	Young	N.S.W.
A & M W **AVONDALE**	F. A. Newman, Avondale, Berringama		VIC
AM **WOODFORD**	J. Donald, Woodford, Dartmoor		VIC.
A M **YAMBLA**	A. Moffatt, Yambla, Mullengandra	Hume	N.S.W.
ANGO	J. V. White, Ango, Blinman		S A.
ANNANDALE	A. H. Biggal, Annandale, Ross	Ross	TAS.
A N **OHIO** **NEW ENGLAND**	J. A. Nivison, Ohio, Walcha	Armidale	N.S.W.
A N S **BALARANG**	Stirton Bros., Balarang, Moree	Moree	N.S.W.
A **OAKLEY RANGE**	J. M. Alison, Oakley Creek, Coolah	Coonabarabran	N.S.W.
A P B **GLENROY**	J. Gordon, Glenroy	Glenroy	S.A.
A P Co **DOONDI**	Australian Pastoral Co., Ltd., Doondi, St. George	St. George	Q.
A P Co **GNOOLOOMA**	Australian Pastoral Co., Ltd., Gnoolooma, Mungindi	St. George	Q.
A P Co **GUMBARDO**	Australian Pastoral Co., Ltd., Bullamon, Holly Mount and Cubbie	St. George	Q.
A P Co **NOONDOO**	Australian Pastoral Co., Ltd., Noondoo, Mungindi	St. George	Q.
A P Co **WARBRECCAN** **MUTTI**	Australian Pastoral Co., Ltd., Warbreccan, Stonehenge	Windorah	Q.

WOOL MARKS.	WOOL GROWERS' NAMES AND ADDRESSES.	PASTORAL DISTRICT.	STATE.
A. PEARCE	A. Pearce, Reedy Creek, Burraga	Carcoar	N.S.W.
A P HEREFORD PARK	J. Rutherford, Hereford	Bathurst	N.S.W.
A P IBELONG	A. Pearce, Ibelong	Jerilderie	N.S.W.
A P L J U G WEE WAA	A. P. Lord, Oceanic View, Wee Waa...	Narrabri	N.S.W.
A P MYALLA	A. Perrottett, Myalla, Narromine	Dubbo ...	N.S.W.
APSLEY	R. J. B. Gaden, Apsley, Wellington ...	Dubbo	N.S.W.
A P YABBA	A. Paton, jun., Yabba, Tallangatta	Tallangatta	VIC.
ARALABAD H B S	H. B. Smith, Aralabad	Gundagai	N.S.W.
A R B CASSILIS	A. R. Busby, Cassilis	Merriwa	N.S.W.
A & R BERCHAM	Arthur and Robertson, Bercham	Dubbo ...	N.S.W.
ARCOONA	Richardson and Gemmell, Arcoona Station	Port Augusta	S.A.
ARDGARTAN	Youngman Bros., Ardgartan, Grassdale		VIC.
ARDMOHR	J. Cameron, Ardmohr, Coleraine	Western District	VIC.
ARDNO	H. J. Filgate, Ardno, Ardno		VIC.
ARGYLE	C. D. Gibbs, Argyle, Wagga	Wagga ...	N.S.W.

WOOL MARKS.	WOOL GROWERS' NAMES AND ADDRESSES.	PASTORAL DISTRICT.	STATE.
A R MUDGEE	A. Rohr, Southwood, Mudgee	Mudgee	N.S.W.
A R P N	A. R. Robertson, Parwan	Central District ...	VIC.
ARRANDOORONG	W. Armstrong, Arrandoorong, Branxholme		VIC.
A R WERIBONE	Goldsbrough, Mort and Co., Ltd., Weribone, Surat	Surat	Q.
A S	A. Sturgeon, Berridale, Cooma	Cooma ...	N.S.W.
A S (in diamond)	A. Snodgrass, Wagga	Wagga	N.S.W.
A S ALLANDALE	Stevenson Bros., Allandale, Warialda	Warialda ...	N.S.W.
A S BAKERS RANGE	Robson Bros., Old Baker's Range, Lucindale		S.A.
A S BERRY JERRY	A. Leitch, Berry Jerry, Wagga	Wagga	N.S.W.
A S B LEIGHWOOD	A. S. Burcher, Leighwood, Golspie	Goulburn ,	N.S.W.
A S CADOGAN	A. Sullivan, Cowga, Gongolgon	Brewarrina	N.S.W.
ASCOT HEATH J P	J. Phillip, Ascot Heath, Dartmoor	...	VIC
A S COWGA	A. Sullivan, Cowga	Brewarrina	N.S.W.
A S D CAMPO SANTO	Capel Bros., Campo Santo, Barraba	Tamworth	N.S.W.
A S GLENELG	A. Shaw, Glenelg, Cowan	Yass	N.S.W.

WOOL MARKS.	WOOL GROWERS' NAMES AND ADDRESSES.	PASTORAL DISTRICT	STATE.
ASHBURTON DOWNS	Throssell and Hancock, Ashburton Downs, Onslow	Onslow	W.A.
ASHE BOGIL RYLSTONE	J. C. Ashe, Bogil, Rylstone ...	Mudgee	N.S.W
ASHFIELD	Union Bank of Australia, Ashfield *via* Coolamon	Wagga	N S.W.
ASHTON GROVE	J. Wood, Ashton Grove, Surat	Surat	Q.
A S JINDABYNE	A. Sturgeon, Jindabyne, Cooma	Cooma ...	N.S.W.
A S SPRING BANK	Molesworth and Ware, Springbank, Charlton ...		VIC.
A ω SWANNELL GRANGE	A. D. Swan, Swannell Grange, Taralga	Goulburn	N.S.W.
A S T INVERGOWRIE NEW ENG	J. L. Mitchell, Invergowrie ...	Armidale	N S.W.
A S TYRVINE	A. Stewart, Tyrvine, Bibbenluke	Bombala	N.S.W.
A T G LOWES PARK	A. J. Gibson, Lowe's Park, Launceston	Launceston	TAS.
A T L WANDA VALE	A. T. Laidlow, Wanda Vale, Pinnacles	Menindie	N.S.W.
A. TOBIN & SONS WINGADEE	A. Tobin and Sons, Wingadee, Coonamble	Coonamble	N.S.W.
A. TOBIN & SONS LILA SPRINGS	A. Tobin and Sons, Lila Springs, Ford's Bridge	Bourke ...	N.S.W.
A T P WILLIMET	Mrs. L. B. Pitman, Willimet	Moree ...	N.S.W.
A T ROCKLANDS	A. Turnbull, Rocklands, Balmoral	Western District...	VIC

WOOL MARKS.	WOOL GROWERS' NAMES AND ADDRESSES.	PASTORAL. DISTRICT.		STATE.
AUSTIN EILYER	A. S. Austin, Eilyer, Lake Bolac	...	...	VIC
AUSTIN LAKE MIDGEON	A. S. Austin, Lake Midgeon	...	...	VIC.
AUSTIN MURGHA	A. Austin, Murgha, Deniliquin	Deniliquin	...	N.S W.
A V E H K	H. Kook and Sons, The Avenue, Darlington Point	Narandera		N.S W.
AVERLEY J S M	J. S. Morrison, Aveley, Balabla	Young ...		N.S W.
AVERY RIO	Avery Bros., Rio and Alroy, Longreach	Longreach		Q.
AVOCA	Cudmore Bros , Avoca, Wentworth	Wentworth	...	N.S.W.
AVONDALE D DOWNS	J. Bignell, Avondale, Cunnamulla	Cunnamulla		Q.
AVONDALE THE ROCK	P. Kerin, Avondale, The Rock	Wagga...		N.S.W.
AVON DOWNS	N.S.W. M. and A. Co., Ltd., Avon Downs, Narrabri	Pilliga ...	...	N.S.W.
A W DEEPWATER NEW ENG	Macansh, Windeyer and Cadell, Allandale and Deepwater	Tenterfield	...	N S.W.
A WEEWONDILLA	H. C. Cooper, Weewondilla, Muttaburra	Muttaburra	...	Q.
AW GEROGERY	M. E. Watson, Gerogery, Albury	Albury ...		N.S.W.
A WILGA DOWNS	Goldsbrough, Mort and Co., Ltd , Wilga Downs Herundale	Cobar ...	...	N S.W.
A W KONNETTA	A. Watson, Konnetta, Robe...	Robe ...	...	S.A.

A

WOOL MARKS.	WOOL GROWERS' NAMES AND ADDRESSES.	PASTORAL DISTRICT.	STATE.
A W **MYALL DOWNS**	Macansh and Cadell, Myall Downs, Yetman	Warialda	N.S.W.
A W **REDWOOD**	A. Waters, Redwood, Cavendish	Western District	VIC.
A W S	A. W. Sands, Euston, Balranald	Balranald	N.S.W.
A W S **BALD RIDGE**	A. W. Stewart, Bald Ridge, Trunkey	Carcoar ..	N.S.W.
A X C	Maginnis and Julian Bros., Bloomfield, Yass	Yass	N.S W.
A X N **GRATTAI**	W. L. Atkinson, Grattai, Mudgee	Mudgee	N.S.W.
A X N **MUDGEE**	A. H. Nevell, Bombandy, Cudgegong...	Mudgee	N.S.W.
A Z	A. Zippie, Millicent, Millicent		S.A.

B

WOOL MARKS.	WOOL GROWERS' NAMES AND ADDRESSES.	PASTORAL DISTRICT.	STATE.
B	C. M. Bowden, Strath Creek, *ria* Broadford, Gippsland	Gippsland	VIC.
BACK YAMMA	J. L. Thatcher, Back Yamma, Parkes	Forbes ...	N.S.W.
BADEN PARK	Bank of N.S.W., Baden Park, Cobar...	Ivanhoe	N.S.W.
BAGOT S	J. A. Chambers, Bagot		S.A.
BAIRNKINE	Grant and Sherriff, Bairnkine, Collarendabri	Walgett	N.S.W.
BALD HILL	W. Firman, Bald Hill, Kalkallo	...	VIC.
BALD HILLS GLENROWAN	R. Twamley, Bald Hills, Glenrowan	Central District	VIC.
BALHAM HILL	J. McCormack, Balham Hill, Molesworth	Central District ...	VIC.
BALLANGEICH	G. Ritchie, Ballangeich, Ellerslie	Western District .	VIC.
BALMORAL	D. Stewart, Balmoral, Fortescue ...	Fortescue ...	W.A.
BALLYMORAN P M	P. Moran, Ballymoran, Wagga ...	Wagga...	N.S.W.
BALLYROE H	H. H. Hacking, Ballyroe, Rockley	Carcoar	N.S.W.
BALOCHILE	J. and D. Smith, Balochile, Coleraine...	Western District.	VIC.
BALOWRIE	D. Halliman, Balowrie, Cootamundra...	Young ...	N.S.W.
BALQUHIDDER Mc G W	W. McGregor, Balquhidder	Western District...	VIC.

16

B

17

B

WOOL MARKS.	WOOL GROWERS' NAMES AND ADDRESSES.	PASTORAL DISTRICT.	STATE.
BAYRICK	R. Turnbull and Co., Bayrick, Augathella	Augathella	Q.
⊞	H. and M. A. Baird, Boco, Nimitybelle	Bombala	N.S.W.
B ✛ B	Bott Bros., Oakbank, Bull Plain	Corowa...	N.S.W.
B **BALDINA**	W. P. Parker, Baldina, Kooringa	Kooringa	S.A.
B B **BALLARD**	Blair Bros., Addington		VIC.
⊞ **BRINDLEY PARK**	J. B. Bettington, Brindley Park, Merriwa	Merriwa	N.S.W.
⟨B⟩ **BINDIE**	E. B. Baker, Bindebango, Mitchell	Mitchell	Q.
B B **MUDGEE**	J. Brien, c/o J. Parkinson, Ben Buckley, Mudgee	Mudgee	N.S.W.
⊞	W. H. Ballantyne, Pine Lodge, Gilgandra	Dubbo ...	N.S.W.
B B R **EMMET DOWNS**	A. and C. W. Busby, Emmet Downs, Isisford ...	Isisford...	Q.
B BROS **MULTAGOONA**	Baird Bros., Multagoona, Mungunyah	Bourke...	N.S.W.
B BROS **WOORAWADIAN**	Binnie Bros., Woorawadian, Walgett ..	Walgett	N.S.W.
B B **STANLEY**	C. Bunn and Co., Stanley, Moree	Moree ...	N.S.W.
⊞ **WARRABAH**	A. B. Bettington, Warrabah, Manilla ..	Tamworth	N.S.W.
B B **WOODVIEW**	Berry Bros., Woodview, Trundle	Forbes ...	N.S.W.

B

WOOL MARKS.	WOOL GROWERS' NAMES AND ADDRESSES.	PASTORAL DISTRICT.	STATE.
B C	B. Cunningham, Stawell, Wimmera	Wimmera	VIC.
B C KERONGA	P. Buckley, Yearman and Keronga, Coonabarabran	Coonabarabran	N.S.W.
B CLOVER	J. Barry, Clover Station, Cunnamulla ..	Cunnamulla	Q.
B C MAYVALE	B. Chambers, May Vale, Barraba	Tamworth	N.S.W.
B CURNAMONA WEST	Canowie Pastoral Co., Ltd., Curnamona West, Hallett	Hallett ...	S.A.
B C WOOLBROOK	B. G. Clements, Woolbrook, Bigga	Carcoar	N.S.W.
B D	W. Morrice, Murramumbla, Dalgety ...	Cooma ...	N.S.W.
B 8 D BROOKWOOD	Mrs. Brooks, Brookwood, Muttaburra...	Muttaburra	Q.
B DERBY	E. Bright, Derby	...	VIC.
B D GLENDILLA	B. Deignan, Glendilla, Cunnamulla	Cunnamulla	Q.
B D J (NEW ENGLAND)	Mrs. Dawson, Armidale	Armidale	N.S.W.
BEALIBA	A. Cameron, Bealiba	Northern District	VIC.
BEDOOBA	Read and Evans, Bedooba, Hillston ...	Hillston	N.S.W.
BEECHAL	Bank of Australasia, Beechal, Charleville	Charleville	Q.
BEEMERY	N.Z L. & M. Co., Ltd., Beemery, Bourke	Bourke...	N.S.W.

B

WOOL MARKS.	WOOL GROWERS' NAMES AND ADDRESSES.	PASTORAL DISTRICT.	STATE.
BELALIE	A. & N.Z. Mercantile Co., Ltd., Belalie, Eungonia	Bourke...	N.S.W.
BELALIE SPRINGS	A. & N.Z. Mercantile Co., Ltd., Belalie, Eungonia	Bourke .	N S.W.
BELAR	H. and R. Campbell, Nevertire	Canonbar	N.S.W.
BELLA VISTA ⬦L⬦	N. McDonald, Bella Vista, Casterton ...	Western District...	VIC.
2 BELLEVIEW	Rev. A. Cameron, Belleview, Matheson	Glen Innes	N.S.W.
BELL VALE YASS	C. H. Barbour, Bell Vale, Yass	Yass	N.S.W.
BELR	H. and R. Campbell, Belaringan, Nevertire	Canonbar ...	N.S.W.
BELTANA	Beltana Pastoral Co., Ltd., Beltana ...	Beltana...	S.A.
BENDUCK	A.M. and A. Co., Ltd., Benduck, Hay...	Hay	N.S.W.
BENEREMBAH	T. Bailey (exors.) Benerembah, Hay ...	Hay ...	N.S.W.
BERAWINIA DOWNS	London Bank of Australia, Berawinia Downs, Wanaaring	Wanaaring ...	N.S.W.
BERINGARRA HD	Darlot Bros., Beringarra, Murgoo	Murgoo ...	W A.
⬦B⬦ **ESHER**	Baynes Bros., Woolscourers, Brisbane ...	...	Q.
BEULAH BEN LOMOND	H. Taylor, Ben Lomond, Ben Lomond	Glen Innes	N.S.W.
B EUROBIN	M. and E. Brennan, Eurobin, Gocup ...	Gundagai	N.S.W.

B

WOOL MARKS.	WOOL GROWERS' NAMES AND ADDRESSES.	PASTORAL DISTRICT.	STATE.
BEVERIDGE TENANDRA PARK	Beveridge Bros., Tenandra Park, Gundagai	Gundagai ...	N.S.W.
BEVERLEY ✳ BURROWA	D. Thompson, Beverley, Burrowa	Young	N.S.W.
◇ B GLENELG	R. E. O'Hara, Glenelg, Inglewood	Inglewood ...	Q.
B H BLOOMFIELD	B. Haydon, Bloomfield, Blandford	Murrurundi ...	N.S.W.
BICKFORD HYNAM	W. and H. Bickford, Hynam	Hynam... ...	S.A.
BIGGA W P	W. Picker, Sandy Creek, Bigga	Carcoar ...	N.S.W.
BILPAH HILLS G T	F. C. Thacker, Bilpah, Glen Thompson		VIC.
BIMBLE W G T	W. G. Taylor, Youie, Bimble and Kialgara, Coonamble	Coonamble ...	N.S.W.
BINDANGO	D. McGregor and McLean, Bindango, Roma	Roma ...	Q.
BING	A. W. Whitney, Coombing Park, Carcoar	Carcoar ...	N.S.W.
BINGLEY	J. and A. P. Bingley, Warrambean North, Shelford	... ...	VIC.
BINNIA	J. McMaster, Binnia, Coolah	Coonabarabran ...	N.S.W.
⌒ B KEEPIT	Dalgety and Co., Ltd., Keepit, Manilla	Tamworth ...	N.S.W.
B K L E GLENDOWDA	J. W. Buckley, Glendowda, Mullaley	Coonabarabran ...	N.S.W.
BLACKBURN YASS	Connell, Harvey and Co., Blackburn, Yass	Yass ...	N.S.W.

B

WOOL MARKS.	WOOL GROWERS' NAMES AND ADDRESSES.	PASTORAL DISTRICT.	STATE.
BLAIR H BROS GOWRIE	S. Hardie, Blairgowrie, Whitton	Narrandera	N S W.
BLAIR & SYME TEMORA	Blair and Syme, Temora, Temora	Wagga...	N.S W.
BLANCH	W. Blanch, Manilla, Tamworth	Tamworth	N.S W.
B LARUNDEL	A. Austin, Larundel, Cargarrie		VIC.
B L EASON	W. J. A. Macpherson, Geegullagong, Burrowa...	Young ...	N S.W.
B L FIG TREE PARK	B. Lavery, Minimay, Goroke...		VIC.
BLINKBONNIE LESLIE	T. Leslie (exors.), Blinkbonnie, Forbes	Forbes	N.S.W.
B & L LISTOWEL DOWNS	Union Bank of Australia, Listowel Downs, Adavale	Adavale	Q.
BLYTHEVALE	W. Weatherley, Blythevale, Streatham		VIC.
B & M BANDON GROVE	Brunner and McNally, Bandon Grove, Toowoomba	Toowoomba	Q.
B MILCHENGOWRIE	J. R. Black, Milchengowrie, Boggabri	Tamworth	N.S.W.
B & M HUNTLY	McKay and Co., Huntly, Capella	Clermont	Q.
B M NARRAN	Jno. Bell, Narran, Cobborah...	Dubbo ...	N.S.W.
B M O	B. M. Osborne, Redbank, Jugiong	Young	N.S.W.
B M O KULKI	B. M. Osborne, Kulki, Jerilderie	Jerilderie	N.S.W.

B

WOOL MARKS.	WOOL GROWERS' NAMES AND ADDRESSES.	PASTORAL DISTRICT.	STATE.
B **N** **FOREST HILL**	T. W. Bull, Forest Hill, Coolamon	Wagga	N.S.W.
>———< **a** **OAK HILLS**	B. and T. Boyton, Oakhills, Nangus	Gundagai	N.S.W.
BOBUNDARA	D. and W. Sellar, Bobundara, Cooma	Cooma ...	N.S.W.
BOGABIGAL	G. Raffan, Bogabigal, Forbes	Forbes ...	N.S.W.
BOGAMILDI	A. M. and A. Co., Ltd., Bogamildi, Wariadda	Wariadda	N.S.W.
BOGOLONG MEIN	J. and A. Love, Bogolong, Bookham ...	Young ...	N.S.W.
BOGOLONG R J	Maginnis and Bookham, Bogolong, Bookham	Young ...	N.S.W.
BOGUNDA	C. Hill and Co., Bogunda, Prarie	Hughenden	Q.
BOLERO	D. T. Wilson, Bolero, Narrandera	Narrandera	N.S.W.
BOLYGAMY	F. J. Scott, Bolygamy, West Wyalong	Condobolin	N.S.W.
BOMERA	Commercial Bank of Australia, Ltd., Bomera, Tambar Springs	Coonabarabran	N.S.W.
(BON ACCORD)	R. Cheney, jun., Bon Accord, Urinquinty	Wagga...	N.S.W.
BOOABULA	J. H. Blackwood, Booabula, Wanganella	Deniliquin	N.S.W.
BOODARIE	H. Richardson and Co., Boodarie, Hedland Point	...	W.A.
BOOK BOOK	E. Ingram, Book Book, Wagga	Wagga ...	N.S.W.

B

WOOL MARKS.	WOOL GROWERS' NAMES AND ADDRESSES.	PASTORAL DISTRICT.	STATE.
BOOKHAM	M. O'Mara, Bookham	Young	N.S.W.
BOOLATHANA J & C B	J. and C. Butcher, Boolathana, Carnarvon	Carnarvon	W.A.
BOOLCARROL $HF \& C^o$	A. E. and M. Co., Ltd., Boolcarrol, Narrabri	Narrabri	N.S.W.
BOONA	L. McLean, Boona West, Condobolin ...	Condobolin	N.S.W.
BOORT	A. D. McWaters, Boort, Cunnamulla	Cunnamulla	Q.
BOORTKOI	E. Manifold, Boortkoi, Hexham	Western District	VIC.
BOOTRA	Taylor and Son, Bootra, Wilcannia	Wanaaring	N.S.W.
BOOYAMURRA S D	Mrs. A. Dean, Booyamurra, Coolah	Coonabarabran	N.S.W.
BORRIYALLOAK E. G. AUSTIN	E. G. Austin, Borriyalloak, Skipton		VIC.
BOUYEO	J. S. Fuller, Beggan Beggan, Murrumburrah	Gundagai	N.S.W.
B OVERTON	G. Blunt, Overton, Muswellbrook	Denman	N.S.W.
BOWEN DOWNS	Scottish Australian Investment Co., Ltd., Bowen Downs, Aramac	Aramac	Q.
BOWES	W. Burges-Bowes, Geraldton	Geraldton	W.A.
BOWNA	A. J. Rial, Bowna, Albury	Albury ...	N.S.W.
BOYD	A. J. and H. W. Stitt, Boyd, Forbes ...	Forbes ...	N.S.W.

B

WOOL MARKS.	WOOL GROWERS' NAMES AND ADDRESSES.	PASTORAL DISTRICT.	STATE.
BOX FARM	E. Wills, Box Farm, Dinyarrak		VIC.
BOXWOOD PARK G C	G. Cary, Boxwood, Bungowannah	Albury	N.S.W.
B P ABEDOAR	B. Proctor, Abedoar, Mungindi	Moree	N.S.W.
BRACKER	Bracker Bros., Warroo, Stanthorpe	Stanthorpe	Q.
BRAEFOOT	H. Scott, Braefoot, Kooringa	Kooringa	S.A.
BRAEMAR	J. E. Pick, Braemar	Braemar	S.A.
BRANGALBAR	B. Blair, Brangalbar, Nyngan	Canonbar	N.S.W.
B R BOLOCO	R. W. Rose, Boloco, Cooma ...	Cooma ...	N.S.W.
BREDBO	J. Clifford, Bredbo, Cooma	Cooma ...	N.S.W.
BREAKFAST CREEK	R. Dwyer, Breakfast Creek, Burrowa ...	Young	N.S.W.
BRIGALOWS COLLINGWOOD	W. F. James, Brigalows, Pilliga	Pilliga ...	N.S.W.
BRINGALBERT	J. D. Laidlow, Bringalbert, Apsley	North-Western District	VIC.
BRIPPICK	J. C. Fitzgerald, Brippick, Nenarpar ...		VIC.
BRISBANE HILL	R. T. Carty, Brisbane Hill, Byaduk	Western District	VIC.
B R N	J. L. Brown, Tondeburnie, Gilgandra ...	Coonabarabran	N.S.W.

B

WOOL MARKS.	WOOL GROWERS' NAMES AND ADDRESSES.	PASTORAL DISTRICT.	STATE.
BRN	J. L. Brown, Tondeburnie, Gilgandra	Coonabarabran	N.S.W.
BROLGAN	Gordon and Williams, Brolgan, Parkes	Forbes	N.S.W.
BRONTE	H. H. Budden, Bronte, Lake Bathurst	Goulburn	N.S.W.
BRONTE Q WATER RESERVE MILLS	H. H. Budden, Bronte, Lake Bathurst	Goulburn	N.S.W.
BROOKONG	A. E. and M. Co., Ltd., Brookong, Urana	Urana ...	N.S.W.
BROOKSTEAD QUEENSLAND	J. Tyson, Doneley, Brookstead, Pittsworth	Toowoomba	Q.
BROOK VALE	J. Leary, Brook Vale, Cumnock	Molong ...	N.S.W.
B ROSSGOLE	J. Blunt, Rossgole, Muswellbrook	Mudgee	N.S.W.
BROWLEY	W. Morrice, Browley, Moss Vale	Berrima ...	N.S.W.
BROWN BOOBOROWIE	J. Lawdon, Booborowie, Kooringa	Kooringa	S.A.
BROWN BOOWILLIA	J. Lawdon, Boowillia, Kooringa	Kooringa	S.A.
BROWNLEE D S	D. Smith, Harrow ...	Western District...	VIC.
BR TIVERTON	R. H. Roberts, Tiverton, Barwang	Young ...	N.S.W.
BRUCE MOUCHAPPIE	J. D. Bruce, Poonindie, Port Lincoln (grown at Hillsea)	Elliston... ...	S.A.
BRUNGAGEE E A F	E. A. Fitzgerald, Brungagee, Book Book	Wagga...	N.S.W.

26

B

WOOL MARKS.	WOOL GROWERS' NAMES AND ADDRESSES.	PASTORAL DISTRICT.	STATE.
BRUNG BRUNGLE S R	R. Ramsden, Brung Brungle, Wannon	Wannon	VIC.
BRYMEDURA	F. E. Churchill, Brymedura, Manildra	Molong	N.S.W.
BRYNOG	D. Ferrier, Brynog, Surat	Surat	Q.
BRYNTIRION T H	F. H. Hutchings (exors.), Lubeck, Wimmera	Wimmera	VIC.
B S 2 NUNEHAM	Mrs. A. M. Cobb, Nuneham, Carcoar	Carcoar	N.S.W.
B TARRION	W. and T. C. Dickson, Tarrion Retreat, Brewarrina	Brewarrina	N.S.W.
B T M Q	H. Batterham, Timor, Blandford	Murrurundi	N.S.W.
BUCKALONG	Garnock Bros., Buckalong, Bombala	Bombala	N.S.W.
BUCKALOW	F. L. Parker (exors.), Buckalow, Broken Hill	Menindie	N.S.W.
BUCKINGBONG	F. Jenkins (exors.), Buckingbong	Narrandera	N.S.W.
BUCKWAROON L Y	Sir J. Lackey, Buckwaroon	Cobar	N.S.W.
BUGILBONE ♧	Queensland Estates, Ltd., Bugilbone	Pilliga	N.S.W.
B U K	Mrs. E. Foot, Winburndale, Daramana	Bathurst	N.S.W.
△ BUKKULLA	H. Wyndham, sen., Bukkulla, Inverell	Glen Innes	N.S.W.
BULGANA J H H	J. H. Holder, Stawell	Western District	VIC.

B

WOOL MARKS.	WOOL GROWERS' NAMES AND ADDRESSES.	PASTORAL DISTRICT.	STATE.
BULGROO	Willis and Co., Bulgroo, Adavale	Adavale ...	Q.
BULLAMON	A. P. Co., Ltd., Bullamon, Mungindie.	St. George	Q.
BULLAWARRIE	L. Livingstone, Bullawarrie, St. George	St. George ...	Q.
BULL BROS BIG RIVER	Bull Bros., Big River, Bingara	Warialda	N.S.W.
BULLENBONG D N	A. Davidson (exors.), Bullenbong, The Rock	Wagga...	N.S.W.
B ULLINA	F. Barry, Termoyne, Ullina ...	Ballarat ...	VIC.
BUMBALONG	A. Peden and Sons, Bumbalong, Colinton	Queanbeyan	N.S.W.
BUN	F. E. Body, Bundemar, Trangie	Dubbo	N.S.W.
BUNDALEER	J. F. Maslin, Bundaleer, Gulnare South	Gulnare	S.A.
BUNGLE GULLY	London Bank of Australia, Ltd., Bungle Gully, Come-by-Chance ...	Pilliga ...	N.S.W.
BUNNA BUNNA	Goldsbrough, Mort and Co., Bunna Bunna, Millie	Narrabri ...	N.S.W.
BUNNAMAGOO	J. H. McIntosh, Bunnamagoo, Rockley	Bathurst ...	N.S.W.
BURBAN GRANGE E S	E. Smythe, Burban Grange ...	Brewarrina	N.S.W.
BURBURGATE	Namoi Pastoral Co., Ltd., Burburgate, Gunnedah	Tamworth ...	N.S.W.
BURBURGATE B U	Namoi Pastoral Co., Ltd., Burburgate, Gunnedah	Tamworth ...	N.S.W.

B

WOOL MARKS.	WOOL GROWERS' NAMES AND ADDRESSES.	PASTORAL DISTRICT.	STATE.
BURBURGATE C C	Namoi Pastoral Co., Ltd., Burburgate, Gunnedah	Tamworth	N.S.W.
BURENDA	Western Queensland Pastoral Co., Burenda, Morven	Angathella	Q.
BURGOON	J. Bruce, Burgoon, Cumnock	Molong ...	N.S.W.
BURN BANK	J. Fry (exors.), Woodstock, Avoca	Avoca	VIC.
BURNIMA H Y	H. T. Edwards, Burnima, Bibbenluke	Bombala	N.S.W.
BURNSIDE C	A. Cameron, Burnside, Glen Thompson	Western District	VIC
BURNSIDE R H	R. Howell (exors.), Geelong.	Geelong	VIC.
BURRANGONG	Barrett and Milrose, Burrangong	Young	N.S.W.
BURRENDONG T C B	T. Campbell, Burrendong	Dubbo	N.S.W.
BURROWA P M G	P. McGrath, Lang's Creek, Burrowa	Young ...	N.S.W.
BURRUMBEEP HILL C C C	J. Cronch, Burrumbeep Hill, Craroona		VIC.
BURRAJAA	Edols and Co., Barrajaa, Corowa	Corowa...	N.S.W.
BURSLEM Q	Wedgewood and Co., Burslem, Muttaburra	Muttaburra	Q.
BURSLEM Q E	Wedgewood and Co., Burslem, Muttaburra	Muttaburra	Q.
BURTA	W. P. McGregor (exors.), Burta, Broken Hill	Menindie	N.S.W.

WOOL MARKS.	WOOL GROWERS' NAMES AND ADDRESSES.	PASTORAL DISTRICT.	STATE.
BUTHERWAH	Mrs. F. E Whitehead, Butherwah, Urana	Urana	N.S.W.
BURTUNDY	E. B. Heaton, Burtundy, Wentworth ...	Wentworth	N.S.W.
BUTE	Roe Brothers, Bute	Bute	S.A.
B V & Co YARDIE	Burt Bros. and Co., Yardie, Ashburton		W.A.
B WALLANGRA	J. R. Black, Wallangra	Warialda	N.S.W.
B WEST BLOWERING	London Bank of Australia, Ltd., West Blowering, Tumut	Gundagai	N.S.W.
BW ORION DOWNS	J. G. H. Wilson, Orion Downs, Rollstone	Springsure	Q.
2 B W TILBUSTER NEW ENG	Warner Bros., Tilbuster, Armidale	Armidale	N.S.W.
B W W W BANDO	H. C. White, Bando, Gunnedah	Tamworth	N.S.W.
B W W W BANDO	H. C. White, Bando, Gunnedah	Tamworth	N.S.W.
B X L	C. Steurs, Bleak House, Birregarria		VIC.
B X MOREA	C. D. Block, Morea, Hamilton, Winchelsea	Western District ..	VIC.
B X OBERNE	C. D. Bardwell, Oberne, Tarcutta	Gundagai	N.S.W.

B

WOOL MARKS.	WOOL GROWERS' NAMES AND ADDRESSES.	PASTORAL DISTRICT.	STATE.
◇ By	Mrs. Bradley (exors.), Bibbenluke	Bombala	N.S.W.
BYGOLOREE	Goldsbrough, Mort and Co., Ltd., Bygoloree, Ungarie	Condobolin	N.S.W.
BYLONG	Nelson and Begbie, Bylong, Richmond	Hughenden	Q.
BY MAILA	G. Busby, Maila, Balladoran	Dubbo ...	N.S.W.
BYNYA	Drysdale and Co., Bynya, Whitton	Narrandera	N.S.W.
BYRNE W	C. Byrne, Byrneville, Dalton	Yass	N.S.W.

C

WOOL MARKS.	WOOL GROWERS' NAMES AND ADDRESSES.	PASTORAL DISTRICT.	STATE.
2 ◇C	T. Gatenby, Fisa, Lake River, Cressy	Cressy	TAS.
◇C	Carr Bros., Tunny Hill, Binda	Carcoar	N.S.W.
◇C	J. L. Currie, Larra, Camperdown	Western District	VIC.
◇C	Hills and Pearse, Caroona, Hallett	Hallett ...	S.A.
△C	W. G. Coutts, Serpentine, Inglewood ...	Bendigo	VIC.
□ C	J. K. Clark, Boggabri, Boggabri	Tamworth	N.S.W.
C A A NEWSTEAD SOUTH NEW ENGLAND	C. A. Anderson, Newstead South, Inverell	Glen Innes	N.S.W.
CAIRNBANK	J. A. Hensley, Cairnbank, Wolseley		S.A.
CALGA	Ryder Bros., Calga, Coonamble	Coonamble	N.S.W.
CALIMO	J. McRae (exors.), Calimo, Deniliquin	Deniliquin	N.S.W.
CALLUBRI	W. H. Armstrong and Brother, Callubri, Dandaloo	Canonbar ...	N.S.W.
CALPERUM	J. H. Robertson, Calperum, Overland Corner		S.A.
CALVERT COLAC	J. Calvert, Irrewarra, Colac . .	Western District...	VIC.
CALVERT WEERING	J. Calvert, Irrewarra, Colac ...	Western District...	VIC.
CAMBRIDGE DOWNS	A.E. & M. Co., Ltd., Cambridge Downs, Richmond	Hughenden	Q.

C

WOOL MARKS.	WOOL GROWERS' NAMES AND ADDRESSES.	PASTORAL DISTRICT.	STATE.
CAMBUSDOON J K	J. Kelly, Cambusdoon, Yerong Creek	Wagga	N.S.W.
CAMDEN	J. M. McA. Onslow, Camden Park, Menangle	Picton	N.S.W.
CAMPBELL FIELDS R D	R. Davison, Campbellfields, Burrowa	Young	N.S.W.
CANALLY	A.M.L. & F. Co., Ltd., Canally, Balranald	Balranald	N.S.W.
CANNAWIGRA	A. K. Hutchinson, Cannawigra, Kingstone	Kingstone	S.A.
CANONBAR	Goldsbrough, Mort and Co., Ltd., Miowera, Nyngan	Canonbar	N.S.W.
CANOWIE	Canowie Pastoral Co., Canowie	Canowie	S.A.
CAPEL GOURNAMA NEW ENGLAND	Capel Bros., Gournama, Warialda	Warialda	N.S.W.
CAPEL PIEDMONT	Capel Bros., Piedmont, Cobbadah	Warialda	N.S.W.
CARAMUT	T. Caley, Caramut, Bundarra	Armidale	N.S.W.
CARANDOTTA	Bank of N.S.W., Carandotta, Boulia	Boulia	Q.
CARDINGTON	Mrs. M. L. Carr, Cardington, Molong	Molong	N.S.W.
CARIGEEN F B	Fitzgerald Bros., Carrigeen, Harrow	Western District	VIC.
CARRAWOBITTY	H. B. Coward, Carrawobitty, Forbes	Forbes	N.S.W.
CARRIGAN	C. Bailey, Carrigan, Trangie	Dubbo	N.S.W.

C

WOOL MARKS.	WOOL GROWERS' NAMES AND ADDRESSES.	PASTORAL DISTRICT.	STATE.
CARROONBOON **D** +	J. Dickson, Carroonboon, Wanganella	Deniliquin	N.S.W.
CARRS PLAINS	H. H. Wettenhall, Carr's Plains, Stawell	Western District	VIC.
CARTER BROS **V** ≡ **LINTON**	Carter Brothers, Linton, Upper Manilla	Tamworth	N.S.W.
CASTLE **STEAD** **C L H**	C. L. Hume, Castlestead, Burrowa	Young ...	N.S.W.
C **AT** **NEW ENGLAND**	Austin Mack, Pallal, Bingara	Moree	N.S.W.
CAVANDALE	McLachlan Bros., Cavandale, Mintaro		S.A.
C B ᗺ	C. Byrne, Byrneville, Dalton	Yass	N.S.W.
C B **BALGALAL**	Corcoran Bros., Corcoran Plains, Burrowa	Young	N.S.W.
C B **COOMA**	Coffey Bros., Tollbar Creek, Cooma	Cooma ...	N.S.W.
C B **CURRACABAH**	C. Binnie, Curracabah, Boggabri	Tamworth	N.S.W.
C B E **INA**	Morgan Bros., Ina, Geeron	Forbes ...	N.S.W.
◇ⓒ **BELLEVUE** **NEW ENG**	Rev. A. Cameron, Bellevue, Matheson	Glen Innes	N.S.W.
ⓒ **BENTLEY**	N. Cameron, Bentley, Deloraine	Deloraine	TAS.
C B **GAMPOLA**	Cooper Bros., Gampola, Stawell	Western District.	VIC.
C B **LAURA**	C. Baker, Laura, Armidale	Armidale	N.S.W.

C

WOOL MARKS.	WOOL GROWERS' NAMES AND ADDRESSES.	PASTORAL DISTRICT.	STATE.
C B LUCKNOW	Fiskin, Banning and Co., Lucknow, Winton	Boulia	Q.
C B N	Sir W. I. Clarke (exors.), Coleran, N. Deniliquin	Deniliquin	N.S.W.
C B NARRANG	R. Christie, Narrang, Dutson, via Sale	Gippsland	VIC.
C ɷ NEW ENG	Haniel and Grills, Kingstown, Armidale	Armidale	N.S.W.
C B O	Curtis Bros., Oaklands, Giffard	Gippsland	VIC.
C B PLAISTOW	C. Bryant, Plaistow, Joyce's Creek	Talbot ...	VIC.
C. BROS WILFORD	J. Cameron, Wilford, Tenterden	Armidale	N.S.W.
C B STANLEY	C. Bunn and Sons, Stanley, Moree	Moree	N.S.W.
C B W B	Cannon Bros., Wallan Billan, Narromine	Dubbo	N.S.W.
C B WINSCOMBE	C. Britten, Winscombe, Uralla	Armidale	N.S.W.
C C	The Australian Mercantile and Agency Co., Ltd., Cowal Cowal, Hillston ...	Hillston	N.S.W.
CC / O (diamond)	W. Coram, Nathalie	North-East District	VIC.
C —— C	C. Chew, Springfield, Stockinbingal	Cooma ...	N.S.W.
C / C C (red)	J. Scott, Korumburra	East District	VIC.
C CALEDONIA	J. Cameron and Co., Caledonia, Aramac	Aramac	Q.

35

C

WOOL MARKS.	WOOL GROWERS' NAMES AND ADDRESSES.	PASTORAL DISTRICT.	STATE.
C ◇ (a) CAMBALONG	R. Campbell, Cambalong, Bombala	Bombala	N.S.W.
C CARLINGFORD	J. J. Christy, Carlingford, Garah	Moree	N.S.W.
C C CHERRY TREE HILL NEW ENG	G. Every, Cherry Tree Hill, Glen Innes	Glen Innes	N.S.W.
C C C W L NEW ENGLAND	J. A. Chisholm, West Lynne, Guyra	Armidale	N S.W.
C C DONORS HILL	A. S. Chirnside and Co., Donors Hill, Norman.	Norman	Q.
C C GORDON DOWNS	South Australian Land, Mercantile and Agency Co., Ltd., Gordon Downs, Capella ...	Clermont	Q.
C C HAMILTON DOWNS	South Australian Land, Mercantile and Agency Co., Ltd., Hamilton Downs, Richmond ...	Hughenden	Q.
C C JINGELLICK	Australian Mercantile and Agency Co., Ltd., Jingellick, Hume	Hume ...	N.S.W.
C C MARY'S MOUNT	Mrs. M. Clonan, Mary's Mount, Gunnedah	Tamworth	N.S.W.
C & Co KENSINGTON	J. Cameron and Co., Kensington, Muttaburra	Muttaburra	Q.
C & Co KENSINGTON DOWNS	J. Cameron and Co., Kensington, Muttaburra	Muttaburra	Q.
OC STONEY CREEK	T. Cash, Stoney Creek, Essington, O'Connell	Bathurst	N.S.W.
C C T	C. Wewell, Jeridgerie North, Coonamble	Coonamble ...	N.S.W.
C D BLOOMFIELD	C. Dowling, Bloomfield, Dalton	Yass ...	N.S.W.
C D F NEW ENG	Fenwick Bros., Europambula, Walcha	Armidale ...	N.S.W.

C

WOOL MARKS.	WOOL GROWERS' NAMES AND ADDRESSES.	PASTORAL DISTRICT.	STATE.
C D J BAN BAN NEW ENG	C. D. Judge, Ban Ban, Ben Lomond	Armidale	N.S.W.
C D NEW ENG	T. Donoghue, Frankfield, Uralla	Armidale	N.S.W.
C E	E. Cusack, Eurowa	North-East District	VIC.
C E HINTON DARLING DOWNS	C. Elborne, Hinton, Dalby	Dalby	Q.
CENTRAL	G. Frew, Central Station, Cobar	Cobar	N.S.W.
C ERINDALE	P. Cummins and Sons, Erindale, Longwood	North-East District	VIC.
C F & Co CONNULPIE DOWNS	C. Fartiere and Co., Connulpie Downs, Tibooburra	Milparinka	N.S.W.
C F F	C. Fletcher, Fentonville and Eagle, Mount Rocky Plain	Cooma ...	N.S.W.
C F POWLETT HILL	C. Fowcett, Glengower	Talbot ...	VIC.
C G RETREAT	Christian and Grice, Retreat, Isisford	Isisford	Q.
C G W BENARBA	C. G. Weston, Benarba North, Moree	Moree	N.S.W.
CHAFFEY MOONBI	W. A. Chaffey, Rock View, Moonbi	Tamworth	N.S.W.
CHAH SING	Grant and Childe, Chah Sing, Moulamein	Moulamein	N.S.W.
CHALLICUM	S. R. Thompson, Challicum, Ballyrogan		VIC.
CHARLEMONT	R. B. Noble, Claremont, Mt. Duneed		VIC.

C

WOOL MARKS.	WOOL GROWERS' NAMES AND ADDRESSES.	PASTORAL DISTRICT.	STATE.
CHARLOTTE VALE	C. H. J. Schmidt and Co., Charlotte Vale, Cunnamulla	Cunnamulla ...	Q.
CHARLTON	Australian Mercantile Land and Finance Co., Ltd., Charlton, Brewarrina ...	Brewarrina ...	N.S.W.
C H CARUNNA	C. Hall, Carunna, Eurelia	Eurelia ...	S.A.
C. H. COX THE OAKS	C. H. Cox, The Oaks, Muswellbrook	Denman ...	N.S.W.
C. HEADLAM EGGLESTON	C. Headlam, Eggleston, Cressy	Cressy	TAS
C HEADLAM W	Headlam's Estate, Eggleston, Campbell Town	Campbell Town ...	TAS.
CHETWYND ⌒	A. Johnson, Chetwynd Estate, Chetwynd	Western District...	VIC.
CHETWYND A J	A. Johnson, Chetwynd Estate, Chetwynd	Western District...	VIC.
CHIDOWLA ⊙	L. Roche, Chidowla, Nanangroe	Gundagai	N.S.W.
CHILLAMURRA	Brown and Haigh, Chillamurra, Port Lincoln	Port Lincoln	S.A.
CHIRK	F. and P. H. Wheaton, Hydon, Redhill		S.A.
CHOCOLYN R H	R. Howell, Chocolyn, Camperdown	Western District...	VIC.
C H THORNEY	Heulen Bros., Thornley, Bathurst	Bathurst	N.S.W.
C H Y G	C. Hazell, Yarran Grove, Nevertire	Canonbar ...	N.S.W.
C J B W R NEW ENGLAND	C. J. Britain, Englefield, Walcha Road	Armidale ...	N.S.W.

C

WOOL MARKS.	WOOL GROWERS' NAMES AND ADDRESSES.	PASTORAL DISTRICT.	STATE.
C J C **DOWNHILL**	J. Connell, Downhill, Yarranbah	Yass	N.S.W.
C J C **PEPPERTON**	C. J. Curtin, Pepperton, Brewarrina	Brewarrina	N.S.W.
C J G **GLENMORE**	W. B. Chomley, Glenmore, Rowsley		VIC.
C & J **GOSDEN**	C. and J. Gosden, Eden Valley		S.A.
C J M **THE CHASE**	C. J. Monk, The Chase, Cuddell Siding	Narrandera	N.S.W.
C K **ALMA**	C. J. Kenny, Alma, Bulyeroi	Dubbo ...	N.S.W.
C & K **ALMA DOWNS**	Cramsie and King, Alma Downs, Richmond	Hughenden	Q.
C K **ROMA DOWNS**	C. S. King, Roma Downs, Roma	Roma	Q.
C L A	Laidlaw Bros., Amphitheatre, Avoca	Avoca	VIC.
CLARE	Fairbairne Pastoral Co., Clare, Aramac	Aramac .	Q.
CLARENDON J W	P. Byrne and Sons, Clarendon, Balranald	Balranald	N.S W.
CLARIS **JUNEE**	J. F. Quilter, Claris Park, Junee	Wagga	N.S.W.
CLAVERTON	W. J. Whitney, (exors.), Claverton Siding, Cunnamulla	Cunnamulla	Q.
CLEAR CREEK	Still Bros., Clear Creek, Limekilns	Bathurst	N S W.
CLEAR HILLS ◇ PH ◇ **JUNEE**	P. Heffernan, Clear Hills, Junee	Wagga	N.S.W.

C

WOOL MARKS.	WOOL GROWERS' NAMES AND ADDRESSES.	PASTORAL DISTRICT.	STATE.
CLEARMONT A H	A. Hare, Clearmont, Wagra	Hay	N.S.W
C L F WARROWIE	C. L. Forrest, Warrowie, Irrewarra	Western District...	VIC.
CLIFFORD	J. Richardson and Sons, Clifford, Yeulba	Roma	Q.
CLIFT BROS BREEZA	Clift Bros., Breeza ..	Tamworth	N.S.W
CLIFTON	S. R. Turner, Clifton, Anakie		VIC.
CLONAGH	W. J. Reid, Clonagh, Cloncurry	Cloncurry	Q.
CLONMORE PARK	J. Dunn, Clonmore Park, Mulwala	Corowa	N.S.W.
CLOVERSIDE	J. Mackay, Cloverside Creek, Louth	Bourke	N.S.W.
C L S WOODSTOCK NEW ENG	C. L. Smith, Edgecliffe, Inverell	Glen Innes	N.S.W.
CLUNIE	D. McGregor, Clunie, Chintin		VIC.
CLUTHA	W. T. Mott, Clutha, Richmond	Hughenden	Q.
CLYDE	W. McLaughlin, Clyde, Garah	Moree	N.S.W.
C. MARINA	W. Taylor, Marina, Euston	Wentworth	N.S W.
C M AVONDALE	F. A. Newman, Avondale, Berringama	Northern District	VIC.
C M 6 BUMBLE	J. Maloney, Bumble, Tycannah	Armidale ...	N.S.W.

C

WOOL MARKS.	WOOL GROWERS' NAMES AND ADDRESSES.	PASTORAL DISTRICT.	STATE.
C MELBA	Edwards Bros., Melba, St. Arnaud	Wimmera	VIC.
C M E L BOXDALE	C. Mill, Boxdale, Barraba	Tamworth	N.S.W.
C MERIVALE	Mrs. Crossley, Merivale	Western District	VIC
C M F YASS CATTLE CAMP	C. McFetters, Cattle Camp, Jeir	Yass	N.S.W.
C MK	C. A. McKenzie, Worrough, Trawool...	North-East District	VIC.
C M QUEENSLAND	Marshall and Slade, Glengallen, Warwick	Warwick	Q.
C M S EULOMO	M. Sawyer, junr., Eulomo, Bethungra	Gundagai	N.S.W.
◇C◇ MYALL PLAINS	Campbell Bros., Myall Plains, St. George	St George	Q.
C N C N	The A.L. & F. Co. of Australia, Ltd., Chillichill, Balranald	Balranald	N.S.W.
C NESTON	J. Coles, Neston, Gundaroo	Queanbeyan	N.S.W.
C NEWMINSTER PARK	R. H. Clarke, Newminster Park, Camperdown	Western District	VIC.
(C) N N	M. Callaghan, Berringa		VIC.
C O B	J. Rutherford, Barrenbilla, Cunnamulla	Cunnamulla	Q.
COBHAM	Goldsbrough, Mort and Co., Ltd., Cobham Lake, Milparinka	Milparinka	N.S.W.
COBRAN	Sir W. J. Clarke (exors.), Cobran, Deniliquin	Deniliquin	N.S.W.

C

| --- | --- | --- | --- |
C O B WARKON	Warkon Station, Ltd., Warkon, Miles	Surat	Q.
COCKETGEDONG	Watt and Thompson (exors.), Cocketgedong, Urana	Urana	N.S.W.
COLANE	Fisher Bros., Colane, Canonbar	Canonbar	N.S.W.
COLBINABBIN	D. Mitchell, Colbinabbin	...	VIC.
COLLERINA	J. Livingstone, Collerina, Bourke	Bourke	N.S.W.
COLLYMONGLE WP * C	G. McLean, Collymongle, Bulyeroi	Walgett	N.S.W.
COLMLEE	R. R. Doyle, Colmlee, Moree	Moree	N.S.W.
COLVINSBY	E. H. Austin, Colvinsby, Dobie's Bridge		VIC.
COMBADELLO	W. and F. A. Moses, Combadello, Moree	Moree ...	N.S.W.
COMMERALGHIP	C. Rowe, Commeralghip, Rokewood		VIC.
CONDAMINE PLAINS DARLING DOWNS	E. S. & A. Bank, Ltd., Condamine Plains, Dalby	Dalby ...	Q.
CONGBOOL	Robertson Bros., Cong Bool, Balmoral	Western District...	VIC.
CONDOBOLIN M F & CO	Australian Estates and Mortgage Co., Ltd., Enm Plains, Condobolin	Condobolin	N.S.W.
CONMURRA W. W.	W. Wager, Conmurra, Lucindale	...	S.A.
CONOBLE	Conoble Pastoral Co., Conoble, Mossgiel	Ivanhoe	N.S.W.

C

WOOL MARKS.	WOOL GROWERS' NAMES AND ADDRESSES.	PASTORAL DISTRICT.	STATE.
CONOOER	T. B. Griffiths, Gawong, St. Arnaud	Wimmera	VIC.
COOGEE	Riverstone Meat Co., Bridge Street, Sydney		N.S.W.
COOINDA B & M	E. Balgarnie, Cooinda, Winton	Winton	Q.
COOK & CO KEERA	T. Cook and Co., Keera, Bingera	Warialda	N.S.W.
COOK & CO SCONE	Cook and Co., Scone, Murrurundi	Murrurundi	N.S.W.
COOK & CO STANTHORPE	Cook and Co., Scone, Murrurundi	Murrurundi	N.S.W.
COOK & CO WOOLSHED	J. Cook and Co., Woolshed, Bingera	Warialda	N.S.W.
COOLABAH K/M	T. W. Kelly, Coolabah, Canonbar	Canonbar	N.S.W.
COOLAMATONG	Mrs. Hepburn, Coolamatong, Berridale	Coonia	N.S.W.
COOLOOTAI	T. Walker (exors.), Coolootai, Warialda	Warialda	N.S.W.
COOLONG R D	R. Dowling, Coolong, Dalton	Yass	N.S.W.
COOLRINGDON	D. Ryrie (exors.), Coolringdon, Cooma	Coonia	N.S.W.
COOMBING PARK LAKESIDE	W. T. Whitney (exors.), Coombing Park, Carcoar	Carcoar	N.S.W.
COONERANG	A. Haylock, Rock Flat, Cooma	Cooma ...	N.S.W.
COONGOOLA	Armstrong Bros., Coongoola Siding, Cunnamulla	Cunnamulla	Q.

C

WOOL MARKS.	WOOL GROWERS' NAMES AND ADDRESSES.	PASTORAL DISTRICT.	STATE.
COONONG	S. McCaughey, Coonong, Urana	Urana ...	N.S.W.
COPPYMURRAMBILLA I B	Brown Bros., Coppymurrambilla, Moree	Moree ...	N.S.W
COOYA POOYA	Mrs. M. Galbraith, Cooya Pooya, Roeburn	Roeburn	W.A.
COOYAL MUDGEE	C. S. Murray, Cooyal, Mudgee	Mudgee ...	N.S.W.
COREA	J. A. Learmonth, Corea, Dunkeld	...	VIC.
COREE	D. McCaughey (exors)., Coree, Jerilderie	Jerilderie	N.S.W.
CORIO	Mrs. J. A. Cotter, Corio, St. George ...	St. George	Q.
CORNALLA	B. Ricketson, Cornalla, Deniliquin	Deniliquin	N.S.W.
CORNELIA CREEK	G. Simmie, Cornelia and Top Creek, Echuca	Northern District	VIC.
CORONA N S W	Goldsbrough, Mort and Co., Corona, Tarawingee	Menindie	N.S.W.
CORRONG	A. and A. Tyson, Corrong, Hay	Hay	N.S.W.
CORROWONG	H. King, Corrowong, Kingsvale	Balranald	N S.W.
COUNSELL LYNDON	F. C. Counsell and Co., Lyndon, Saltern	Barcaldine	Q.
COWL COWL	Australian Mercantile and A. Co., Ltd., Cowl Cowl, Hillston...	Hillston	N.S.W.
COWLEY	E. McNeile, Cowley, Charleville	Charleville	Q.

C

WOOL MARKS.	WOOL GROWERS' NAMES AND ADDRESSES.	PASTORAL DISTRICT.	STATE.
COWAL NORTH	Low Bros., Cowal North, Marsden	Forbes	N.S.W.
C O Y ENSAY	J. McCoy, Ensay, Gippsland...	Gippsland	VIC.
C P A	C. Purcell, Woodalga, Adelong	Gundagai	N.S.W.
C P & Co MOSSGIEL	C. Powell and Co., Moanguii, Mossgiel	Ivanhoe	N.S.W
C P E LTD RICHLANDS	Camden Park Estate, Richlands, Taralga	Goulburn	N.S.W.
C PINDARI	P. C. and J. Campbell, Pindari, Inverell	Glen Innes	N.S.W.
C P S ROSEWOOD	C. S. Perrottet, Rosewood, Trangie	Dubbo ...	N.S.W.
C R B W NEW ENGLAND	C. R. Blaxland, Wollun, Armidale	Armidale	N.S.W.
CROMER	W. H. Larcomb, Petavel Railway Station, Geelong ...	Western District..	VIC.
CROXTON EAST -÷- P M	P. Matuschka, Croxton East...	Western District	VIC.
C R P N NARRACOORTE	Manager Narracoorte Station, Narracoorte	South-Eastern District	S.A
CRUTTENDEN	T. O. Nourilam, Cruttenden, Berthbell		TAS.
C & R WATERLOO	J. Sanderson and Co., Woolscourers, Spring Street, Sydney ...		N.S.W.
C R W B PARK ILLABO	C. R. Westmacott, Bethungra Park, Illabo	Gundagai	N.S.W.
C SATIMER	R. S. Bree, Satimer, Coleraine	Wannon	VIC.

WOOL MARKS.	WOOL GROWERS' NAMES AND ADDRESSES.	PASTORAL DISTRICT.	STATE.
C & S F	Clarke and Spicer, Fermoy, Winton	Winton...	Q.
C & S **FERMOY**	Clarke and Spicer, Fermoy, Winton	Winton	Q.
C S G	C. Smith, Nandillyan Heights, Molong	Molong...	N.S.W.
C X S **GLENISLA**	S. Carter, Glenisla, Brimpean		VIC.
C S **MUSSEN**	C. Stairs, Willow Tree, Murrurundi	Tamworth	N.S.W.
C S **NEW ENGLAND**	C. Smith, Uralla, Armidale ...	Armidale	N.S.W.
C & T D **UCOLTA**	E. E. Kernott (manager), Ucolta Station, Ucolta		S.A.
C ⊢ E **SOBRAON** **NEW ENG**	C. Thorpe, Sobraon, Damaresq	Armidale	N.S.W.
C **T H**	R. W. Corney, Tulse Hill, Coleraine	Wannon	VIC.
C T V	Chateau Tahbilk Co., Tahbilk	North-Eastern District	VIC.
CUBA	J. McGaw (exors.), Kooba, Darlington Point	Narrandera	N.S.W.
CUDAL **M M**	H. A. Taylor and Co., Cudal, Molong...	Molong... ...	N.S.W.
CUDDELL	Rial Bros., Cuddell, Narrandera	Narrandera	N.S.W.
CUDMORE & SONS **TARA**	Cudmore and Sons, Tara, Saltern	Barcaldine	Q.
CULDABURRA	P. Hillam, Culdaburra, Baroota		S.A.

C

WOOL MARKS.	WOOL GROWERS' NAMES AND ADDRESSES.	PASTORAL DISTRICT.	STATE.
CULGOA W N W	A J.S. Bank, Culgoa, Brewarrina	Brewarrina	N S W.
CULLEN LA PLATA	G. T. Cullen, La Plata, Blackall	Blackall	Q
CUMBAMURRA T R	E. Brown, Cumbamurra, Binalong	Young	N S W.
C U PINE HILLS	E. S. M. Edgar, Pine Hills, Harrow		VIC
CURLUE HILL L MC K	L. McKenna, Curlew Hill, Dunkeld	Hamilton	VIC.
CURNAMONA	Canowie Pastoral Co., Ltd., Curnamona	North-Eastern District	S.A.
CURRAWILLINGHI	Peel River L. and M. Co., Currawillinghi, Hebel	St. George	Q.
CUTHERO J X P	S. Smith, Cuthero, Broken Hill	Menindie	N S.W.
C WARADGERY	G. G. Claughton, Waradgery, Hay	Hay	N.S.W.
CURRAGUNDI	Australian Mercantile and A. Co., Ltd., Curragundi, Moree ...	Moree	N.S.W.
C W C JUNEE	C. W. Crawley, Mount Christo, Junee	Wagga	N.S.W.
C W L & Co COREENA	Coreena Pastoral Co., Coreena, Barcaldine	Barcaldine	Q.
Ⓒ WOGOOLA	Cameron and Clark, Wogoola, Onslow	Onslow	W.A.
C W ROCKY PLAIN	T. W. Beglemann, Rocky Plain, Berridale	Cooma	N S.W.
C W S MUNGADAL	C. W. Simson, Mungadal, Hay	Hay	N.S.W.

C

WOOL MARKS.	WOOL GROWERS' NAMES AND ADDRESSES.	PASTORAL DISTRICT.	STATE.
C W W **BROOMFIELD**	C. W. White, Broomfield, Muswellbrook	Denman	N.S.W.
C X **BULLIO**	W. J. Cordeaux (exors.), Bendooley, Berrima	Berrima	N.S.W.
C X C **LONG PARK**	M. Carroll, Long Park, Boree Creek	Urana	N.S.W.
C X J **WARRADERRY**	W. Jones, junr., Warraderry, Grenfell	Forbes ...	N.S.W.
C Y **2**	C. Young, Hilltop, Garland ...	Carcoar	N.S.W.
C y	The Collaroy Co., Ltd., Collaroy, Merriwa	Merriwa	N.S.W.
C Y **C. OTWAY**	The Collaroy Co., Ltd., Collaroy, Merriwa	Merriwa	N.S.W.
C Y **DOWNS**	E. J. Cary, The Downs, Terry-hie-hie...	Moree ...	N.S.W.
C Y **GOBARRALONG**	J. M. Carberry, Cotway, Gobarralong	Gundagai	N.S.W.
C Y **HILLTOP**	C. M. Young, Hilltop, Garland	Carcoar	N.S.W.
C Y **LAGOON CREEK**	N. Carberry, Lagoon Creek, Gobarralong	Gundagai	N.S.W.

D

WOOL MARKS.	WOOL GROWERS' NAMES AND ADDRESSES.	PASTORAL DISTRICT.	STATE.
D	H. C. Taylor, Dobikin, Woolabra	Narrabri	N.S.W.
] D	A. Downward, Mornington ...	Eastern District	VIC.
D A B GUNDAGAI	D. and A. McGruer, Dobikin, Woolabra	Narrabri	N.S.W.
DAGWORTH	Manager Dagworth Resumption, Winton	Winton...	Q.
DAIRY PARK	Mrs. S. M. Molloy, Dairy Park, Mandurama	Carcoar	N.S.W.
DAISY PLAINS	E. Rees, Daisy Plains, Booligal	Balranald	N.S.W.
DALBY DOWNS D D	Queensland Cattle Co., Dalby Downs, Dalby	Dalby	Q.
DALNESS	D. McKinnon, Dalness, Evandale	Evandale	TAS.
D A POMEROY	A. A. Dalgleish, Pomeroy, Woore	Goulburn	N.S.W.
DALYENONG C	Cameron Bros., Dalyenong, Emu Railway Station		VIC.
D A MORTAT	T. Robertson and Brothers, Mortat, Goroke	W. Wimmera	VIC.
DANEDITE	J. H. Hindlaugh, Danedite, Weerite ...		VIC.
DANEDITE M	J. H. Hindlaugh, Danedite, Weerite		VIC.
DANGELONG	G. King and Co., Dangelong, Cooma ...	Cooma ...	N.S.W.
DARBALARA W B S	W. B. Smith, Darbalara, Gundagai	Gundagai	N.S.W

4

D

WOOL MARKS.	WOOL GROWERS' NAMES AND ADDRESSES.	PASTORAL DISTRICT.	STATE.
DARLING TALGAI DOWNS	Queensland Cattle Co., Talgai, Clifton	Warwick	Q.
DARR RIVER DOWNS	Taylor, Fiskin and Co., Darr River Downs, Muttaburra	Muttaburra	Q.
DAVIS BROS SPRING CREEK	Davis Bros., Spring Creek, Cootamundra	Young ...	N.S.W.
D B	Dennis and Wettenhall, Woorneoort ...	...	VIC.
DB	Dawson Bros., Glenlea, Condobolin	Condobolin	N.S.W.
D B	Doyle Bros., Muckerawa, Brewarrina...	Brewarrina	N.S.W.
D BANEEDA	R. Donaldson, Baneeda, Tambo	Tambo ...	Q.
D B G BERKELEY	D. B. Girst, Berkeley, Richmond	Hughenden	Q.
D 5 B NOORINDOO	A. A. Dangar, Noorindoo, Surat	Surat ...	Q.
D. BROS K	Daniel Bros., Kulpara	Kulpara	S.A.
D. BROS Mᵀ ELGIN	C. Dahlenburg, Mt. Elgin, Nhill	Wimmera	VIC.
D B T B T	D. B. Foster, Wombat, Young	Young ...	N.S.W.
D C	D. Clancy, Henty, Albury	Albury ...	N.S.W.
D C ARARAT	D. Canty, Ararat	Western District...	VIC.
D C AVOCA	A. D. Vanrenem, Avoca Forest, Logan		VIC.

D

WOOL MARKS.	WOOL GROWERS' NAMES AND ADDRESSES.	PASTORAL DISTRICT	STATE.
D C **BOWAKA**	H. G. Nosworthy, Bowaka, Lucindale...	Lucindale	S.A.
D C & C **OAKDALE**	D. C. Dearman, Oakdale, Way	Way	S.A.
D C **DUNAN**	D. Cameron, Dunan, Henty ...	Western District...	VIC.
D C **MOREDUN**	D. Cregan, Moredun, Ben Lomond	Armidale	N.S.W.
D & Co **DEEP WATER**	Macansh, Windeyer and Cadell, Deepwater, Tenterfield	Tenterfield	N.S.W.
D C & S F **REDCLIFFE**	Docker, Clark and Smith, Redcliffe, Hughenden	Hughenden	Q.
D C **ST ANDREW PARK**	D. Campbell, St. Andrew Park, Coonamble	Coonamble	N.S.W.
D C **S** **TANGLEY**	J. Stewart, Tangley, Guyra ...	Armidale	N.S.W.
D **CULLENGORAL**	A. M. Rouse, Cullengoral, Gulgong	Mudgee	N.S.W.
D D & Co **KERRIBREE**	A. & N.Z.M. Co., Ltd., Kerribree, Ford's Bridge	Bourke...	N.S.W.
D D **C** **ROSEVALE**	A. Dalziel, Rosevale, Louther	Bathurst	N.S.W.
D D **KARA**	Donelan Bros., Kara, Western District	Western District...	VIC.
D D & W L Co **AYRSHIRE DOWNS**	Darling Downs and Western Land Co., Ayrshire Downs, Winton	Winton ..	Q.
D D & W L Co **JIMBOUR**	Darling Downs and Western Land Co., Jimbour, Macalister	Dalby	Q.
D D & W L Co **WESTLAND**	Darling Downs and Western Land Co., Westland, Longreach ...	Longreach	Q.

D

WOOL MARKS.	WOOL GROWERS' NAMES AND ADDRESSES.	PASTORAL DISTRICT.	STATE.
DECAMERON	W. Williamson (exors.), Elmhurst	Western District ..	VIC.
DEEPDENE	O. S. Scale, Yea, Anglesey ...	Anglesey	VIC.
DELATITE R I C	E. H. McCartney, Delatite, Mansfield...	North-Eastern District	VIC.
DELEGATE $\overline{\text{WW}}$	J. and A F. Jeffreys, Delegate Station, Delegate	Bombala	N.S.W
DELLAPOOL	H. W. Stanghton, Dellapool, Narrandera	Narrandera	N.S.W.
D E McL GLENELG	D. E. McLaughton, Glenelg, Adelaide		S.A.
DENILIQUIN PARK T MILLEAR	T. Millear (exors.), Wanganella Estate, Deniliquin	Deniliquin	N.S.W.
DERRA	Capel Bros., Derra Derra, Bingara ...	Warialda	N.S.W.
DERRENGULLEN YASS	A. F. Lloyd, Derrengullen, Yass	Yass	N.S.W.
DERRINAL	A. Chisholm, Derrinal, Camperdown	Camperdown ...	VIC.
DERRYMORE	T. Dwyer, Derrymore, Young	Young ..	N.S.W.
D E S MOORAMONG	D. E. Stoddart, Mooramong, Skipton ..	Western District	VIC.
DEVON PARK	J. White, Devon Park, Dunkeld	Western District...	VIC.
D F	D. Fraser, Eulo, Darlington Point ...	Narrandera	N.S W.
D F ✳	R. and D. Ferguson, Flowerdale, Broadford ...	North-Eastern District	VIC.

D

WOOL MARKS.	WOOL GROWERS' NAMES AND ADDRESSES.	PASTORAL DISTRICT.	STATE.
D F D	D. F. Dunnett, Penong, Denial Bay	Denial Bay	S A.
D F **F** **FOR GLEN**	Messrs. Finlayson, Forglen, Armidale	Armidale	N.S.W.
D F **GOLDEN VALLEY**	D. Flannery, Golden Valley, Burrowa	Young ...	N.S.W.
D H P **WIRRILLA**	D. H. Power, Wirrilla, Manoora	Manoora	S A.
DILLALAH	W. Peterson (exors.), Dillalah, Charleville	Charleville ...	Q.
DIMORA	T. F. Knox, Dimora, Richmond	Hughenden	Q.
DINBY	C. E. Taylor, Dinby, Baradine	Pilliga	N.S.W.
DINGI DINGI	S. F. Gentle, Dingi Dingi, Stockinbingal	Wagga ...	N.S.W.
D I W **GOWANG**	D. I. Watt, Gowang, Coolah	Coonabarabran	N.S.W.
D I W **ULINDA**	D. I. Watt, Ulinda, Coolah ...	Coonabarabran	N.S.W.
D I W **YARRAGRIN**	D. I. Watt, Yarragrin, Coolah	Coonabarabran	N.S.W.
D **ſ** **DILGA**	D. Johnson, junr., Dilga, Molong	Molong	N.S.W.
D JH **MIDDALYA**	D. J. Hearman, Middalya, via Carnarvon	Carnarvon	W.A.
D J **NEW ENG**	L. Jurd, Bundarra, Armidale	Armidale	N.S.W.
D L **BALMAIN**	D. J. Lowe, Balmain, Grauan	Warialda	N.S.W.

D

WOOL MARKS.	WOOL GROWERS' NAMES AND ADDRESSES.	PASTORAL DISTRICT.	STATE.
D L **CALOOLA**	R. G. Hassall, Caloola, Braidwood	Braidwood	N.S.W.
D L **EUROKA**	Dalgety and Co., Ltd., Euroka, Walgett	Walgett	N.S.W.
D L **LUMLEY**	D. Leahy, Lumley Park, Bungendore...	Goulburn	N.S.W.
CL **MYALL PARK**	S. Donaldson, Myall Park, Gunnedah...	Tamworth ...	N.S.W.
D L N **MUNDINE**	P. Dillon, Mundine, Boggabilla	Warialda ...	N.S.W.
D M	D. Mairs, Balnarring, Mornington	Mornington	VIC.
◇**D**◇ **MADERTY**	T. Dean, Maderty, Coonabarabran	Coonabarabran ...	N.S.W.
D & M **BULGANORAMINE**	J. D. Mackay, Bulganoramine, Tomingley	Dubbo ...	N.S.W.
D McD **MIDDLE CREEK**	D. McDonald, Middle Creek...		VIC.
D M K	D. Cameron, Buddah Park, Trangie ...	Dubbo ..	N.S.W.
CM **KAYUGA**	D Macintyre, Kayuga, Muswellbrook	Murrurundi	N.S.W.
D M K **PIBBON**	C. McKellar, Pibbon, Mundooran	Coonabarabran	N S.W.
D + M **TERICA**	R. McLeod, Terica, Stanthorpe	Stanthorpe	Q.
D M **MAC VILLE**	D. McAlary, Macville, Warren	Coonamble ...	N.S.W.
D M P	J. McPherson, Springfields, Bundilla ...	Coonamble ...	N.S.W.

D

| --- | --- | --- | --- |
D **MUCKERAWA**	Doyle Bros., Muckerawa, Brewarrina	Brewarrina	N.S.W.
D O B **WHEEO**	J. A. Crow, Glenfernie, Wheeo	Yass	N.S.W.
D **O M**	D. O Mahoney, Trowel Creek, Nyngan	Cobar ...	N.S.W.
D **OMEO**	E O'Rourke, Omeo, Benambra	Benambra	VIC.
DON	E. D. Donkin, Mandama, Temora	Wagga ..	N.S.W.
DOOGALOOK	Hamilton Bros., Doogalook, Homewood	Homewood	VIC.
2 **DOOGALOOK**	Hamilton Bros., Doogalook, Homewood	Homewood	VIC.
DOONA	Mrs. Boyd, Doona, Yerong Creek	Wagga... ...	N.S.W.
DOWNIE	J. Downie, Glenelg, Macquarie Plains	Macquarie	TAS.
D P	Manager, Bowman's Forest	North-Eastern District	VIC.
D & P	W. Duffield (exors.), Koonoona, Kooringa	Kooringa ...	S.A.
D P **GREENBANK**	Prowse Bros., Greenbank, Adelong	Gundagai ...	N.S.W.
D P K O **WARRANA**	D. P. Keogh (exors.), Warrana, Coonamble	Coonamble ...	N.S.W.
D R	D. Ross, Forest Vale, via Wellington ..	Dubbo	N.S.W.
D R **B**	D. Rankin, Pineleigh, Bungarby	Cooma ..	N.S.W.

D

WOOL MARKS.	WOOL GROWERS' NAMES AND ADDRESSES.	PASTORAL DISTRICT.	STATE.
D R BLACKWOOD	R. Ritchie, Blackwood, Penshurst	Western District	VIC.
D R LYSTER FIELD	Roach Bros., Lysterfield, Coolamon	Wagga...	N.S.W.
D ROSEDALE	D. Dawson, Rosedale, Moree	Moree ...	N.S.W.
DROUBALGIE MB	Martin Bros., Droubalgie, Forbes	Forbes ...	N.S.W.
D S GLENORCHY	D. Swan, Glenorchy, Inverell	Glen Innes	N.S.W.
D S KANGIARA	D Stewart, Kangiara, Tangmangaroo	Yass	N.S.W.
D S W KILCUMMIN	Australian Estates and Mortgage Co., Ltd., Kilcummin, Clermont	Clermont	Q.
D S W TERRICK	Australian Estates and Mortgage Co., Ltd., Terrick Terrick, Blackall	Blackall	Q.
ɑT	T. Donoghue, Summer Hill, Burragorang	Picton ...	N.S.W.
D T C	G. Chirnside, Werribee	Werribee	VIC.
D T N	H. Dutton, Anlaby Estate, Kapunda	Kapunda ...	S.A.
DUERAN	D. Mitchell, Dueran, Mansfield	Eastern District	VIC.
DUNGALEAR	J. A. Campbell, Dungalear, Walgett ...	Walgett ...	N.S.W.
DUNRAVEN	Coldham Bros., Dunraven, Saltern	Barcaldine ...	Q.
DUNROBIN	W. R. M. Bethune, Dunrobin, Ouse ...	Ouse ...	TAS.

D

WOOL MARKS.	WOOL GROWERS' NAMES AND ADDRESSES.	PASTORAL DISTRICT.	STATE.
DUNROBIN A S M	A. S. M. Dunrobin, Casterton	Western District	VIC.
DURHAM COURT B NSW	W. Baldwin, Durham Court, Mandla	Tamworth	N.S.W.
DURHAM DOWNS	Flower Bros., Durham Downs, Yeulba	Roma	Q.
D V S PUEN BUEN	J. H. Davis, Puen Buen, Scone	Murrurundi	N.S.W.
D V S TUREE VALE	J. H. Davis, Turee Vale, Cassilis	Merriwa	N.S.W.
D WERRINA	M. Doyle, Werrina, Moree	Moree ...	N.S.W.
D WINTON	Doyle Bros., Winton	Winton...	Q.
D W WURROIT	R. Whitehead, Wurroit, Warrnambool	Western District...	VIC.
D W NEW ENGLAND	D. Williams and Sons, Reedy Creek, Boorolong	Armidale	N.S.W.
D X M	D. and D. McLeish, Murrindindi, Yea	North-Eastern District	VIC.
D YANKO	Sir S. Wilson (exors.), Yanko, Jerilderie	Jerilderie	N.S.W.
D Y ERINS VALE	Manager, Erin's Vale, Stradbrook		VIC.

WOOL MARKS.	WOOL GROWERS' NAMES AND ADDRESSES.	PASTORAL DISTRICT.	STATE.
E	Barron and Taylor, Cunabunda, Brewarrina	Brewarrina	N.S.W.
E A B NEW ENG	E. A. Barnes, Sunnyside, Woolbrook...	Armidale	N.S.W.
E. A. CREED WARMATTA	Mrs. W. C. Creed, Warmatta, Berrigan	Jerilderie	N.S.W.
E & A C WILGA PLAINS	Clemson Bros., Wilga Plains, Condobolin	Condobolin	N.S.W.
EAGLES NEST	J. Howard, Eagle's Nest, Carnsdale ...	Albury ...	N.S.W.
E A H EVERMORE	E. A. Holcombe, Evermore, Wee Waa	Pilliga ...	N.S.W.
EAST LODDON (blue)	J. Ettersbank, East Loddon, Serpentine Creek...	Central District ...	VIC.
E A S NARROOGAL	E. A. Smith, Narroogal, Wellington ...	Molong...	N.S.W.
m B E B B F F G	J. Smith, Allowrie, Cullinga .. Eve Brothers, Woolscourers, Botany	Young ...	N.S.W N.S.W.
E B BINALONG	E. Brown, Cumbamurra, Binalong	Young	N.S.W.
E . B KULPARA	E. Brooks, Kulpara	Kulpara	S.A.
E B N	E. B. Nosk, Montajup	Western District	VIC.
E B N MANILLA	Barling Bros., Manilla, Upper Manilla	Tamworth	N.S.W.
ɘ B PASCOE VALE	G. Bull and Sons, Pascoe Vale, Booroopki	Western District...	VIC.

E

WOOL MARKS.	WOOL GROWERS' NAMES AND ADDRESSES.	PASTORAL DISTRICT.	STATE.
E B R	Evans Bros., Redcamp	North-Eastern District	VIC.
E B WOOLOOGA	E. Booker, Woolooga, Gympie	Gympie	Q.
E C BEVLY	E Clemeshaw, Beverley, Yarraman	Tamworth	N.S.W.
E C & Co BIMBAH	R. H. Edkins, Bimbah, Longreach	Longreach ...	Q.
E C & Co BIMBAH ILFRACOMBE	Edkins, Campbell and Co., Bimbah, Longreach	Longreach	Q.
ECHO HILLS	W. J. Reid (exors.), Echo Hills, Moonbi	Tamworth	N.S.W.
E C MONTANA	Miss M. Clark, Montana, Carcoar	Carcoar ...	N.S.W.
E C NEW ENGLAND	E. Cahill, Salisbury Plains, Uralla	Armidale	N.S.W.
E D	E. Dowling, Ross ...	Ross	T.AS.
EDDINGTON	N.Z. & A. Land Co., Ltd., Eddington, Richmond	Hughenden	Q.
EDGAR	Edgar Bros., Harrow	Western District	VIC.
EDGARLEY	T. Millear, Edgarley, Wickliffe Road		VIC.
EDGECOMBE	J. Cruise, Edgcombe, Berrigan	Jerilderie	N.S.W.
E E	T. Shaw, Camperdown	Western District	W.A.
m E 3 w REDBANK	E. Francis, Redbank, Strathford	Gippsland	VIC.

WOOL MARKS.	WOOL GROWERS' NAMES AND ADDRESSES.	PASTORAL DISTRICT.	STATE.
EEYEUK	A. Dennis, Eeyeuk, Kolora		VIC.
EGAN **Z**	J. Egan, Bonegilla	North-Eastern District	VIC.
E G B	Sweeney Bros. and Connor, Alberton, Gippsland	Gippsland	VIC.
E G B **BEXLEY**	E. G. Blume, Bexley, Longreach	Longreach	Q.
E G H **POMONA**	E. G. Harvey, Pomona, Wellington	Dubbo	N.S.W.
E H **C**	E. Hain, Hainfield, Cooma	Cooma ...	N.S.W.
E H **CARABOBOLA**	T. A. Heriot (exors.), Carabobola, Culcairn	Hume ...	N.S.W.
E H **INNISFAIL**	E. Hill, Innisfail, Longwood	North-Eastern District	VIC.
E H **T**	E. H. Turner, Wooloowarree, Gunning	Yass	N.S.W.
E H T & Co **BATHURST**	E. H. Treweeke (exors.), Clifton Grove, Orange	Bathurst	N.S.W.
E H ♡ **THUGGA**	J. W. E. Heriot, Thugga, Germanton...	Hume ...	N.S.W.
E H **WATTLE** **GROVE**	L. Howard, Wattle Grove, Judd's Creek	Bathurst	N.S.W.
E J **CADOW**	Jones Bros., Cadow, Warroo	Forbes	N.S.W.
E J L **BERRIWA**	E. J. Lowe, Berriwa, Gulgong	Mudgee	N.S.W.
E J L **MYALLS**	C. Lloyd, Myalls, Coonamble	Coonamble	N.S.W.

WOOL MARKS.	WOOL GROWERS' NAMES AND ADDRESSES.	PASTORAL DISTRICT.	STATE.
E J R	E. J. Rogers, Charlotte West, Brisbane	Brisbane	Q.
E K	E. A. Kinsey, Barrie Park, Moama	Deniliquin	N.S.W.
E K BOWEN PARK	Mrs. E. Kearney, Cudal, Forbes	Forbes	N.S.W.
E K N	Hon. C. Young, Nymagee, Hillston	Hillston	N.S.W.
E L B	J. M. McBride, Kooringa	Kooringa	S.A.
ELDER	N. G. Elder, The Meadows, Rokewood	Rokewood	VIC.
ELDERSLIE	Robertson Bros., Elderslie, Apsley	North-Western District	VIC.
ELLANGOWAN DARLING DOWNS	A.S. & A. Bank, Ltd., Ellangowan, Clifton	Warwick	Q.
ELLISVALE S.B WHEEO	Sullivan Bros., Ellisvale, Wheeo	Yass	N.S.W.
ELMINA F 7 ⊁	Fletcher Bros., Elmina, Morven	Bollon ...	Q.
ELSINORA ✝ THURLOE DOWNS	Goldsbrough, Mort and Co., Ltd., Elsinora, Wannaring	Wannaring	N.S.W.
ELVERSTON F ⊂ 7	J. Rooks, Elverston, Charleville	Charleville	Q.
E M B WARGUNDY	Bowman Bros., Wargundy, Gulgong	Mudgee	N.S.W.
ƎM COLLINGWOOD	E. Murphy, Collingwood, Cullinga	Young	N.S.W.
EMILY PARK	J. and F. G. Coleman, Emily Park, Ben Lomond	Glen Innes	N.S.W.

WOOL MARKS.	WOOL GROWERS' NAMES AND ADDRESSES.	PASTORAL DISTRICT.	STATE.
E M MUNGIE	Miss E. A O'Mara, Mt. Pleasant, Delegate	Cooma	N.S.W.
E. MORRIS KAPPAWANTA	T. Morris, Kappawanta, Way	Way	S.A.
EMU PLAINS URANA	Mrs. E. Wakeley, Emu Plains, Urana	Urana	N.S.W.
E NARRAGOLONG	E. Hallam, Narragolong, Dalton	Yass	N.S.W.
ш NARRAGOLONG	E. Hallam, Narragolong, Dalton	Yass	N.S.W.
E N BLYTHEWOOD	E. Nixon, Blythewood, Wallabadah	Tamworth	N.S.W.
E N DUNDEE	E. White, Dundee Vale, Wandsworth	Armidale	N.S.W.
ENGLEFIELD	Chrystal and Gotch, Englefield, Balmoral	Western District	VIC.
E. NICHOLAS	G. Nicholas, Cawood, Ouse	Ouse	TAS.
ENNERDALE	J. Robertson, Ennerdale, Streatham	...	VIC.
E N TIARA	E. Norton, Tiara, Walcha	Armidale	N.S.W.
ENSAY	T. McHamilton, Ensay, N. Gippsland	Gippsland	VIC.
E O PALESTHAN	E. J. Owen, Palesthan, Condobolin	Condobolin	N.S.W.
E PARR	E. Parr, Graman, Warialda	Warialda	N.S.W.
E P B GULLY PLAINS	E. P. Berriman, Gully Plains, Moira	Deniliquin	N.S.W.

WOOL MARKS.	WOOL GROWERS' NAMES AND ADDRESSES.	PASTORAL DISTRICT.	STATE.
E P N	P. Nobelly, Baradine, Coonabarabran	Coonabarabran	N.S.W.
(ER)	E. Reseigh, Avon Plains	Western District	VIC.
ERAMBIE	G. H. Hebden, Erambie, Molong	Molong	N.S.W.
EREMERAN	Goldsbrough, Mort and Co., Ltd., Eremeran and Dine Dine, Nymagee ...	Condobolin	N.S.W.
E R LOGAN	H. Reid, Logan, Evandale	Evandale	TAS.
ERROWANBANG	G. and C. Hebden, Errowanbang, Carcoar	Carcoar	N.S.W.
ERUDINA	W. H. James, Erudina	Erudina	S.A.
ESDAILE J H E	J. H. Edwards, Esdaile, Clear Lake		VIC.
E S DRYSDALE EUROA	E. S. Drysdale, Euroa, Ballangeich	North-Eastern District	VIC.
E SILVERWOOD	E. G. Edgar, Silverwood, Kar's Springs	Merriwa	N.S.W.
E & S PINE DEANE	D. Pabot, Pine Deane, The Rock	Wagga ...	N.S.W.
E S YARRAN PARK	F. J. Smith, Yarran Park, Whitton	Narrandera	N.S.W.
E T LANGULAC	E. Twomey, Langulac, Penshurst	Western District	VIC.
ETONA Q,LAND	W. Cumming, Etona, Morven	Morven ...	Q.
ETTRICK	H. Duff and Co., Ettrick, Condon	Condon.	W.A.

WOOL MARKS.	WOOL GROWERS' NAMES AND ADDRESSES.	PASTORAL DISTRICT.	STATE.
ETTRICK	J. McLarty, Ettrick, Heywood	Western District	VIC.
EULONG	J. Rand, Eulong, Forbes	Forbes ...	N.S.W.
EURABBA	J. Hitchens, Eurabba, Moree	Moree	N.S.W.
EURACK	R. B. Chirnside, Mount Rothwell, Little River...	Western District	VIC.
EURAMBEEN	Beggs Brothers, Eurambeen	Western District	VIC.
EURAMBEEN EAST	F. Beggs, Eurambeen East, Beaufort...	Western District	VIC.
EUREKA	H. Hughes, Eureka, Quondong, Broken Hill	Menindie	N.S.W.
EURELLA FITZROY DOWNS	F. Dunsmuir, Eurella, Fitzroy Downs	Roma	Q.
EURIE EURIE NAMOI	T. A. Sturton, Eurie Eurie, Walgett ..	Walgett	N.S.W.
EURIMBLA	W. Rutter, senr., Eurimbla, Cumnock	Molong	N.S.W
EURIMBURRA S . H B	S. H. Belcher, Eurimburra, Reid's Flat ...	Carcoar	N.S.W.
EUROKA	Dalgety and Co., Ltd., Sydney		N.S.W.
EUSTON	W. Taylor, Euston, Balranald	Balranald	N S.W
EVANS	R. Francis, Evans, Hamilton	Hamilton	TAS.
E V CONJI	E. Vickery and Sons, Conji, Walcha Road	Armidale	N.S.W.

E

WOOL MARKS.	WOOL GROWERS' NAMES AND ADDRESSES.	PASTORAL DISTRICT.	STATE.
E V **KANIMBLA**	E. Vickery and Sons, Kanimbla, Little Hartley	Bathurst	N.S.W.
E V **MUNGYER**	E. Vickery and Sons, Mungyer, Millie	Moree	N.S.W.
E V **NEW ENG**	E. Vickery and Sons, Conji, Walcha Road	Armidale	N.S.W.
E V **NOWLEY**	E. Vickery and Sons, Nowley, Narrabri	Pilliga ...	N.S.W.
E W **MARKDALE**	Julia Wells, Markdale, Binda	Carcoar	N.S.W.
E W & N **N**	E. and W. Naughton, Deniliquin	Deniliquin	N.S.W.
E Y N	T. Staughton (exors.), Melton, Bacchus Marsh	Central District ...	VIC.

F

WOOL MARKS.	WOOL GROWERS' NAMES AND ADDRESSES.	PASTORAL DISTRICT.	STATE.
◇F◇	G. H. Armytage, Balmoral	Western District...	VIC.
F 2	M. Fitzpatrick, Wattle Vale, Kobyboyn	North-Eastern District	VIC.
F A F M. CAMP	F. A. Fernor, Main Camp, Rouchel	Murrurundi	N.S.W.
F & A G MOREE	F. and A. Glennie, Norwood, Moree	Moree ...	N.S.W.
FAIRFIELD	J. E. Shephard, Fairfield, Carnsdale ...	Albury ...	N.S.W.
FAIRGRASS	S. Brien, Fairgrass, Freshwater Creek	Western District	VIC.
FAIRLIE D M B GRANGE	D. McBean, Fairleigh Grange, Jerilderie	Jerilderie	N.S.W.
FAMILY HOME	J. Theeuf and Sons, Family Home, Hughenden	Hughenden	Q.
F A NARADA	F. Armitage, Narada, Anakie		VIC.
F B B BEENAH	F. B. Bloomfield, Beenah, Canonbar	Canonbar	N.S.W.
F B Mt H	F. Broadribb, Mount Hope, Ladysmith	Wagga	N.S.W.
F BROS BENDENINE	Friend Bros., Bendenine, Binalong	Young ...	N.S.W.
F BROS COLANE	Fisher Bros., Colane, Canonbar	Canonbar	N.S.W.
F BROS MERRIMBA	J. W. Fisher, Merrimba, Warren	Coonamble	N.S.W.
F. BROS WILLAWA	G. Flynn, Willawa, Carinda...	Walgett	N.S.W.

F

WOOL MARKS.	WOOL GROWERS' NAMES AND ADDRESSES.	PASTORAL DISTRICT.	STATE.
F B S KABELLA	F. B. Suttor, Kabella, Stuart Town	Molong...	N S.W.
F B S REDBANK	F. B. Suttor, Redbank, Stuart Town ...	Molong...	N.S.W.
F B TALLAGEIRA	Fraser Bros., Tallageira, Francis	Francis	S.A.
F C C PIEDMONT	Capel Bros., Piedmont, Cobbadah	Warialda	N.S.W.
F C SHEPTON HILL	F. Chasey (exors.), Shepton Hill, Happy Valley	Grenville	VIC.
F DALMALLY	D. Fletcher, Dalmally, Cooinda and Brucedale, Roma	Roma ...	Q.
F D SHEEP STATION	P. Dwyer, Sheep Station Creek, Binalong	Young ...	N.S.W.
F E MERRIWA	G. Evans, Merriwa, Boggabilla	Warialda	N.S.W.
FERNLEE	Scottish-Australian Investment Co., Fernlee, Bollon	Bollon	Q.
F F RIVER VIEW	D. Findlayson and Bros., Riverview, Oban	Glen Innes	N.S.W.
F F WOOLBROOK	F. W. Fairbairne, Woolbrook, Teesdale	Western District	VIC.
F G	F. F. Gibson, Caragabal, Grenfell	Forbes	N.S.W.
F GLENORCHY	D. Swan, Glenorchy, Inverell	Glen Innes	N.S.W.
F G PRESTON	F. C. Griffen, Preston, Mansfield	North-Eastern District	VIC.
F H B T RAINWORTH	F. H. B. Turner, Rainworth, Springsure	Springsure	Q

F

WOOL MARKS.	WOOL GROWERS' NAMES AND ADDRESSES.	PASTORAL DISTRICT.	STATE.
F H C TARA	F. H. Cornish, Tara, Brewarrina	Brewarrina	N.S.W.
F H DUNGOWAN	J. and D. Maher, Dungowan Creek, Dungowan	Tamworth	N.S.W.
F H H CLEAR SPRINGS	F. H. Holman, Clear Springs, Lankey Creek, Germanton	Hume	N.S.W.
(F) **HILLGROVE**	F. J. Fahey, Hillgrove, Burrowa	Young ...	N.S.W.
⟨FH⟩ **MERINO DOWNS**	H. McLeod and Hindson, Merino Downs, Henty	Western District	VIC.
FIELD GARVAN PARK	R. Field (exors.), Garvan Park, Avoca	North-Western District	VIC.
F & J G ALAGALA	F. J. Gillanders, Alagala, Narromine	Dubbo ...	N.S.W.
F J H MT COOPER	F. J. Hobson, Mt. Cooper, Holt's Flat	Bombala	N.S.W.
F J MOUNT VIEW	F. Johns, Mount View, Hillston	Hillston	N.S.W.
⌐ᒣ	G. M. Finlay, Thornthwaite, Scone	Murrurundi	N.S.W.
F L BUNDARBO	F. Lenane, Mount Pleasant, Dudauman	Young	N.S.W.
FLEMING BROS DOREEN	Fleming Bros., Doreen, Narrabri	Narrabri	N.S.W.
FLEMINGTON J P J B	J. P. Bell, Flemington, Walgett	Walgett	N.S.W.
F MANSFIELD	J. Forest, Mansfield	North-Eastern District	VIC.
F M MUDGEE	F. McGrath, Highland Home, Mudgee ...	Mudgee	N.S.W.

WOOL MARKS.	WOOL GROWERS' NAMES AND ADDRESSES.	PASTORAL DISTRICT.	STATE.
F M NATIONDALE	F. Myers, Port Elliston, West Coast ...	West Coast	S.A.
F M Y NORTHAMPTON	F. Murphy and Sons, Northampton, Tambo	Tambo ...	Q.
F OBERN	C. D. Bardwell, Obern, Tarcutta	Gundagai	N.S.W.
FONTENOY NEW ENG	J. P. Cunneen, Fontenoy, Walcha Road	Armidale	N.S.W.
FORDON ◇ D C	C. Cameron, Fordon, Evandale	Evandale	TAS.
FORESTFIELD J L	Lockie Bros., Forestfield, Strathdownie	Strathdownie	VIC.
FORESTVALE J X S	J. Snodgrass, Forestvale, Albury Road	Wagga ...	N.S.W.
FORT BOURKE	M. P. Fitzgerald and Co., Bourke	Bourke ...	N.S.W.
FOUR BOB CAMP U B	Union Bank of Australia, Ltd., Four Bob Camp, Condobolin ...	Condobolin	N.S.W.
FOUR MILE CREEK ⌒	Rial Bros., Four Mile Creek, Germanton	Hume ..	N.S.W.
F O X WILBEROI	Fox Bros., Wilberoi, Boggabri	Tamworth	N.S.W.
FRANKFIELD E H	Watson and Johnson, Frankfield, Gunning	Yass	N.S.W.
℞ COLLINGWOOD	D. Fletcher, Bolagula, Coonamble	Coonamble	N.S.W.
F R M NEW ENG	F. R. Mackenzie, Green Bank, Ben Lomond	Glen Innes	N.S.W.
FRODSLEY	T. H. Parker, Frodsley, Fingal	Fingal ...	TAS

WOOL MARKS.	WOOL GROWERS' NAMES AND ADDRESSES.	PASTORAL DISTRICT.	STATE.
F R W HARBEN VALE	R. W. and C. E. White, Harben Vale, Blandford	Murrurundi ...	N.S.W.
F & R. W. KIRBY	F. and R. W. Kirby, Frankestone, Collarendabri	Walgett	N.S.W.
F R W MIHI	R. W. C. E. and J. H. White, Rockwood, Uralla	Armidale ...	N.S.W.
F&S GLENBROOK	Fazakerley and Shepherd, Woolscourers, Botany		N.S.W.
F S R WALCHA	F. Schrader, Walcha, Armidale	Armidale ..	N.S.W.
F SWAMP OAK	W. T. Lee, Swamp Oak, Limbri	Tamworth	N.S.W.
F S WHEEO	Bank of N.S.W., Wheeo, Yass	Yass	N.S.W.
F U DUNDEE	E. White, Dundee Vale, Wandsworth	Armidale	N.S.W.
FURRACABAD H L Co LTD	The Haymarket Land Co., Ltd., Furracabad, Glen Innes	Glen Innes ...	N.S.W.
F W A	F. W. Armytage, Woolamanuter, Lara	Geelong	VIC
F W A NOCOLECHE	F. W. Armytage, Nocoleche, Wanaaring	Wanaaring ...	N.S.W.
F W B D	F. W. Bacon, Dumble, Goodooga	Brewarrina ...	N.S.W.
F W B DUMBLE	F. W. Bacon, Dumble, Goodooga	Brewarrina ...	N.S.W.
F W B DUMBLE LAKESIDE	F. W. Bacon, Dumble, Goodooga	Brewarrina	N.S.W.
F W K EWENMAR	F. Knynett, Ewenmar, Trangie	Dubbo	N.S.W.
F W MULLION	C. W. Walker, Ledgerton, Yass	Yass	N.S.W.
F W R	F. W. Rynill, Winmininnie ...	Winmininnie	S.A.

G

WOOL MARKS.	WOOL GROWERS' NAMES AND ADDRESSES.	PASTORAL DISTRICT.	STATE.
G A	Mrs. E. G. Ashwin, Capel's Crossing ...	North-Eastern District	VIC.
G (in circle)	J. Green, Bordertown	Bordertown	S.A.
G A H UKOLAN	G. A. Higgins, Ukolan, Manilla	Tamworth	N.S.W.
G A L	H. Jugall and Sons, Inglewood, Wallabadah	Tamworth	N.S.W.
GALA	E. Currie, Gala, Lismore	Lismore	VIC.
GALONG Y N	M. Hickey, Galoog, Galong	Young . .	N.S.W.
GAMBOOLA	W. A. Smith (exors.), Gamboola, Molong	Molong...	N.S.W.
7 GAPP CREEK	A. A. Huggins, Omeo, Gippsland	Gippsland	VIC.
C A P WEEBO	G. A. Patterson c/o Bank of N.S.W , Sydney		N.S.W.
GARANGULA	J. W. and A. W. Macansh, Garangula, Murrumburrah ...	Young	N.S.W.
G A R HOWLONG	Johnson and Vickars, Woolscourers, Sydney		N.S.W.
GAZETTE	Cross and Co., Gazette, Penshurst	Western District...	VIC.
G B ADAVALE	Goldsbrough, Mort and Co., Ltd., Adavale, Parkes	Forbes ...	N.S.W.
G BANNOCKBURN	Richmond and Scott, Bannockburn, Inverell	Glen Innes	N.S.W.
G B FLORIDA	A.M.L. & F. Co., Ltd., Florida, Nyngan	Cobar	N.S.W.

WOOL MARKS.	WOOL GROWERS' NAMES AND ADDRESSES.	PASTORAL DISTRICT.	STATE.
◇ G B ◇ GLEN GLEESON	Bostock Bros., Glengleeson, Broadwater	Port Fairy ...	VIC.
G B LAURA	G. Baker, Laura, Armidale ...	Armidale	N.S.W.
G B ORRIE COWRIE	G. Brooks, Orrie Cowrie, Warooka	Warooka	S.A.
G B R DANDALOO	G. B. Richardson, Kelvin, Dandaloo	Dubbo	N.S.W.
G B ROSENTHOL	Burgess Bros., Mountside, Dalveen	Warwick	Q.
◇ G B ◇ ROTHERWOOD	Bowman Bros., Rotherwood, Tarago	Goulburn	N.S.W.
◇ G - B ◇ TERRIE-HIE-HIE	J. R. Black and Co., Terrie-Hie-Hie, Moree	Moree	N S.W.
◇ G ◇ BUNDALEER	C. R. Goode, Bundaleer, Jamestown	Jamestown	S.A.
◇ G CO ◇	L. McBean Grant (exors.), Butherwah, Urana	Urana ..	N.S.W.
G C COVE	G. Carmichael, Cove, Dinyarrak	...	VIC.
G C CUDGELO	Mrs. Campbell, Cudgelo, Cowra	Carcoar ...	N.S.W.
G C DUNTROON	G. Campbell (exors.), Duntroon, Queanbeyan	Queanbeyan	N.S.W.
G C F BURRUMBEEP	G. C. Forbes (exors.), Burrumbeep, Maroona	Ararat	VIC.
G C JERULA	Mrs. J. B. Campbell, Jerula, Cowra ...	Carcoar ...	N.S.W.

G

WOOL MARKS.	WOOL GROWERS' NAMES AND ADDRESSES.	PASTORAL DISTRICT.	STATE.
G C HAZEL GREEN	G. Cook, Hazel Green, Wandsworth	Glen Innes	N.S.W.
G C ROSEBROOK	Carter Bros., Rosebrook, Horsham	Western District	VIC.
G C & S ♡ ELLERSLIE	G. Coutts and Sons, Ellerslie, Fernihurst	North-Eastern District	VIC.
G C STRATHDOWNIE	A. H. Brown, Strathdownie		VIC.
G C WAKEFIELD	G. Croxon, Wakefield, Isisford	Isisford	Q.
G D B MYALL	G. D. Boyle, Myall Lake, Mundi, Menindie	Menindie	N.S.W.
G D HAZELDELL	C. and J. Dennis, Hazeldell, Temora	Wagga...	N.S.W.
G D N CONMURRA	H. A. Morris, Conmurra, Reedy Creek		S.A.
GEANMONEY	Goldsbrough, Mort and Co., Ltd., Geanmoney, Coonamble	Coonamble	N.S.W.
G E K STONEY CREEK NEW ENG	G. E. Kemp, Stoney Creek, Tingha	Armidale	N.S.W.
GENANAGIE	Watt and Gilchrist, Genanagie, Parkes	Forbes	N.S.W.
GERALDRA	W. H. & G. D. Davidson, Geraldra, Cootamundra	Young	N.S.W.
GERALGAMBETH W P	W. Patterson, Geralgambeth, Harefield	Wagga ...	N.S.W.
G EUSTON	W. Taylor, Euston, Balranald	Balranald	N.S.W.
G F BARCALDINE	Fairbairn Pastoral Co., Barcaldine Downs and Home Creek, Saltern	Barcaldine	Q.

G

WOOL MARKS.	WOOL GROWERS' NAMES AND ADDRESSES.	PASTORAL DISTRICT.	STATE.
G F **BEACONSFIELD**	S. Fairbairn, Beaconsfield, Ilfracombe	Barcaldine	Q.
G F **BIMERAH**	Fairbairn Pastoral Co., Bimerah, Longreach	Longreach	Q.
G F **CORRINGLE**	G. Frost, Corringle, Mewburn	Young	N.S.W.
G F G **MOURA**	G. F. Giles, Moura, Parkes ...	Forbes ...	N.S.W.
G F **LARA**	J. L. Currie, Lara, Camperdown	Camperdown	VIC.
G F **LOGAN DOWNS**	F. W. Fairbairn, Logan Downs, Clermont	Clermont	Q.
G F **PEAK DOWNS**	Fairbairn Pastoral Co., Peak Downs, Capella	Clermont	Q.
G F **THIRKELL**	G. F. Thirkell, Darlington Park, Macquarie River		TAS.
G F **WHITEWOOD**	G. G. Fisher, Whitewood, Canonbar	Canonbar	N.S.W.
G F **WOLFGANG**	Fairbairn Pastoral Co., Wolfgang, Nebo	Clermont	Q.
G G **BASIN CREEK**	G. Gollan, Basin Creek, Wallabadah	Tamworth	N.S.W.
G G **BURRANGONG**	Barrett and Melrose, Burrangong, Young	Young ...	N.S.W.
G G **HARROW**	J. M. O'Rourke, Harrow	Western District...	VIC.
G G **MOUNTAIN HOME**	G. Golding, Mountain Home, Forbes	Forbes	N.S.W.
G G **MT CONE**	Gebhardt Bros., Mackerode, Kooringa	Kooringa	S A.

G

WOOL MARKS.	WOOL GROWERS' NAMES AND ADDRESSES.	PASTORAL DISTRICT.	STATE.
G & G **MYALLA**	Glasson and Glasson, Myalla, Woodstock	Carcoar	N.S.W.
G & G **S**	Glasson and Glasson, Stanfield, Carcoar	Carcoar	N.S.W.
G H **APSLEY**	G. Hackett, Apsley, Perth	Bathurst	N.S.W.
G H G **IANDRA**	Hon. G. H. Greene, Iandra, Young	Young ...	N.S.W.
G H G **MT ORIEL**	Hon. G. H. Greene, Mt. Oriel, Young	Young	N.S.W.
G. H. JENKINS **HERBERT PARK** **ARMIDALE** **NEW ENGLAND**	G. H. Jenkins, Herbert Park, Armidale	Armidale	N.S.W.
G & H S **BATHURST**	H. C. Suttor, Brucedale, Peel	Bathurst	N.S.W.
G H & S **BLAINA**	J. A. Hayward, Blaina, Longreach	Longreach	Q.
G & H S **CURRANYALPA**	H. C. Suttor, Curranyalpa, Louth	Cobar	N.S.W.
G H **TYNTYNDER**	Holloway Bros., Tyntynder, Swan Hill	Northern District	VIC.
G H **X**	G. Hunt, Forest Lodge, Wee Waa	Pilliga ...	N.S.W.
G I B	Gibson and Co., Burrumbuttock, Albury	Albury ...	N.S.W.
GIDLEY	W. F. Rutledge, Gidleigh, Bungendore	Queanbeyan	N.S.W.
G I E **OLLERA**	G. J. and E. Everett, Ollera, Guyra	Armidale	N.S.W.
GILL **MOONBI**	R. Gill, Moonbi, Tamworth	Tamworth	N S.W.

G

WOOL MARKS.	WOOL GROWERS' NAMES AND ADDRESSES.	PASTORAL DISTRICT.	STATE.
GINGIE	Richmond and Scott, Gingie, Walgett	Walgett	N.S.W.
G J F QUONDONG	Furner Bros., Quondong, Coolamon	Wagga	N.S.W.
G J M OURA	G. J. Mulholland, Oura, Wagga	Wagga	N.S.W.
G J MYLORA	J. J. Garry, Mylora, Binalong	Young ...	N.S.W.
G. JURD MOREE	G. Jurd, Blairmore, Moree	Moree	N.S.W.
G J WEST QUARTER	G. Johnstone, West Quarter, Augathella	Augathella	Q.
G K	G. Killen, Gunyamma, Moree	Moree	N.S.W.
G K JENNAWARRA	G. Krogen, Jennawarra, Croxton East		VIC.
⟨GL⟩	G. Lee, Merriwee, Condobolin	Condobolin	N.S.W.
G L BEEAC	A. and J. Long, Shatherie, Weering		VIC.
GLEN	J. W. Chisholm, Kobyboyn, ría Seymour	Central District	VIC.
GLENBROOK	J. W. Johnston, Glenbrook, Cooma	Cooma	N.S.W.
GLENCOE	G. C. Coulson, Glencoe, Longford	Gippsland	VIC.
GLENELG W W P	W. W. Priddle, Glenelg, Grenfell	Forbes ...	N.S.W.
GLENETIVE D Mc	D. McCorkindale, Narcen	Western District...	VIC.

WOOL MARKS.	WOOL GROWERS' NAMES AND ADDRESSES.	PASTORAL DISTRICT.	STATE.
GLENFINE	W. I. Rowe, Glenfine, Capellear		VIC.
GLENGOWER	A. Clarke, Glengower, Campbelltown	Central District	VIC.
GLENHOPE	J. Gemmell, Glenhope, Coolamon	Wagga	N.S.W.
GLENHOPE ✹	J. Gemmell, Glenhope, Coolamon	Wagga	N.S.W.
GLEN INNES R A E WILLAROO	A. Rae, Willaroo, Moree	Moree	N.S.W.
GLENISLA J BUTLER	J. Butler, Glenisla, Brimpaen		VIC.
GLENISLA J R S	J. R. Stahorn, Glen Isla, Tomingley	Dubbo	N.S.W.
GLENLOATH	W. Peters, Glenloath Railway Station		VIC.
GLENMORE E E C	E. E. Campbell, Glenmore, Moonan Flat	Murrurundi	N.S.W.
GLENORCHY A J	J. McNichol, Glenorchy, Merino	Western District	VIC.
GLENROCK 9 7	I. Coleman, Glenrock, Gundaroo	Queanbeyan	N.S.W.
GLEN RONALD ✹	The Manager, Glen Ronald, Glenthompson	Western District	VIC.
GLENSLOY A Mc F	J. H. McFarlane, Glensloy, Young	Young	N.S.W.
GLENTREE C N	J. C. Noble, Glentree, Modewarre	...	VIC.
GLENTURRET	W. W. Murray, Glenturret, Truro	Truro	S.A.

WOOL MARKS.	WOOL GROWERS' NAMES AND ADDRESSES.	PASTORAL DISTRICT.	STATE.
GLENVALE	G. T. East, Glenvale, Warwick	Warwick	Q.
GLENWOOD	D. O'Brien, Glenwood, Hawkesdale	Western District...	VIC.
GLENWOOD H S MUDGEE	N. H. Smith, Glenwood, Spicer's Creek	Mudgee	N.S.W.
GLENWYLLYN	D. McKellar, Glenwyllyn, Stawell	Western District...	VIC.
GLENYON	R. McLeod, Glenyon, Stanthorpe	Stanthorpe	Q.
G L G	A. Park (exors.), Klori, Tamworth	Tamworth	N.S.W.
G L G N E	A. Park (exors.), Alexander Park, Longford, Bendemeer	Armidale	N.S.W.
⟨G L⟩ LEEHOLME	G. Lee, Leeholme, Kelso	Bathurst	N.S.W.
G L LORD CLYDE	G. Leishman, Lord Clyde, Ullina	Ullina	VIC.
GLOBE HILL	McRae and Halpen, Globe Hill, Onslow	Onslow ..	W.A.
G L T NAVARRE	G. L. Thompson, Navarre	North-Western District	VIC.
G L WAGRA	G. W. Last, junr., Wagra, Tumut	Gundagai	N.S.W
G MASSY	G. Massy, Burrorumba, Gunderoo	Queanbeyan ...	N.S.W.
G Σ BALD HILL	F. S. Manglesdorf, Bald Hill, North Berry Jerry	Wagga	N.S.W.
G M B NEW ENGLAND	G. Manuel, Beaconsfield, Yarrowyck	Armidale	N.S.W.

G

WOOL MARKS.	WOOL GROWERS' NAMES AND ADDRESSES.	PASTORAL DISTRICT.	STATE.
G M **BURRUM**	G. Maconochie, Burrum	Western District	VIC.
G M **COONAMBLE**	G. Moran, Wentworth, Coonamble	Coonamble	N.S.W.
G M G **GULGO**	D. Scott, Mowabla and Gulgo, Condobolin	Condobolin	N.S.W.
G M **GLENMONA**	G. Mills, Glen Mona, Bung Bong	North-Western District	VIC.
G ⵯ **MORVEN**	J. R. Phillip, Morven, Branxholme	Western District	VIC.
G M **RAVENSWORTH**	W. H. Mackay, Ravensworth Station, Ravensworth	Denman	N.S.W.
G M **ROSEBANK**	G. R. and A. Melrose, Rosebank, Mt. Pleasant .	Mt. Pleasant	S.A.
G M **SWEDES FLAT**	G. Mackin, Swede's Flat, Bordertown	Border District	S.A.
G **MT BATTERY**	J. C. H. Graves, Mt. Battery, Mansfield	North-Eastern District	VIC.
G ⵯ **V ▭**	G. Matchett, Morven and Bald Hills, Grenfell	Forbes ...	N.S.W.
GNALTA	Goldsbrough, Mort and Co., Gnalta, White Cliffs	Wilcannia	N.S.W.
GNARPURT	J. C. Manifold, Gnarpurt, Lismore	Camperdown	VIC.
G N **MANILLA**	G. Nixon, Upper Manilla, Upper Manilla	Tamworth	N.S.W.
GNOTUK	J. H. and G. R. Hope, Gnotuk, Camperdown	Western District . .	VIC.
GOBALG **◇**	M. Carberry, Gobarralong, Wagga	Wagga	N.S.W.

G

WOOL MARKS.	WOOL GROWERS' NAMES AND ADDRESSES.	PASTORAL DISTRICT.	STATE.
GOBBAGUMBALIN A B	A. Booth (exors.), Gobbagumbalin, Wagga	Wagga	N.S.W.
GOBLUP A M N	A. M. Nicolson, Goblup, Broomehill	Broomehill	W.A.
G & O. CULLODEN	Govett and Orr, Culloden, Muttaburra	Muttaburra	Q.
G O DIRNASSEER	G. Osborne, Dirnasseer, Junee Reefs ...	Wagga	N.S.W.
GOGELDRIE	Waugh, Stanbridge and Waugh, Gogeldrie, Whitton	Narrandera	N.S.W.
GOLDEN HILLS	Union Bank of Australia, Golden Hills, Temora	Wagga ...	N.S.W.
GOLDSWORTH V NEW ENG	R. Vickers, Goldsworth, Uralla	Armidale	N.S.W.
GOL GOL	J. H. Patterson, Gol Gol, Balranald	Balranald	N.S.W.
GOOL BURRA J S	J. C. H. Schmidt, Goolburra, Cunnamulla	Cunnamulla	Q.
GOOLGUMBLA	S. McCaughey, Goolgumbla, Jerilderie	Jerilderie ...	N.S.W.
GOOLHI	N.S.W. M. Loan and Agency Co., Ltd., Goolhi, Gunnedah	Tamworth	N.S.W.
GOONAL	Watt and Co., Goonal, Moree	Moree	N.S.W.
GOONOO GOONOO PR L & M C	Peel River L. & M. Co., Ltd., Goonoo Goonoo, Tamworth	Tamworth	N.S.W.
GORDON MANAR	W. F. Gordon, Manar Station, Manar	Braidwood	N.S.W.
GOREE	A. D. and J. Robertson, Goree, Narrandera	Urana	N.S.W.

G

WOOL MARKS.	WOOL GROWERS' NAMES AND ADDRESSES.	PASTORAL DISTRICT.	STATE.
GORIAN	Capel Bros., Gorian, Pilliga ...	Pilliga	N.S.W.
GORRINN	J. and A. Richardson, Gorrinn, Dobie's Bridge ...		VIC.
GOWAN ⟨M⟩	Sutherland and Co., Gowan, Freemantle	Bathurst	N.S.W.
GOWRY H O BURROWA	H. Ovens, Mattarai, Burrowa	Young ...	N.S.W.
G P B NEW ENG	G. Painter, Bundarra, Armidale	Armidale	N.S.W.
G PHELPS LOCHINVAR	G. Phelps, Lochinvar, Pilliga	Pilliga ...	N.S.W.
G P W O B C	G. P. Wilson, Big Springs, Wagga Wagga	Wagga ...	N.S.W.
GRASSDALE	Black Bros. and Smith, Grassdale		VIC.
G ⌣R CASSILIS	G. Piper, Cassilis, Cassilis	Merriwa	N.S.W.
G R BUCKIE	G. Raffan, Buckie, Warialda	Warialda	N.S.W.
GREENBANK H A	H. Albion, Greenbank, Cunnamulla	Cunnamulla	Q.
GREENBANK J C W	J. C. Watson, Greenbank, Young	Young ...	N.S.W.
GREENHILL	A. Anderson, Greenhill, Newlyn	North-Western District	VIC.
GREENHILLS VICTORIA	O'Keefe Bros., Green Hills, Winslow ...	Western District	VIC.
GREEN VALE	W. J. Austin, Green Vale, Wickliffe Road Railway Station ...	Wimmera	VIC.

G

WOOL MARKS.	WOOL GROWERS' NAMES AND ADDRESSES.	PASTORAL DISTRICT.	STATE.
GRENVILLE P P	P. Mullavey, Grenville, Bowna P.O.	Albury ...	N.S.W.
GREYLANDS C R	C. Rhodes, Greylands, Henty	...	VIC.
G R GUNDAROO	Mary Reynolds, Gundarooie, Temora ...	Wagga...	N.S.W.
G R J FERNDALE	G. R. Jackson, Ferndale, Molanga	ria Albury	N.S.W.
G R L Y	J. Simson (exors.), Gurley, Narrabri ...	Narrabri	N.S.W.
GROGAN	J. Cronin, Grogan, Grogan ...	Young ...	N.S.W.
GROGANVILLE W G ?	W. J. Grogan, Groganville, Tangmangaroo	Yass	N.S.W.
GROONGAL	S. R. L. Learmouth, Groongal, Carrathool	Hay	N.S W.
G S F FLODDEN FIELDS	C. G. Smith, Flodden Field, Coonamble	Coonamble	N.S.W.
G S K B K Q'LAND	G. Sinclair, c/o Commercial Bank, Sydney, N.S.W.		N.S W.
G S LONG PLAIN	Sedgwick Bros., Long Plain, Corowa...	Corowa...	N.S.W.
G. SMITH CORNUCOPIA	G. Smith, Cornucopia, Narromine	Dubbo	N.S.W.
G S NEW ENG	G. Smith, Gwydir, Uralla	Armidale ...	N.S.W
G T BLACK SPRINGS	G. Thompson, Black Springs, Cootamundra	Gundagai ...	N.S.W.
G T W	G. T. Woolaston, Somerton, Carroll	Tamworth ...	N.S.W.

G

WOOL MARKS.	WOOL GROWERS' NAMES AND ADDRESSES.	PASTORAL DISTRICT.	STATE.
GUISELEY	J. S. Gordon, Guiseley, Walgett	Walgett	N.S.W.
GUMBLE P R	P. R. Robinson, Gumble Station, Gumb'e	Molong	N S.W.
GUM CREEK	J. J. Duncan, Gum Creek, Hanson	Hanson...	S.A.
GUMMIN	V. J. Dowling, Gummin Gummin, Gilgandra	Coonabarabran	N.S.W.
GUMS	A. K. Ross, The Gums, Penshurst	Western District	VIC
GUMS W D D	W. D. Davies, The Gums, Casterton	Western District...	VIC.
GUNBAR	Armstrong Bros., Gunbar Station, Gunbar	Hillston	N.S.W.
GUNBOWER	S. Booth, Gunbower, Minchca	Eastern District ...	VIC.
GUNDABOOKA	T. Robertson and Bros , Gundabooka, Bourke ...	Bourke...	N.S.W.
GUNDARE	A. B. Campbell, Gundare, Coolah	Coonabarabran ...	N.S.W.
GUNN	J. Gunn, Boolarwell, Goondiwindi	Goondiwindi	Q.
GUNNINGBAR	W. Hay, Gunningbar, Warren	Canonbar	N.S.W.
GUNNING EAST	G. Raffan, Gunning East and Bogabigal, Forbes	Forbes ...	N.S.W.
GUNTAWANG MUDGEE	R. and E. G. Rouse, Guntawang, Gulgong	Mudgee	N.S.W.
ĜW	A. S. Webb, Young	Young ...	N.S.W.

G

WOOL MARKS.	WOOL GROWERS' NAMES AND ADDRESSES.	PASTORAL DISTRICT.	STATE.
G W B MANNANARIE	G. W. Brooks, Mannanarie, Kulpara ...	Kulpara ...	S.A.
G W H HILLVIEW	J. and G. Hamel, Hillview, Uralla	Armidale	N.S.W.
G W J EUROBA	G. W. Johnston, Euroba, Merrindee ...	Dubbo ...	N.S.W.
G W K CHISWICK	E. G. Keith and F. H. S. Keith, Chiswick, Ross	Ross	TAS.
G W L FERNHILL	J. Goodfellow, Fernhill, Lyndhurst	Carcoar	N.S.W.
G W YAMBACOONA	Goldsbrough, Mort and Co., Yambacoona, Brewarrina	Brewarrina	N.S.W.
GWYDER	R. E. Chapman, Gwyder Park, Uralla	Armidale	N.S.W.
GX MUDGEE	A. W. and V. D. Cox, Mudgee	Mudgee ...	N.S.W.

H

WOOL MARKS.	WOOL GROWERS' NAMES AND ADDRESSES.	PASTORAL DISTRICT.	STATE.
H	Capt. A. J. Robertson, Traversdale, Forbes	Forbes ...	N.S.W.
(H)	D. Haigg, Yackandandah	North-Eastern District	VIC.
H & A B CORADGERY	H. and A. Balcombe, Coradgery, Parkes	Forbes ...	N.S.W.
H A CURRA	Arthur and Sons, Curra, via Parkes	Forbes ...	N.S.W.
HADDON RIGG	T. Kenny, Haddon Rigg, Warren	Coonamble	N.S.W.
H A E IVANHOE	H. H. Evans (exors.), Ivanhoe, Keyneton	Keyneton	S.A.
HANDLEY A K	A. Kilpatrick, Handley, Albury	Albury ...	N.S.W.
⟨HAP⟩ GUNNEGULDRIE	H. A. Preston and Co., Gunneguldrie, Euabalong	Condobolin	N.S.W.
HAPPY J. TRIPP VALLEY	J. Tripp, Happy Valley, Aberdeen	Murrurundi	N.S.W.
HAREFIELD W McN	W. McNickle, Harefield	Wagga . .	N.S.W.
HARLAND HILLS	S. Turner, Harland Hills, Dergholm ...	Western District ..	VIC.
HARLAND HILLS ⌒ T	S. Turner, Harland Hills, Dergholm ...	Western District...	VIC.
HARTWOOD	Blackwood Bros , Hartwood, Jerilderie	Jerilderie	N.S.W.
HARVEY PARK	F. Beasley, Harvey Park, Mingelo	Molong...	N.S.W.
HAWKER BUNGAREE	Hawker Bros., Bungaree, Clare	Clare	S.A.

WOOL MARKS.	WOOL GROWERS' NAMES AND ADDRESSES.	PASTORAL DISTRICT.	STATE.
HAWKER CARRIEWERLOO	J. McGilp (Manager), Carriewerloo, Port Augusta	Port Augusta ...	S.A.
HAWTHORNE	R. Jones, Hawthorne, Binnaway	Coonabarabran ...	N.S.W.
HAWTHORNE R J	R. Jones, Hawthorne, Binnaway	Coonabarabran	N.S.W.
HAZELWOOD F B G	Mrs. R. Glasson and Co., Hazelwood, Blayney ..	Carcoar... ...	N.S.W.
H B ARUNDEL	H. Broomfield, Arundel, Howlong	Albury	N.S.W.
H & B BALGOWNIE DARLING DOWNS	Mrs. Hogarth, Balgownie, Pittsworth...	Toowoomba	Q.
H B BALLYGLUNIN PARK	H. O'Brien Blake, Ballyglunin Park, Horsham	Horsham	VIC.
H B BUSHY CREEK	F. Beggs, Bushy Creek, Glenthompson	Western District...	VIC.
H BEATTIE MT AITKEN	H. Beattie, Mt. Aitken, Buttlejorrk	Central District ...	VIC.
(I) BELUBLA	N. Thornley (exors.), Belubla, Tocumwal	Deniliquin	N.S.W.
H B EVERLEIGH	C. Beames, Everleigh, Tooraweenah ...	Coonabarabran	N.S.W.
H B HOME PLAIN	Haynes Bros., Home Plain, Parkes	Forbes ...	N.S.W.
H B JUBILEE PARK	H. Brown, Jubilee Park, Kotupna ...	Northern District	VIC.
(H) BOIKERBERT	W. T. Hoare and Co., Boikerbert, Apsley	Western District...	VIC.
H & B O OAKWOOD	Oakwood Pastoral Co., Oakwood, Augathella	Augathella ...	Q.

H

WOOL MARKS.	WOOL GROWERS' NAMES AND ADDRESSES.	PASTORAL DISTRICT.	STATE.
H BROS CAREUNGA	W. McLaughlin, Careunga, Garah	Moree	N.S.W.
H BROS & Co EMU FLAT	F. W. Reynolds, Emu Flat, Binalong	Young ...	N.S.W
H B SALISBURY NEW ENG	H. Bourke, Salisbury Plains, Uralla	Armidale	N.S.W.
H B SYDENHAM	H. J. Bager, Sydenham, Surat	Surat	Q.
H BURNEWANG	H. Holmes, Burnewang, Elmore	Bendigo	VIC.
H BUTLER LAGOON	H. Butler, Woolbrook, Lagoon	Armidale	N.S.W.
H B VALEHEAD	H. C. Betts, Valehead, Molong	Molong...	N.S.W.
H — C	H. Chew, Stoneridge, Young	Young ...	N.S.W.
H C COTWAY	J. M. Carberry, Cotway, Gobarralong	Gundagai	N.S.W.
H & C D WALLA WALLA	J. H. Douglas, Walla Walla, Culcairn	Albury ...	N.S.W.
H C GLENRIDDLE	H. Crowley, Glenriddle, Barraba	Tamworth	N.S.W.
H C (red) H P	H. Cameron, Terang	Western District..	VIC.
H C H YARRAFORD	H. C. Holmes, Yarraford, Glen Innes	Glen Innes	N.S.W
H C M BAILEY	Haynes Bros., Bailey Park, Boggabri...	Tamworth	N.S.W.
H C M BOLOCO	H. C. Merrett, Carroll's Corner, Boloco	Cooma	N.S.W.

WOOL MARKS.	WOOL GROWERS' NAMES AND ADDRESSES.	PASTORAL DISTRICT.	STATE.
H C NEW ENG	H. Cameron, Breelong, Yarrowych	Armidale ...	N.S.W.
H COWABEE	J. Hannah, Cowabee, Coolamon	Wagga	N.S.W.
H & Co WELBONDONGAH	Hebden and Co., Welbondongah, Moree	Moree ...	N.S.W.
H & Co WILLAMURRA	W. Hoskins, Willamurra, Brewarrina	Brewarrina	N.S.W.
H C P	Heslop and Co., Powlett River, Western Port	Gippsland	VIC.
H C S TOWER HILL	J. Phillimara, Tower Hill, Illowa		VIC.
H C T GLENMORE	H. C. Taylor, Dobikin, Woolabra	Narrabri	N.S.W.
H C URAWILKIE	H. Campbell, Urawilkie, Coonamble	Coonamble	N.S.W.
H C WOODSTOCK	H. Colless, Woodstock, Moocalta Siding	Bourke ..	N S.W.
H DAISYBURN (red)	E. Haywood, Daisyburn, Seymour	Central District ...	VIC.
H D COBRAM	H. Dick, Cobram ...	Northern District	VIC.
⟨H&D⟩ ETON VALE	A. Hodgson and Sons, Eton Vale, Cambooya ...	Toowoomba	Q.
H DINGEE	Hunter Bros., Dingee, Elmore	Northern District	VIC.
H D MONTREAL	H. Dyball, Montreal, Cooma	Cooma	N.S.W.
HD OULNINA	W. H. Duncan, Oulnina	North-Eastern District	S.A.

H

WOOL MARKS.	WOOL GROWERS' NAMES AND ADDRESSES.	PASTORAL DISTRICT.	STATE.
H E B **A**	H. E. Bird, Amphitheatre	North-Western District	VIC.
H E B **THALGARRAH**	H. E. Bigg (exors.), Thalgarrah, Armidale	Armidale	N.S.W.
H **E HANN** **COURALIE** **PARK**	E. Hann, Couralie Park, Terry-Hie-Hie	Moree ...	N.S.W.
H E H **OLRIGG**	H. E. Holmes, Olrigg, Craigieburn	Central District	VIC.
H E K **EGELABRA**	H. E. Kater, Egelabra, Warren	Canonbar	N.S.W.
H E S **ECHO**	H. E. Suttor, Echo, Hill End	Mudgee	N.S.W.
H F **COOMA**	H. Fittness, Pleasant View, Moonbah...	Cooma ...	N.S.W.
H F **GLENEARN**	Elder, Smith and Co., Glenearn, Surat	Surat	Q.
H F **RYLSTONE**	H. Farelly, Mountain View, Carwell Railway Station	Mudgee	N.S.W.
H F W **ULUMBARELLA**	McDouall Bros., Ulumbarella, Barraba	Moree ...	N.S.W.
H F **X**	Mrs. F. M. Edwards, Attunga, Tamworth	Tamworth	N.S.W.
H G **BIMBI**	A. Ganet, Bimbi, Grenfell	Forbes ...	N.S.W.
ⓗ **BORAMBLE**	G. Hosking, Boramble, Mundooran	Coonabarabran	N.S.W.
H G **GRAGIN**	Gordon Bros , Gragin, Warialda	Warialda	N.S.W.
H **GLENPEDDER**	A. M. Hamilton, Glen Pedder, Greendale	Bacchus Marsh	VIC.

WOOL MARKS.	WOOL GROWERS' NAMES AND ADDRESSES.	PASTORAL DISTRICT.	STATE.
H GORAH	Mrs. J. C. C. Hannah, Gorah, Bagaldi	Coonabarabran	N.S.W.
H G & P MARRA	Hay, Graves and Paxton, Marra, Wilcannia	Wilcannia	N.S.W.
H G & P TALYEALYE	Hay, Graves and Paxton, Marra, Wilcannia	Wilcannia	N.S.W.
H G R & Co SHIRLEY	H. G. Roberts and Co., Shirley, Longreach	Longreach	Q.
H. HAY COLLENDINA	H. Hay, Collendina, Corowa...	Corowa...	N.S.W.
H & H BEANBAH	Messrs. Haynes and Hann, Beanbah, Coonamble	Coonamble	N.S.W.
H H B GLENCOE	H. H. Barton, Glencoe, Roma	Roma ...	Q.
H H DUNDEE	W. Sweeney, Dundee, Windellama	Goulburn ...	N.S.W.
H H W	H. H. Wettenhall, Warncoort	Western District ..	VIC.
HH WATTAWELLA	Hall Bros., Watta Wella, Stawell	Western District.	VIC.
HIGHBURY	R. Salmon, Highbury, Quorn	Quorn	S.A.
HIGH ★ FIELDS	Union Bank of Australia, Highfields and Sunny Hills, Longreach ...	Longreach	Q.
HILLSIDE J B	J. Berryman, Hillside, Moira	Deniliquin ...	N.S.W.
H ILLYRIA	M. Hardiman, Illyria, Burrowa	Young	N.S.W.
H J A DOON	H. J. Almond, Bonnie Doon ..	Mansfield ...	VIC.

H

WOOL MARKS.	WOOL GROWERS' NAMES AND ADDRESSES.	PASTORAL DISTRICT.	STATE.
H J B **LAWRENNY**	H. J. Brock, Lawrenny, Ouse	Ouse	TAS.
H J D **BALD HILL**	H. J. Dennis, Bald Hills		S.A.
H **JUNEE**	I. W. Hammond (exors.), Wyoming, Old Junee	Wagga ...	N.S.W.
H **C** **YAMMATREE**	H. Jenkins, Yammatree, Bethungra	Gundagai	N.S.W.
H **KEMPFIELD**	J. R. Hailstone, Kempfield, Trunkey ...	Carcoar ...	N.S.W.
H K **GARRAWILLA**	H. H. Kelly, Garrawilla, Gunnedah	Coonabarabran	N.S.W.
H K **K V**	H. King, Kingsvale, Young ...	Young	N.S.W.
H K **NARRAWA**	H. Kensit, Narrawa, Goulburn	Goulburn	N.S.W.
H K **WILDO**	H. Kurtzmann, Wildo, Mansfield	Mansfield	VIC.
H L A **A**	Dr. H. L. Atkinson, Raywood	Northern District	VIC.
H L A **BARWONLEIGH**	A. F. Kelly, Barwonleigh, Inverleigh...	Western District...	VIC.
H L A **R**	D. H. L. Atkinson, Ravenswood	Central District	VIC.
H L Co LD	Haymarket Land Co., Ltd., Furracabad, Glen Innes	Glen Innes ...	N.S.W.
H L Co LD **FURRACABAD**	Haymarket Land Co., Ltd., Furracabad, Glen Innes	Glen Innes ...	N.S.W.
H L **EUROOL**	H. C. and J. C. Lewis, Eurool, Collarendabri	Walgett ...	N.S.W.

H

WOOL MARKS.	WOOL GROWERS' NAMES AND ADDRESSES.	PASTORAL DISTRICT.	STATE.
H L N **ORROROO**	H. L. Nant, Orroroo (grown near Pt. Augusta)	Port Augusta ...	S.A.
H **MANAR**	W. F. Gordon, Manar, Braidwood	Braidwood ...	N.S.W.
H M **COMBADELLO**	W. and F. A. Moses, Combadello, Moree	Moree	N.S.W.
H M **D S O**	W. T. Hoare and Co., Apsley	Western District...	VIC.
H **MITIAMO PARK**	W. J. Hill, Mitiamo Park, Mitiamo	Bendigo	VIC.
H M L **WARRA**	Mrs H. McLean, Warra Warra, Glenorchy	Wimmera	VIC.
H M **NOMBI**	H. Moses and Son, Nombi, Mullaley	Coonabarabran	N.S.W.
H M **OREGON**	Misses McMillan, Oregon, Warialda	Warialda	N.S.W.
H M T **KENILWORTH**	H. M. Terry (exors.), Kenilworth, Yass	Yass	N.S.W.
H N **B Y**	H. Norton, Boomey, Molong	Molong...	N.S.W.
⟨H⟩ **NEW ENGLAND**	A. E. Hayes, Stoney Batter, Uralla	Armidale	N.S.W.
H O	H. Oliver, Mallow Grove, Bayney	Carcoar	N.S.W.
H O **BANGAROO**	H. Osborne, Bangaroo, Canowindra	Carcoar	N.S.W.
H O C **B**	H. O. Carter, Winston, Moss Vale	Berrima	N.S.W
H O C **I**	H. O. Carter, Winston, Moss Vale	Berrima ...	N.S.W.

H

WOOL MARKS.	WOOL GROWERS' NAMES AND ADDRESSES.	PASTORAL DISTRICT.	STATE.
HOL BROS RAYLEIGH	W. and J. F. Holcombe, Rayleigh, Pilliga	Pilliga	N.S.W.
HOLLYMOUNT	J. A. Mayer, Hollymount, Pyalong	Central District	VIC.
HOLM	W. R. Podger, Holm Chase, Colac	Western District	VIC.
H O L WEETAWAA	W. R. Holcombe, Weetawaa, Wee Waa	Pilliga ...	N.S.W.
HOME FLAT	G. Jackson, Home Flat, Dara Dara	Hume ...	N.S.W.
HOPE PARK J M	J. Mibus, Hope Park, Hochkirch	Western District	VIC.
HOPE W W	R. C. H. Hope, Wolta Wolta, Clare	Clare	S.A.
HORSE (WOOL) SHOE	W. D. Crozier, Horseshoe, Wentworth, River Murray	Wentworth ...	N.S.W.
HORTON VALE F D	F. T. Philpot, Horton Vale, Cunnamulla	Cunnamulla	Q.
H P B & Co COONIMBIA	H. P. Blake and Co., Coonimbia, Merrigal	Coonamble ...	N.S.W.
H P JOHNS CREEK	H. Pearson, John's Creek, Aberfoyle, Guyra	Armidale	N.S.W.
HP KIANDRA	H. Pearse, Racecourse, Kiandra	Cooma ...	N.S.W.
H P MELTON PARK	H. Patterson, Melton Park, Bacchus Marsh	Central District ...	VIC.
HP NEW ENGLAND	H. Pearson, John's Creek, Glen Innes	Glen Innes ...	N.S.W.
H P TIVERTON	H. Peters, Tiverton, Mullaley	Tamworth	N.S.W.

H

WOOL MARKS.	WOOL GROWERS' NAMES AND ADDRESSES.	PASTORAL DISTRICT.	STATE.
H P **WAGRA**	H. H. Pearse, Wagra, Tallangatta	North-Eastern District	VIC.
H R **BLACK CREEK**	W. J. Foster (exors.), Black Creek, Blackville	Tamworth	N.S.W.
H **REEDY CREEK**	J. Huggins, Reedy Creek, Hinnomungie	Gippsland	VIC.
H **REST DOWN**	J. P. Hearne, Restdown, Rochester	Northern District	VIC.
H R **HANLETH**	H. Reid, Hanleth, Evandale	Evandale	TAS.
H R **LOGAN**	H. Reid, Logan, Evandale	Evandale	TAS.
H R R **GLENROY ESTATE** **W H H**	W. B. Sells (exors.), Glenroy Estate, Second Valley	Glenroy	S.A.
H R **SCONE**	T. Ring, Bingston, Woodland, Scone...	Murrurundi	N.S.W.
H S **ARAPILES**	Sudholz Brothers, Natimuk Station, Natimuk ...	Horsham	VIC.
H S **G H** **A**	Sharp and Sons, Green Hills, Adelong	Gundagai	N.S.W.
H **80**	H. Steer, Mahonga Park, Mahonga	Urana	N.S.W.
H S **REDCLIFFE**	M. Scott, Redcliffe, Florieton	Florieton	S.A.
H **STREAMVILLE**	E. Hammond, Streamville, Mt. Macdonald	Carcoar	N.S.W.
H T B	H. T. Beresford, Homewood, Dalton ..	Yass	N.S.W.
H T **GREENDALE**	O. E. Hudson, Greendale, Germanton...	Hume	N.S.W.

94

WOOL MARKS.	WOOL GROWERS' NAMES AND ADDRESSES.	PASTORAL DISTRICT.	STATE.
HUDOR	J. I. Good, Hudor, Glenthompson	Western District	VIC.
HUGHENDEN	R. Gray, Hughenden Station, Hughenden	Hughenden	Q.
HUGHES PARK	J. J. Duncan, Hughes Park, Watervale	Watervale	S.A.
HULME ⌒ & ⌒ SONS	G. Hulme and Sons, High Plain, Germanton	Hume	N.S.W.
HUME EURALIE	F. W. Hume, Tarengo, Burrowa	Young ...	N.S.W.
HUMMOCKS	R. B. Smith, Hummocks, Snowtown		S.A.
HUTT RIVER	C. Maslin, Hutt River, Yacka		S.A.
H V Z HUNTERS VALE	J. Corbett, Hunter's Vale, Moonan Brook	Murrurundi	N.S.W.
H W	Mrs. H. Wells, River Bend, Ashford ...	Tenterfield	N.S.W.
H W C BROOKLYN	H. W. Curtis, Brooklyn, Armidale	Armidale	N.S.W.
H W LAKE VIEW	A. & J. Robertson, junr., Lake View, Dundonnell	Dundonnell	VIC.
H W NUMBLA	H. Withers, Numbla, Dalgety	Cooma ...	N.S.W.
◇HY◇ **BURNIMA**	H. T. Edwards, Burnima, Bibbenluke	Bombala ...	N.S.W.
HYDE PARK	M. McLean (Manager), Hyde Park, Cavendish...	Western District...	VIC.
HYDON	F. and P. H. Wheaton, Hydon, Red Hill		S.A.
◇HY◇ **MERIANGAH**	H. T. Edwards, Burnima, Bibbenluke	Bombala	N.S.W.

WOOL MARKS.	WOOL GROWERS' NAMES AND ADDRESSES.	PASTORAL DISTRICT.	STATE.
I A P BEN BUCKLEY MUDGEE	I. A. Parkinson, Ben Buckley, Mudgee	Mudgee	N.S.W.
I B D	Dulhunty and Deakin, Kiloola, Peel	Bathurst	N.S W.
IBBOTT THURLOO	J. A. Ibbott. Thurloo, Coonamble	Coonamble	N.S.W.
IBBOTT ORWELL	J. A. Ibbott, Thurloo, Coonamble	Coonamble	N.S.W.
I C A C HILL NEW ENGLAND	Mrs. J. Coventry, Camperdown, Armidale	Armidale	N.S.W.
I C BARWON VALE	Collins and Sons, Barwon Vale, Walgett	Walgett	N.S W.
I C CAMPERDOWN NEW ENGLAND	Mrs. J. Coventry, Camperdown, Armidale	Armidale	N.S.W.
COPPABELLA	J. Maher, Coppabella, Bookham	Young ...	N.S.W.
I D BORAMBOLA	Goldsbrough, Mort and Co., Ltd., Borambola, Wagga	Wagga ...	N.S.W.
ID BORAMBOLA	Goldsbrough, Mort and Co., Ltd., Borambola, Wagga	Wagga...	N.S W.
ID BYWONG	Goldsbrough, Mort and Co., Ltd., Bywong, Queanbeyan	Queanbeyan ...	N.S.W.
ID RETREAT	Youngman Bros., Retreat, Casterton ...	Western District...	VIC
I E P CHATHAM	I. E. Peynton, Chatham, Augathella ...	Augathella ...	Q.

I

WOOL MARKS.	WOOL GROWERS' NAMES AND ADDRESSES.	PASTORAL DISTRICT.	STATE.
I H M WOODLANDS	I. H. Moss, Woodlands, Dandaloo	Dubbo	N.S.W.
I J S	I. J. Sloam, North Lagoon, Cowra	Carcoar	N.S.W.
ILLUNIE	M. I. Brown, Crowther Crowther, Young	Young ...	N.S.W.
I M P NERRIN NERRIN	Mrs. W. McPherson, Nerrin Nerrin, Streatham	Western District...	VIC.
I M WAGRA	Moyle Bros., Wagra, Tallangatta	North-Eastern District	VIC.
INGLEBY	O. J. Armytage, Ingleby, Winchelsea ...	Western District...	VIC.
INGLEBY	J. Rawson, Ingleby, Tallarook	Wagga...	N.S.W.
INGLEVALE	J. Newman, Inglevale, Grenfell	Forbes ...	N.S.W.
I N HAMPSHIRE	I. Noble, Hampshire, Idaville	Merriwa ...	N.S.W.
INNISHOWEN H H	W. Barklemore, Inneshowen and Pulpulla, Cobar	Cobar ...	N.S.W.
I N O	J. Hume, Collingwood, Gunning	Yass	N.S.W.
I + N PARK HILL	H. Ball, Park Hill, Myaring...	... ...	VIC.
IONA	P. Barry, Iona, Trangie	Dubbo	N.S.W.
IRONBONG	M. O'Brien, Ironbong, Bethungra	Wagga... ...	N.S.W.

WOOL MARKS.	WOOL GROWERS' NAMES AND ADDRESSES.	PASTORAL DISTRICT.	STATE.
IRVING **T**	R. T. Irving, Mt. Tenandra, Gulargambone	Coonabarabran	N.S.W.
ISIS DOWNS	O. Smith and Co., Isis Downs, Isisford	Isisford ..	Q.
I S **KIACATOO**	A. & N.Z.M. Co., Ltd., Kiacatoo, Condobolin	Condobolin	N.S.W
I S **WHEEO**	Bank of N.S.W., Wheeo, Yass	Yass	N.S.W.
I W **B**	I. Winter, Tulcumbah, Carroll	Tamworth	N.S.W.
I W **T**	I. Winter, Tulcumbah, Carroll	Tamworth	N.S.W.

WOOL MARKS.	WOOL GROWERS' NAMES AND ADDRESSES.	PASTORAL DISTRICT.	STATE.
◇ ?	R. H. D. Jones, Toorawandi, Coonabarabran	Coonabarabran	N.S.W.
J A B	J. A. Badgery, Arthursleigh, Moss Vale	Goulburn	N.S.W.
J A B	J. A. Buckland, Pine Ridge, Gulgong	Coonabarabran	N.S.W.
J A B BURRA	J. A. Badgery, Burra, Queanbeyan	Queanbeyan	N.S.W.
J A BEREMBED	Andrew Bros., Berembed, Grong Grong	Wagga...	N.S.W.
J A D	J. Arch, Dubbo	Dubbo ...	N.S.W.
J A D GLEN INNES	J. A. Davidson, Glen View, Glen Innes	Glen Innes	N.S.W.
J A DUNALAN	J. Allen, Dunalan, Wolseley	Wolseley	S.A.
J A F CRAWNEY	J. Foggarty, Crawney, Nundle	Tamworth ...	N.S.W.
J A F ROSEWOOD	J. A. Fowler, Rosewood, Monteagle	Young ...	N.S.W.
J A G BRAEHOUR	J. A. Gunn, Braemar and Broadbin, Borambola	Wagga	N.S.W.
J A H CHEVIOT HILLS	J. A. Hutton, Cheviot Hills, Penshurst	Western District...	N.S.W.
△ J A HUMULA	J. Angel, Humula Station, Humula	Hume	N.S.W.
JAMES MELROSE	J. Melrose, Hallett..	Hallett ..	S.A.
JAMES MELROSE HALLETT	J. Melrose, Hallett...	Hallett ..	S.A.

WOOL MARKS.	WOOL GROWERS' NAMES AND ADDRESSES.	PASTORAL DISTRICT.	STATE.
J A MONA	J. Alexander, Mona, Boomi	Moree	N.S.W.
JANDRA	M. Robertson and Co., Jandra, Bourke	Bourke	N.S.W.
J A N WHEATLEY	J. A. Nickoll, Wheatley, Shelbourne ...	Bendigo	VIC.
J A PINE HILL	J. Anderson, Pine Hill, Moama	Deniliquin	N.S.W.
J A ROCKY CREEK	J. Arndell, Rocky Creek, Moree	Moree	N.S.W.
JASPER BULLAGREEN	Jasper T. Jones, Bullagreen, Coonamble	Coonamble	N.S.W.
J A TOOLONG	G. Sharpe, Toolong, Port Fairy	Western District...	VIC.
J A WAGGA WAGGA	J. Anderson, Yerong Creek, Yerong	Wagga...	N.S.W.
2 J A W OMEO	J. Williams, Hinnomungie, Omeo	Gippsland	VIC.
J A YARRAN VALE	J. Anderson, Yarran Vale, Darlington Point	Narrandera	N S.W.
J B	Mrs. J. Balderstone, Bindegambil, Tooraweenah	Coonabarabran	N.S.W.
J B A	J. Bell and Sons, Archdale, Bealiba	Northern District	VIC.
J B ARMIDALE	J. Baker, Rose View, Abington	Armidale	N.S.W.
J B BARRABA	J. Broadbeck, Millie Creek, Barraba ...	Tamworth ...	N.S.W.
J3 BARRY	W. H. Brayshaw, Barry, Nundle	Armidale ...	N.S.W.

WOOL MARKS.	WOOL GROWERS' NAMES AND ADDRESSES.	PASTORAL DISTRICT.	STATE.
J B B **D** **NEVERTIRE**	J. B. Burgman, Danbury, Nevertire	Dubbo	N.S.W.
J B **BELLEVUE**	F. J. Bowhay, Bellevue, Yeoval	Molong	N.S.W.
J B **BONE BONE**	W. Buckley, Bone Bone, Mundooran	Coonabarabran	N.S.W.
J B **BOREAMBLE**	J. Brett, Boreamble, Coolamon	Condobolin	N.S.W.
J B **△ ◇ VIEW**	J. Bolan and Co., Bell View, Balmoral	Western District	VIC.
J B **CURRAGH**	J. Brett, Curragh, Coolamon	Condobolin	N.S.W.
J B D	J. B. Donkin, Lake Cowal, Forbes	Forbes	N.S.W.
J B D **PURNAMOOTA**	J. B. Davidson, Purnamoota, Broken Hill	Menindie	N.S.W.
J B D & SONS **THULE**	J. B. Docker and Sons, Thule, Cobar	Cobar	N.S.W.
J B G **MOUNT STRUAN**	J. B. Gill, Mt. Struan, Casterton	Western District	VIC.
J B G **RUNNYMEDE**	J. B. Gill, Runnymede, Casterton	Western District	VIC.
J B **HILL CREST**	J. Barry, Hill Crest, Myrtle Ville	Goulburn	N.S.W.
J B **HUGUNDRA**	J. Blyton, sen., Rock Lodge, Cooma	Cooma	N.S.W.
J B **LANE**	J. B. Lane, Rose Hill, Orange	Bathurst	N.S.W.
J B **LITTLE PLAINS**	Barton Bros., Little Plains, Frogmore	Young	N.S.W.

WOOL MARKS.	WOOL GROWERS' NAMES AND ADDRESSES.	PASTORAL DISTRICT.	STATE.
J B LODGE	J. Blyton, sen., Rock Lodge, Cooma	Cooma	N.S.W.
J B M KILGOWLA	J. B. Manning and Son, Kilgowla, Moree	Moree ...	N.S.W.
J B M MUNKORA	J. B. Makin, Munkora, Wolseley	Wolseley	S.A.
J B ◆ **M V**	J. Berryman, Myall View, Gilgandra	Dubbo	N.S.W.
J BOXSELL CHERRY GROVE	J. Boxsell, Cootamundra, Wallendbeen	Young	N.S.W.
J B P MERRI MERRI	J. B. Peacock, Merri Merri, Bourbah ..	Coonamble ...	N.S.W.
J B R KEELENDI	J. B. Rundle, Keelendi, Pilliga	Pilliga	N.S.W.
J. BROS BEEFWOOD	Jamieson Bros., Beefwood, Moree	Moree ...	N.S.W.
J BRUCE G	J. Bruce, Germanton, Hume	Hume	N.S.W.
J B WAPPAN	A. F. Bon, Wappan, Bonnie Doon	Mansfield	VIC.
J3 W BRUNDAH	J. Q. and P. Wood, Brundah, Grenfell	Forbes	N.S.W.
J B WOLLENGOUGH	Johns Bros., Wollengough, Ungarie ...	Condobolin ...	N.S.W.
J C	J. Charleson, Allendale, Ballarat	Ballarat ...	VIC.
J C ⚓	J. Chisholm, Kobyboyn	North-Eastern District	VIC.

WOOL MARKS.	WOOL GROWERS' NAMES AND ADDRESSES.	PASTORAL DISTRICT.	STATE.
J ◇ C	J. Clifford, Bredbo, Cooma	Cooma ...	N.S.W.
J C BLACK FLAT	J. Commins, Black Flat, Michelago	Queanbeyan	N.S.W.
J C BULLIO	J. Chalker, Bullio, Bannaby...	Goulburn	N.S.W.
J C B WILLANA	J. C. Brown, Willana, Frances	Frances	S.A.
J O C	J. Connell, Cootamundra, Young	Young ...	N.S.W.
J C & Co BIRELLAN	J. Clements and Co., Birellan, Greenmantle	Carcoar	N S.W.
J C & Co GLENDON NEW ENG	Cramsie and Co., Glendon, Glen Innes	Glen Innes	N.S.W.
J C CONDAH	J. Cowan, Condah ...	Western District	VIC.
J C O SPRINGVALE	J. Corcoran, Springvale, Bombala	Bombala	N.S.W.
J C E	C. Sinnot, Armstrongs	Western District...	VIC.
J C EMILY PARK BEN LOMOND	J. and F. G. Coleman, Emily Park, Ben Lomond	Glen Innes	N.S.W.
J C GBRL	J. Carberry, Gobarralong, Gundagai ..	Gundagai	N.S.W.
J C INGLEWOOD	J. Chirnside, Inglewood, Bombala	Bombala	N.S.W.
J C JIMENBUAN	Crisp Bros., Jimenbuan, Cooma	Cooma ...	N.S.W.
J C K	J. Coffey, Kewell	Horsham	VIC.

WOOL MARKS.	WOOL GROWERS' NAMES AND ADDRESSES.	PASTORAL DISTRICT.	STATE.
J C KERI	J. Cumming (exors.), Keri Keri, Moulamein	Moulamein ...	N.S.W.
J C L	W. Jackman, Clear Lake, Horsham	Horsham	VIC.
J C LONGFORD	C. W. Rye, Longford, Cooma	Cooma ...	N.S.W.
J C ◇M BLAND	Chisholm Bros., Bland, Temora	Wagga...	N.S.W.
J C MEMSIE	J. Catto, Bridgewater	Bendigo	VIC.
J C M GLENMOAN	Manchee Bros., Glen Moan, Willow Tree	Tamworth ...	N.S.W.
J C ◇M KIP	C. K. Chisholm, Raeburn, Goulburn	Goulburn	N.S.W.
◇JC M LERIDA	A. B. Chisholm, Carrawarra, Goulburn	Goulburn	N.S W.
J C MOGONG	J. Carter, Mogong, Canowindra	Molong	N.S.W.
J C ◇M RAEBURN	C. K. Chisholm, Raeburn, Breadalbane	Goulburn	N.S.W.
J C MT PLEASANT	J. Collett, Mt. Pleasant, Gunning	Yass	N.S.W.
J C NEW ENG	J. Cameron, Wilford, Guyra... ...	Armidale ...	N.S.W.
J C NUMBY	J. Cummings, Rockwood, Reid's Flat ...	Young	N.S.W.
J. COX MANGOPLAH	J. Cox, Mangoplah, Wagga...	Wagga... ...	N.S.W.
J C REIDS FLAT	J. Clements, Reid's Flat, Young	Young	N.S.W.

WOOL MARKS.	WOOL GROWERS' NAMES AND ADDRESSES.	PASTORAL DISTRICT	STATE.
J C **RICES FLAT**	J. Collison, Rice's Flat, Yass	Yass	N.S.W.
J C **ROSSMORE**	M. Carey, Rossmore, Haydonton	Murrurundi	N.S.W.
J C & S	Cooper and Son, Cullingral, Merriwa...	Merriwa	N.S.W.
L C S **MOUNT ADRAH**	A. and L. Crain, Mt. Adrah...	Gundagai	N.S.W.
J C S **WARRANGONG**	J. C. Syme, Warrangong, Cowra	Young	N.S.W.
J C **TOLLBAR**	Coffey Bros., Tollbar, Cooma	Cooma	N.S.W.
J C T **STANHOPE**	W. J. W. Irving (exors.), Stanhope, Rushworth	North-Eastern District	VIC.
J D	J. Donoghue, Plain Camp, Tambar Springs	Tamworth	N.S.W.
△ J D	J. M. O'Rourke, Harrow	Western District	VIC.
J D **BALOWRA**	J. Dalton, Balowra, Nymagee	Hillston	N.S.W.
J D **BANAR**	J. Dawson, Banar, Condobolin	Condobolin	N.S.W.
J D **BRIBEREE**	Bank of N.S.W., Briberee, Young	Young	N.S.W.
J D & Co **RICHMOND**	P. K. F. Miller (Manager), Richmond Station, Rathscar		VIC.
△ **J DENT**	J. Dent, Eualdrie, Grenfell	Forbes	N.S.W.
J DENT	J. Dent, Ooma, Forbes	Forbes	N.S.W.

WOOL MARKS.	WOOL GROWERS' NAMES AND ADDRESSES.	PASTORAL DISTRICT.	STATE.
J D **HAPPY VALLEY**	J. R. Derrick, Happy Valley, Mundarlo	Gundagai	N.S.W.
J D H **BOGALARA**	J. D. Hill, Bogalara, Bookham	Young	N.S.W.
J D M **BUMBALDRY**	J. McMahon, Bambaldry, Grenfell	Forbes	N.S.W.
J D **M** **MILLIE**	A. Buchanan, Millie, Pilliga	Pilliga	N.S.W.
J D **NETLEY**	J. Dunn, Netley, Menindie	Menindie	N.S.W.
J D **PINE HILLS**	J. Donaldson, Pine Hills, Warialda	Warialda	N.S.W.
J D **ROUGHWOOD**	J. Dickie (exors.), Roughwood, Jerilderie	Jerilderie	N.S.W.
J D S	J. D. Scott, Fernbank, Gippsland	Gippsland	VIC.
J D **TAHARA**	J. Dolile, Tahara	Normanby	VIC.
J — D **ULUMBIE**	J. H. Doyle, Ulumbie, Walgett	Walgett	N S.W.
J D **WEEBO** **PARK**	J. D. Dunn, Weebo Park, Bungowannah	Albury	N.S.W.
J D **YEUMBURRA**	Maria Duff, Yeumburra, Yass	Yass	N.S.W.
J D **Z Z**	J. Drummond, Walwa, Tallangatta	North-Eastern District	VIC.
J E **BALOWRA**	J. English, Balowra, Marengo	Young	N.S.W.
J E B **FAIRFIELD**	J. E. Butler, Fairfield, Coonamble	Coonamble	N.S.W.

J

WOOL MARKS.	WOOL GROWERS' NAMES AND ADDRESSES.	PASTORAL DISTRICT.	STATE.
J E COOBANG	J. Ewan, Coobang, Parkes	Forbes ...	N.S.W.
J E COOBANG LAKESIDE	J. Ewan, Coobang, Parkes	Forbes	N.S.W.
J E CUMNOCK	J. Egglestone, Cumnock, Molong	Molong...	N.S.W.
JEDBURGH	G. H. Burcham, Jedburgh, Warren	Coonamble	N.S.W.
J E GROVE HILL	J. Elliott, Grove Hill, Forbes	Forbes	N.S.W.
J E GUNNINGBLAND	J. Ewan, Gunningbland, Bogan Gate	Forbes	N.S.W.
J E NEILA	J. Ewan, Neila, Cowra	Young ...	N.S.W.
J E NEILA LAKESIDE	J. Ewan, Neila, Cowra	Young ...	N.S.W.
J E W BILLENBAH	J. E. Warby, Billenbah, Narrandera	Narrandera	N.S.W.
J E WINMERE	J. Eckersley, Winmere, St. Arnaud	Kara Kara	VIC.
J F	J. Fowler, Coolegong, Young	Young	N.S.W.
J F BASIN FARM KOORINGA	J. Ford, Basin Farm, Kooringa	Kooringa	S.A.
J F BYADUK	Fraser Bros., Byaduk, Hamilton	Western District	VIC.
J -- F DALMORE,	J. H. Fairfax, Dalmore, Longreach	Longreach	Q.
J F D NAMOI	J. H. Fitzgerald, Huntsgrove, Manilla	Tamworth	N.S.W.

WOOL MARKS.	WOOL GROWERS' NAMES AND ADDRESSES.	PASTORAL DISTRICT.	STATE.
J F DUNTULUM	J. Faucett (exors.), Duntulum, Clunes	Talbot ...	VIC.
J F COOLEGONG	J. Fowler, Coolegong, Monteagle	Young	N.S.W.
J F E KIAMERON	Mrs. M. A. Egan, Kiameron, Mt. Harris	Canonbar	N.S.W.
J F EMBY	Fisher and Co., Emby and Tooloon, Gulargambone	Coonamble	N.S.W.
J. F. GAGE SYNNOT	J. F. Gage, Synnot	Synnot ...	TAS.
J F G SHIEL	J. F. Glasson, Shiel, Woodstock	Carcoar	N.S.W.
J F H TEMI	J. Hoddle, Temi, Ardglen	Tamworth	N.S.W.
J F KENTUCKY	J. Fletcher, Kentucky, Uralla	Armidale	N.S.W.
J F MENENIA	Ferguson and Powell, Menenia, Maroona	Ararat	VIC.
J F M WATERVIEW	J. F. Male, Waterview, Goolagong	Forbes ...	N.S.W.
J F N	J. Fell, Tungamah...	Benalla	VIC.
J F OGILVIE	J. Fingleton, Ogilvie, Moree...	Moree ...	N.S.W.
J FOSTER MERLIN	Fenwicke and Gill, Merlin, Walcha	Armidale	N.S.W.
J F QUANDONG PARK	Furner Bros., Quandong, Coolamon	Wagga...	N.S.W.
J FRAMPTON	McClintock Bros., Frampton, Cootamundra	Wagga	N.S.W.

WOOL MARKS.	WOOL GROWERS' NAMES AND ADDRESSES.	PASTORAL DISTRICT.	STATE.
J F **ROSEMOUNT**	W. Franklin, Rosemount, Jugiong	Gundagai	N.S.W.
J F **SUNNYRIDGE**	J. Fagan, Sunnyridge, Mandurama	Carcoar	N.S.W.
J F **WALBUNDRIE**	W. Kiddle, Walbundrie, Walbundrie	Albury ...	N.S.W.
J G **AUBURN**	E. Gorman, Auburn, Berrigan	Jerilderie	N.S.W.
J **G** **BELLEVUE**	J. Bacon, Bellevue, Oatlands	Oatlands	TAS.
J G **BRINGELONG**	J. Glasson, Bringelong, Blayney	Bathurst	N.S.W.
J G B **WILLOW BANK**	W. Henderson, Willow Bank, Bung Bong Railway Station ...	Talbot ...	VIC.
J G **COLANE PARK**	J. Gillett, jun., Colane Park, Coonamble	Coonamble	N.S.W.
J G E **BLACK SPRING**	J. G. Evans, Black Spring, Narrawa ...	Goulburn	N.S.W.
J G **GARA**	A. Glass, Gara, Metz	Armidale	N.S.W.
J & G **GARDENIA**	James and Gard, Gardenia, Ivanhoe	Ivanhoe ...	N.S.W.
J G **GLEN OAK**	J. Geddes, Glen Oak, Upper Manilla ...	Tamworth	N.S.W.
J G G **MUDGEE**	J. G. Golden, Collingwood, Mudgee	Mudgee	N.S.W.
J G **INJEMIRA**	J. Good, Injemira, Winslow and Grassmere	Warrnambool	VIC.
J G L	J. G. Lloyd, Umeralla, Cooma	Cooma	N.S.W.

WOOL MARKS.	WOOL GROWERS' NAMES AND ADDRESSES.	PASTORAL DISTRICT.	STATE.
J G M	J. G. Moseley, Clear View, Port Augusta	Port Augusta ...	S.A.
J G M	J. G. Mack, Lismore, Camperdown	Western District...	VIC.
J G MYATHONG	J. Glenn, Myathong, Jerilderie	Jerilderie	N.S.W.
J G P H NEW ENG	J. Grieve, Pine Hill, Woolbrook	Armidale	N.S.W.
J GREEN OAK PARK PEARCE	J. Green, Oak Park, Pearce...		S.A.
J Gs	J. Geddes, Woorndoo, Hampden	Western District...	VIC.
J G THE GROVE	J. Glen, The Grove, Winton	Winton	Q.
J G T O P	J. G. Terry, Oulnina Park, Mannahill	Mannahill	S.A.
J G WEE WAA	J. Gray, Wee Waa, Pilliga	Pilliga	N.S.W.
J G W GLENTHORPE	J. G. Wilmott, Glenthorpe, Bullarah	Moree ...	N S.W.
J G W S	J. G. Williams, Leasingham	Leasingham	S.A.
J H B KOORONG	J. H. Baird, Koorong, Bombala	Bombala	N.S.W.
J H BONEGILLA PARK	J. Hoddonett, Bonegilla Park, Bonegilla	...	VIC.
J H BROADMEAD	J. Harris, Broadmead, Macalister	Dalby ...	Q.
J H B TYCANNAH	W. J. Gall, Tycannah, Moree	Moree	N.S.W.

WOOL MARKS.	WOOL GROWERS' NAMES AND ADDRESSES.	PASTORAL DISTRICT.	STATE.
JHC	J. Hurley, Killanear, Burrowa	Young	N.S.W.
J H C HOWLONG	A Macvean, Howlong, Howlong	Albury	N.S.W.
JHD	J. S. Downing, Rockleigh		S.A.
J H D I	J. H. Doyle, Moermein, Scone	Murrurundi	N.S.W.
J H G HOLYROOD	J. H. George and Sons, Holyrood, Burrumbuttock	Albury	N.S.W.
J H GLENLEIGH	O. J. Hore, Glenleigh, Bowna	Albury	N.S.W.
J H H	J. Housion, Hay	Hay	N.S.W.
J H H	J. H. Hynes, Palmer	Palmer	S.A.
J H H	J. Housion, Hay	Hay	N.S.W.
J H H OOLLINGWOOD	J. H. Hume, Collingwood, Gunning	Yass	N.S.W.
J H H ELLEN VALE	J. H. Hayward, Ellenvale, Windorah	Windorah	Q.
ꝀK	H. J. Kelk, Wyoming, *via* Wandsworth	Glen Innes	N.S.W.
ꞁH KORALEIGH	J. Henderson, Koraleigh, Tongala Railway Station	Northern District	VIC.
J H K RONG	J. H. Kendall, Flowerpot Valley, The Rock	Wagga	N.S.W.
J H M KOOLUNGA	J. H. Maslin, Koolunga, Gulnare South	Gulnare	S.A.

J

WOOL MARKS.	WOOL GROWERS' NAMES AND ADDRESSES.	PASTORAL DISTRICT.	STATE.
J H M **MAROONAH**	J. H. Maslin, Maroonah	Maroonah	W.A.
J H **MOLTON**	J Halse, Molton, T.P.O. No. 2, N. W. Line, Moree	Moree	N.S.W.
JHM **SWANBROOK**	Munsie Bros., Swanbrook, Inverell	Glen Innes	N.S.W.
J H O B **HATTON**	J. H. O'Brien, Hatton, Warren	Coonamble	N.S.W.
JH **OVERDALE**	J. Holden, Overdale, Stawell	Western District	VIC.
J H **S**	J. Hurst, Romsey	Central District ...	VIC.
J H S **NEW ENG**	J. H. Stier Milady's Creek, Walcha	Armidale ...	N.S.W.
JH **STRUAN**	J. Huxley, Struan, Merino	Western District...	VIC.
J H S **YATHONG**	J. H Spiller, Yathong, Yarragundry	Wagga	N.S.W.
J H S **Y Y**	J. H. Spiller, Yarragundry, Wagga	Wagga... ...	N.S.W.
J H **WALWA**	Mr. Watson, Walwa, Walwa Creek	...	VIC.
J H **WHITE HALL** **GLYNWYLLN**	J. Hutchings, White Hall, Stawell	Western District...	VIC.
JIMENBUAN **C**	Crisp Bros., Jimenbuan, Cooma	Cooma	N.S.W.
JINGELLIC	A. M. & A. Co., Ltd., Jingellic, Hume	Hume ...	N.S.W.
JIREENA	H. Tall, Jireena, Prairie Creek	Hughenden	Q.

WOOL MARKS.	WOOL GROWERS' NAMES AND ADDRESSES.	PASTORAL DISTRICT.	STATE.
J I SANDSIDE	J. Innis, Sandside, Narrandera	Narrandera	N.S.W.
J 3 ISIS	Oliver Smith and Co., Isis Downs, Isisford	Isisford...	Q.
J I TOMBONG	J. Ingram, Tombong, Delegate	Bombala	N.S.W.
L 7 CUDGEGONG	J. Jennings, Toolamanang, Cudgegong	Mudgee	N.S.W.
J J H ROSEFIELD	J. J. Hughston, Rosefield, Burrowa	Young	N.S.W.
J J J FOXDOWN	J. Goodwin, Foxdown, Tangmangaroo	Yass	N.S.W.
J J K DOODLE COOMA WEST	J. J. Keighran, Doodle Cooma, Henty	Albury ...	N.S.W.
J J M LAWLOIT	J. J. Meagher, Lawloit, Miram Piram	North-Western District	VIC.
J J ROSEHILL	J. Jones, Rosehill, Jericho ...	Jericho...	TAS.
J JURD MOREE	J. Jurd (exors.), Watercourse, Moree...	Moree	N.S.W.
J. J. WARBY B	J. J. Warby, Mungindi, Moree	Moree ...	N.S.W.
J J W T H	J. J. Worthington, Thorn Hill, Frampton	Gundagai	N.S.W.
JK	R. R. Keynes, Keyneton	Keyneton	S.A.
J K ASCOT VALE	J. Kenorthy, Ascot Hill, Broken Hill...	Menindie	N.S.W.
JKF KINGLEBILLA	J. K., J. P. & J. H. Fleming, Kinglebilla, Bollon	Bollon	Q.

J

WOOL MARKS.	WOOL GROWERS' NAMES AND ADDRESSES.	PASTORAL DISTRICT.	STATE.
J K F ULAH	J. K. Fleming, Ulah, Walgett	Walgett ...	N.S.W.
J K M DRYSDALE	J. K. Moreton, Drysdale, Ballangeich	Warrnambool	VIC.
K NARRAWA	Mrs. C. Kelly, Narrawa, Young	Young	N.S.W.
J K P WARWILLAH	J. K. Palmer, Warwillah, Hawkesdale	Western District...	VIC.
J K WOODLAWN	Kelly Bros., Woodlawn, Purnim	Warrnambool	VIC.
J L	J. Lennard, Breeza, Tamworth	Tamworth	N.S.W.
J L B	J. L. Brown, Tondebucnic, Gilgandra...	Coonabarabran	N.S.W.
J C LARRA	J. L. Currie, Larra, Camperdown	Western District...	VIC
J L CLELAND	J. Lander, Cleland, Ballon	Bollon	Q.
J L C SPRINGBANK	Molesworth and Ware, Springbank, Charlton	N.N.W. District ...	VIC.
J L DUNDONNELL	J. Lamont, Dundonnell Station, Dundonnell		VIC.
J L E B MUDGEE	J. Lee, Burrendong, Mudgee	Mudgee	N.S.W.
J L GLENFERN	J. Lovegrove, Glenfern, Yarraman	Tamworth	N.S.W.
J L GLENGARRY	J. W. Lamb, Glengarry, Kangaroo Point	Glen Innes	N.S.W.
J L HARTWOOD	J. Lynch, Hartwood, Narromine	Dubbo ...	N.S.W.

114

WOOL MARKS.	WOOL GROWERS' NAMES AND ADDRESSES.	PASTORAL DISTRICT.	STATE.
⬦JL⬦ HAZELDEAN	A. J. Litchfield, Hazeldean, Cooma	Cooma ...	N.S.W.
J L LAKE WALLACE	Fenton and Phillip, Lake Wallace South, Eden-hope...	Lake Wallace	VIC.
J L M INVERGOWRIE	J. L. Mitchell, Invergowrie, Armidale	Armidale	N.S.W.
J L MUDGEE	J. Lloyd, sen., Coomber, Rylstone	Mudgee	N.S.W.
⬦J L P L⬦	J. and P. Lang, Tocumwal, Deniliquin	Deniliquin	N.S.W.
J L R P	J. Lamrock, Cosgrove, Gippsland	Gippsland	VIC.
J L RYLSTONE	J. Lloyd, jun., Kilgoola, Rylstone	Mudgee	N.S.W.
J L TARA HALL	Lawer Bros., Tara Hall, Merriwa	Merriwa	N.S.W.
J L WAGGA	J. Lockett, Clebury Road, Wagga	Wagga...	N.S.W.
J L WALLALOO	The Manager, Wallaloo, St. Arnaud	Avoca	VIC.
J L WILPENA	Mr. Lewis, Wilpena	Wilpena	S.A.
J L YUMA	J. Lauders, Yuma, Coonamble	Coonamble	N.S.W.
J M	J. Moir and Co., 58 Margaret Street, Sydney		N.S.W.
J M A	J. McAlister, Daisy Hill, Wollumbi	Armidale	N.S.W.
◁J M▷ ANAMA	J. Maitland, Anama, Rochester	Rochester	S.A.

J

WOOL MARKS.	WOOL GROWERS' NAMES AND ADDRESSES.	PASTORAL DISTRICT.	STATE.
J M B **CLARENDON**	P. Byrne and Sons, Clarendon, Balranald	Balranald	N.S.W.
J M **B** **MUDGEE**	J. Murray, Beaudesert, Gulgong	Mudgee ...	N.S.W.
J M **CURRAJONG**	J. Moncrieff, Currajong, Lockhart	Urana ...	N S.W.
J M D **EDLIN VALE**	J. McDonald, Edlin Vale, Broken Hill	Menindie	N.S.W.
J M D **MOONAN**	J. D. McCallum, Bell Brook, Moonan Flat	Murrurundi	N.S.W.
JMD **URIARRA**	J. McDonald, Uriarra, Queanbeyan	Queanbeyan ...	N.S.W.
J M **FERNLEA**	A. Hardie, Fernlea, Crossley	Warrnambool ...	VIC.
J M **G F**	J. Mitchell, Lower Bethunga	North-Eastern District	VIC.
⊃ M **9** **GNOULAMEIN**	J. Moloney, Gnoulamein, Tycannah ...	Moree ...	N.S.W.
J M **GOOMBARGANA**	A. Balme, Goombargana Station, Goombargana	Albury	N.S.W.
J M I **BURRUM**	J. McIntosh, Burrum	Western District...	VIC.
J M **IRONMONGIE**	E. O'Meara, Ironmongie, Dalgety	Cooma	N.S W.
J M **J** **BRUSHY CREEK**	J. Jackson, Brushy Creek, Guyra	Armidale	N.S.W.
J M **JEWS LAGOON**	M. J. Murphy, Jews Lagoon, Bulyeroi	Pilliga	N.S.W.
J M **LANARK**	J. Mahon, Lanark, Morangorell	Young ...	N.S.W.

WOOL MARKS.	WOOL GROWERS' NAMES AND ADDRESSES.	PASTORAL DISTRICT.	STATE.
J M **L B**	J. Mitchell, Bethanga	North-Eastern District	VIC.
J M L **H. VALLEY**	Mrs. M. Locker, Happy Valley, Adaminaby	Cooma	N S W
J M **LODDON**	W. L. Reid, Loddon, Durham Ox	Gunbower	VIC.
J M McB **OUTAALPA**	J. M. McBride, Outaalpa, O'Lara		S.A.
J M **MELROSE**	J. Mogollin and Bros., Melrose, Longreach	Longreach	Q.
J M **M** **MORANGHURK**	R. A. Molesworth, Moranghurk, Lethbridge	Geelong	VIC.
J M **MOONAN**	J. Muller, Moonan, Moonan Flat	Murrurundi	N.S.W.
J M M **ROCKGEDGIEL**	McMaster Bros., Rockgedgiel, Bundella	Coonabarabran	N.S.W.
J M M **WEETALABAH**	McMaster Bros., Weetalabah, Coolah...	Coonabarabran	N.S.W.
J M **N** **MOUNT NAPIER**	A. J. Simpson, Mt. Napier, Hamilton...	Western District	VIC.
J M **OAKFIELD**	J. Miller, Oakfield, Miller	Dubbo ...	N.S.W.
J M **Q**	J. Metham, Borambil, Quirindi	Tamworth	N.S.W.
J M R **B C** **NEW ENG**	J. Maher, Woolbrook, Armidale	Armidale	N S W
J M S	J. M. Simmons, Drung Drung, Horsham	Wimmera	VIC.
J M S **BURINDI**	J. M. Simpson, Burindi, Barraba	Tamworth	N.S.W.

WOOL MARKS.	WOOL GROWERS' NAMES AND ADDRESSES.	PASTORAL DISTRICT.	STATE.
J M 7 SPRING CREEK	J. Medway, Spring Creek, Dalton	Yass ...	N.S.W.
J M TABLETOP	J. Mitchell, Table Top Station, Table Top	Albury	N.S.W.
J M TIMOR	A. Martin, Mountain View, Timor	Murrurundi	N.S.W.
J M TRIDA NEW ENG	J. Mannel, Trida, Armidale ...	Armidale	N.S.W.
J MURRAY CAPPEEDEE	W. A. Murray, Cappeedee, Hallett	Hallett ...	S.A.
J MURRAY RHINE PARK	J. Murray, Rhine Park, Eden Valley	Eden Valley	S A.
J M Y C K	J. Moffat and Sons, Yarrowyck, Armidale	Armidale	N.S.W.
J M Y Y	J. Morris, Yanac-a-Yanac, Nhill	Wimmera	VIC.
J McC B	J. McCalman, Ballagreen, *via* Warren	Coonamble	N.S.W.
J McC L	J. McC. Laug, Horseshoe Bend, Barudine	Coonabarabran	N.S.W.
J McC WESTBANK	J. McConochie, Westbank, Kariah		VIC.
J McD	P. J. C. McDouall, New Frengh, Whittingham...	Singleton ...	N.S.W.
J McD ELMHURST	J. McDonald, Elmhurst	Wimmera	VIC.
J McD MARYVALE	J. McDonald, Maryvale, Streaky Bay...		S.A.
J McD YABBA	J. McDonald, Yabba, Tallangatta		VIC.

WOOL MARKS.	WOOL GROWERS' NAMES AND ADDRESSES.	PASTORAL DISTRICT.	STATE.
J M C **GLENWOOD**	J. McCarty, Glenwood Hall, Gundaroo	Queanbeyan	N.S.W.
J Mc H **SPRING GULLY**	J. McHugh, Spring Gully, Bundarra ...	Armidale	N.S.W.
J McM **AMAROO**	J. McMahon, Amaroo, Orange	Bathurst	N.S.W.
J McM **BUMBALDRY**	J. McMahon, Bumbaldry, Grenfell	Forbes ...	N.S.W.
J Mc N **LONDON BRIDGE**	J. and P. McNamara, London Bridge, Queanbeyan	Queanbeyan	N.S.W.
J McPH **CORRUMBENE**	J. McPherson, Corrumbene	Western District	VIC.
J McPHEE	J. McPhee, Trunkey	Carcoar	N.S.W.
J N	J. Neman, Robe	Robe	S.A.
J N **BANDON**	J. Newell, Bandon, Forbes	Forbes	N.S.W.
J N **BOLARO**	J. Nott, Bolaro, Cobbora	Dubbo ...	N.S.W.
J N **FASSIFERN**	J. Newoon, Fassifern, Barnawatha	North-Eastern District	VIC.
J N **K**	J. Nooman, Gulnare	Gulnare	S.A.
J N **MUDGEE**	J. Niven, Springridge, Gulgong	Mudgee	N.S.W.
J N **NAREEN**	C. Elliott, Nareen Station, Nareen		VIC.
J N S **GLENCOE**	J. N. Swinson, Glencoe, Coolah	Coonabarabran	N.S.W.

WOOL MARKS.	WOOL GROWERS' NAMES AND ADDRESSES.	PASTORAL DISTRICT.	STATE.
J O	J. Dunnet, Denial Bay	Denial Bay	S.A.
J O C HOVELLS CREEK	J. O'Connor, Hovell's Creek, Frogmore	Young	N.S.W.
JOHN GRANT BELUBULA	J. Grant, Belubula, Canowindra	Molong...	N.S.W.
J O L MILLTHORPE	J. J. O'Leary, Limestone Creek, Millthorpe	Bathurst	N.S.W.
JONES BACK MERIGAL	A. E. Jones, Back Merrigal, Merrigal...	Coonamble	N.S.W.
JONES BULLAGREEN	J. T. Jones, Bullagreen Station, Bullagreen	Coonamble	N.S.W.
JONES MERIGAL	T. Jones, Merrigal, Gularganbone	Coonamble	N.S.W.
JONES MUNNELL	A. N. Jones, Munnell, Gilgandra	Coonamble	N.S W.
J P	J. Parkin, Pine Grove, Kingstown	Ballarat	VIC.
J P C AVYMORE	J. P. Carrigan, Avymore, Boggabilla ...	Warialda	N.S.W.
J P CLUNES	G. Fraser, Clune's Estate, Clunes	Carcoar	N S.W.
J P DALE	J. Packer, Bethanga	North-Eastern District	VIC.
J PEACOCK WARRAGAN	J. Peacock, Warragan, Walgett	Walgett	N.S.W.
ᒍP **ELMS**	J. Potter, The Elms, Stawell	Wimmera	VIC.
J P **EUBELLA**	J. F. Perpement, The Nutshell, Somerton	Tamworth	N.S.W.

WOOL MARKS.	WOOL GROWERS' NAMES AND ADDRESSES.	PASTORAL DISTRICT.	STATE.
J P **EULELLA**	J. F. Perpement, Eulella and Wynilla, Woolomin	Tamworth	N.S.W.
J P G I **NEW ENG**	J. Pomroy, Stonehenge, Glen Innes	Glen Innes ...	N.S.W.
J P **GREG GREG**	J. Pierce, Greg Greg, Hume...	Hume	N S.W.
J P I A **SCONE**	J. Ashford, Woodlands, Scone	Murrurundi ...	N.S.W.
J P **JOUNAMA**	Mrs. J. Pethers, Jounama, Yarraugobilly	Gundagai	N.S.W.
J P **LORRAINE PARK**	J. J. Porter, Lorraine Park, Heyfield ...	Gippsland ...	VIC.
J P **MELTON**	J. Pratley, Melton Estate, George's Plains	Bathurst	N.S.W.
J P **MYALL PARK**	J. Patrick, Myall Park, Gilgandra	Coonamble	N.S.W.
J P **PINE GROVE**	Mrs. W. L. Pearce, Pine Grove, Jerilderie	Jerilderie	N.S.W.
J P R **BURROWA**	J. P Ryan, Rockview, Burrowa	Young ...	N.S.W.
J P R **WRAYBURNE**	J. P. Radford, Wrayburne, Wee Waa	Pilliga ...	N.S.W.
J P S **COOMA**	J. Murdock, Peter's Park, Bungarby ...	Bombala ...	N.S.W.
J P S M	P. Phillip, St. May's, Clear Lake	Western District	VIC.
J P X △	J. Pingelby, Yarraman, Tamworth	Tamworth ...	N.S.W.
J P X △ **YARRAMAN**	J. Pingelby, Yarraman, Tamworth	Tamworth ...	N.S.W.

J

WOOL MARKS.	WOOL GROWERS' NAMES AND ADDRESSES.	PASTORAL DISTRICT.	STATE.
J R	J. Rogerson, Pearsley Hall, Inverell	Glen Innes	N.S.W.
J R B	J. R. Bidgood (exors.), Lochiel	... ...	S.A.
J R BURNSIDE	J. Ferry (Manager), Burnside, Bannockburn, Gheringhap	Western District ...	VIC.
JR C B	J. R. Carter, Talbalba, Bourke	Bourke ...	N.S.W.
J R HAMPDEN	J. Ralston, Hampden, Nile	Evendale	TAS.
J R KIMO	J. Robinson, Kimo, Gundagai	Gundagai	N.S.W.
J R L E	J. R. Learmonth, Ellengowan, McArthur	Western District ...	VIC.
J R L ASTON	J. R. Logan, Aston, Bombala	Bombala	N.S.W.
J R L WIRRAH	J. R. Lomax, Wirrah, Mungindi	Moree	N.S.W.
J R MAYFIELD	J. and R. E. Roberts, Mayfield...	Braidwood	N.S.W.
J R MINTO	J. Rutherford, Minto, Bibbenluke	Bombala	N.S.W.
J R M ROSEPOINT	J. R. Murphy, Rosepoint, Cookardinia	Albury ...	N.S.W.
J R MUDGEE	J. Reid, Hill End, Mudgee ...	Mudgee	N.S.W.
J R MUNDAREE	J. Rigney, Mundaree, Coonamble	Coonamble	N.S.W.
J R N	J. Robertson, Wallen Wallen, Lent	... ...	VIC.

WOOL MARKS.	WOOL GROWERS' NAMES AND ADDRESSES.	PASTORAL DISTRICT.	STATE.
J R **P H**	J. Ryan, Pine Hill, Jerilderie	Jerilderie	N.S.W.
J R P **MORVEN**	G. Matchett, Morven Station, Morven	Albury ...	N.S.W
J. R. ROSS **BANGO** **YASS**	J. R. Ross, Bango, Yass	Yass	N.S.W.
J **R W**	R. J. Whipp, Crosses' Station, Bannaby, Taralga	Goulburn	N.S.W.
⬦JR⬦ **WALBUNDRIE**	W. Kiddle, Walbundrie, Henty	Albury ...	N.S.W.
J R **WATERVALE**	J. Rumble, Watervale, Harden	Young ...	N.S.W.
(**J S**)	J. Stewart, Cullingeria, Reefton	Young	N.S.W.
J̅ S̅	Riley, Newman & Co., Macquarie Street, Sydney		N.S.W.
J S **BYGOO**	Stewart and Sons, Bygoo, Narrandera	Narrandera	N.S.W.
JSC **CARDUNGLE**	J. Crowley, Cardungle, Trundle	Forbes ...	N.S.W.
(**J S**) **CULLINGERIA**	J. Stewart, Cullingeria, Reefton	Young ...	N.S.W.
J S **D** **DRUNGALEAR**	Mrs. M. A. Simpson, Drungalear, Warren	Coonamble	N.S.W.
J S D **GOONOO GOONOO**	Mrs. A. Dunbar, Corora, Goonoo Goonoo	Tamworth	N.S.W.
J S **GRAHAM**	J. Smith, Graham, Reid's Flat	Young ...	N.S.W.
J S **HILLTOP**	A. Sturgeon, Hilltop, Jindabyne	Cooma	N.S.W.

J

WOOL MARKS.	WOOL GROWERS' NAMES AND ADDRESSES.	PASTORAL DISTRICT.	STATE.
J S I M D C	J. Sevil, Glasston, Willow Tree	Tamworth ...	N.S.W.
J S INVERARY	F. W. Stewart, Inverary, Branxholme	Western District ...	VIC.
J S KIRAWA	Mrs. E. Siddins, Kirawa, Ashley	Moree	N.S.W.
J SLO BRIDGEWATER	J. Sloman, Bridgewater, Dundee	Molong...	N.S.W.
J SLO DUNDEE	J. Sloman, Bridgewater, Dundee	Molong...	N.S.W.
J SMART GREEN HILLS	J. Smart, Green Hills, Nangus	Gundagai	N.S.W.
J S MARYVALE	J. Smith, Maryvale, Narrawa	Young	N.S.W.
J S MOORLANDS	J. Simpson, Moorlands, Walgett	Walgett ...	N.S.W.
J S NANGARAH	J. Spencer, Nangarah, Barraba	Tamworth	N.S.W.
J S REIDS VALE	J. Smith, Reid's Vale, Narrawa	Young ...	N.S.W.
J S R GUMS	J. S. Ross, North Gums, Penshurst	Warrnambool	VIC.
J STEEL WALCHA	Steel Bros., Craigend, Walcha	Armidale ...	N.S.W.
J S WONNAMINTA K Y	A.M.L. & F. Co., Ltd., Wonnaminta and Nundoro, Broken Hill	Milparinka ...	N.S.W.
J T B NEW ENGLAND	J. T. Bell, Bellmont, Black Mountain...	Armidale ...	N.S.W.
J T C	J. T. Chew, Danabilla, Bendick Morell	Young ...	N.S.W.

J

WOOL MARKS.	WOOL GROWERS' NAMES AND ADDRESSES.	PASTORAL DISTRICT.	STATE.
J T ERIN	Turner Bros., Erin, Narrabri	Narrabri	N.S.W.
J T GLENALVON	J. Taylor, jun., Glenalvon, Murrurundi	Murrurundi	N.S.W.
T H MERRIWA	J. T. Howard, Muni Vale, Merriwa	Merriwa	N.S.W.
J T MITCHELLS CREEK	T. Tehan, Mitchell's Creek		VIC.
J T M S B O	J. T. Mortlock, Bellilingra Platform, via Cooma	Cooma ...	N.S.W.
J & T M TARA	H. Murray, sen., Tara, Louth	Bourke .	N.S.W.
J TREVELYAN	J. Glasson, Trevelyan, Blayney	Carcoar	N.S.W.
J T ROUND PLAIN	A. G. Thompson, Round Plain, Halfield	Balranald	N.S.W.
J T 2 SPRING PARK	J. Tunney, Spring Park, Monteagle	Young ...	N.S.W.
J V MUDGEE	J. M. Vitnell, Mount Hope, Guntawang	Mudgee	N.S.W.
J W B HINNOMUNGIE	J. W. Brumley, Hinnomungie, Omeo ...	Gippsland	VIC.
J W B NEWINGTON	J. W. Buchanan, Newington, Wallendbeen	Young . .	N.S.W.
J W B POOLAMACCA	J. W. Brongham, Poolamacca, Broken Hill	Menindie	N.S.W.
J. W. B. RIDGE	J. W. Bowman, The Ridge, Rosedale...	Gippsland	VIC.
J W C PRIMROSE	J. W. Clark, Primrose Farm, Bourke...	Bourke...	N.S.W.

WOOL MARKS.	WOOL GROWERS' NAMES AND ADDRESSES.	PASTORAL DISTRICT.	STATE.
J & W C SPRING HILL	J. and W. Crick, Spring Hill, Gymbawen, Goroke	W. Wimmera	VIC.
J W C YASS	J. Carey, Cave Valley, Yass...	Yass	N.S.W
J WEATHERLY	J. Weatherly, Hillgay, Coleraine	North-Western District	VIC.
J WELSH TRINKEY	J. Welsh, Trinkey, Boggabilla	Warialda	N.S.W.
J W G T RIDGELANDS	J. W. G. Taylor, Ridgelands, Scone	Murrurundi	N S.W.
J W MT WELLS	J. Wells, Mt. Wells, Blanket Flat	Carcoar...	N.S.W.
J W MULLA CREEK	D. G. Ware, Mulla Creek, Moonbi	Tamworth	N.S.W
J WOODLANDS	H. D. Howard, Woodlands, Bigga	Carcoar	N.S.W.
J W ROCKLANDS	J. Wheelihan, Rocklands, Murrurundi	Murrurundi	N.S.W
J W S NEW ENG	J. Winter, Stonehenge, Glen Innes	Glen Innes	N.S.W.
J W S NEWHAVEN	J. W. Smith, Newhaven, Narramine ...	Dubbo ...	N.S.W.
JW SPRING RIDGE	J. and W. Smith, Spring Ridge, Moulamein	Moulamein	N.S.W.
J. W. SPRINGVILLE	J. Whiteman, Springville, Narrabri	Narrabri	N.S.W.
J W SUNNYSIDE	J. Whitten, Sunnyside, Tamworth	Tamworth	N.S.W.
J W TASMANIAN	J. Wardlaw, Pastoralist, Tasmania		TAS.

J

WOOL MARKS.	WOOL GROWERS' NAMES AND ADDRESSES.	PASTORAL DISTRICT.	STATE.
J & W W	J. and W. Webb, Fairlight, Queanbeyan	Queanbeyan	N.S.W.
J W WARGE ROCK	J. Williamson and Son, Warge Rock, Parkes	Forbes	N.S.W.
J X P POLIA	Pile Bros., Polia, Pooncairn, Wentworth	Wentworth	N.S.W.
J X THERRIBRI	W. F. Jaques, Therribri, Boggabri	Narrabri	N.S.W.
J YOUNG	W. James, Hazeldean, Stockinbingal	Young	N.S.W.

K

WOOL MARKS.	WOOL GROWERS' NAMES AND ADDRESSES.	PASTORAL DISTRICT.	STATE.
K	W. Kirkley, Glen Prairie, Moree	Moree ...	N.S.W.
K	H. J. Moore, North Hamilton	Western District	VIC.
K	W. T. Knowling, Rupanyup, Wimmera	Wimmera	VIC.
K ADELAIDE VALE	A. O'Keefe, Adelaide Vale, Axedale	Bendigo	VIC.
KADINA	C. S. McPhillamy, Kadina, Alectown...	Molong	N.S.W.
KADLUNGA	F. W. Weston (Manager), Kadlunga, Mintara	Mintara	S.A.
KADNOCK	Edgar Bros., Kadnock, Harrow	Hamilton	VIC.
KALADBRO	M. M. McKinnon, Kaladbro, Strathdownie		VIC.
KALANGAN	A. D. Middleton, Kalangan, Galong	Young ...	N.S.W.
KALENO	W. H. Fletcher, Kaleno, Cobar	Cobar	N.S.W.
KAL KAL TEMORA	G. J. Howard, Kal Kal, Temora	Wagga	N.S.W.
KALLARA	C. and S. Officer, Kallara, Louth	Wilcannia	N.S.W.
KAMILAROI Ⓢ Ⓢ	W. S. Sims, Kamilaroi, Millie	Moree ...	N.S.W.
KANGAROOBIE J D O	J. Dalton, Kangaroobie, Mullion's Creek	Bathurst	N.S.W.
KANGATONG N̄	Hon. N. Thornley, Kangatong, Hawkesdale	Warrnambool	VIC.

K

WOOL MARKS.	WOOL GROWERS' NAMES AND ADDRESSES.	PASTORAL DISTRICT.	STATE.
KANIMBLA **E V**	E. Vickery and Sons, Kanimbla, Little Hartley	Bathurst	N.S.W.
KARABEAL **T W H**	T. and W. Higgins, Karabeal, Dunkeld	Wannon	VIC.
K **ARDELL**	M. J. Kerin, Ardell, Balderodgery	Molong...	N.S.W.
KAROOLA	T. Knight, Karoola, Guyra	Armidale	N.S.W.
⬦K⬦ **BROOKFIELD**	T. Cruice, Brookfield, Beaufort	Glen Innes	N.S.W.
⬦K⬦ **BUDDAH GROVE**	J. S. and W. Kirby, Buddah Grove, Collarendabri	Walgett	N.S.W.
K B **W C**	J. W. R. Koppman, Windy Corner, Umeralla ...	Cooma ...	N.S.W.
K **CARINGLE**	J. S. Kirkup, Bundabulla, via Brewarrina	Brewarrina	N.S.W.
K **COOLAC**	E. J. Keane, Mooney Mooney, Coolac...	Gundagai	N.S.W.
K **CORNHILL**	R. McKenzie, Cornhill, Mansfield	Mansfield	VIC.
K **DOLGELLY**	J. Keen, Dolgelly, Moree	Moree ...	N.S.W.
KELVIDON **F S**	F. Scott, Kelvidon, Wee Waa	Narrabri	N.S.W.
KENILWORTH	Philip and Fenton, Kenilworth, Cavendish	Hamilton	VIC.
KENSINGTON **K BROS**	Kennedy Bros., Kensington, Come-by-Chance ..	Coonamble	N.S.W.
KENTUCKY	J. G. Gray, Kentucky, Corowa	Corowa...	N.S.W.

K

WOOL MARKS.	WOOL GROWERS' NAMES AND ADDRESSES.	PASTORAL DISTRICT.	STATE.
KERARBURY	J. S. Horsfall & Co., Kerarbury, Darlington Pt.	Narrandera	N.S.W.
KERR	A. Kerr, Springvale, Nareen		VIC.
KEWITA	G. H. Hope, Toora, Gippsland	Gippsland	VIC.
KEYTAH	P. H. O'Brien, Keytah, Moree	Moree	N.S.W.
K F CONINGDALE	Mrs. K. Finlayson, Coningdale, Armidale	Armidale	N.S.W.
K GLENMORE	W. Keen, Glenmore, Moree ...	Moree ...	N.S.W.
KIAH LAKE	E. J. Allen, Kiah Lake, Berridale	Cooma	N.S.W.
KIAORA MONARA	S. B. Beard, Kiaora, Cooma...	Cooma	N.S.W.
KILLALOOLAH H C R	H. C. Rogers, Killaloolah, Dubbo	Dubbo	N.S.W.
KILLEN	G. H. Chomley, Killen, Longwood	N.N.E. District	VIC.
KILLEN RIVERSLEA	E. Killen, Riverslea, Mt. McDonald	Young	N.S.W.
KILLINGWORTH	C. G. Morrison, Killingworth, Yea ...	Central District ...	VIC.
KIL TAMMIT	A. J. and W. Kilpatrick, Tammit, Euston	Balranald ...	N.S.W.
KIMBOLTON	W. C. Hamilton, Kimbolton, Axedale...	Bendigo ...	VIC.
KINCHEGA	H. W. Hughes, Kinchega, Broken Hill	Menindie ...	N.S.W.

K

WOOL MARKS.	WOOL GROWERS' NAMES AND ADDRESSES.	PASTORAL DISTRICT.	STATE.
KINGSTON PARK	A. Haylock, Kingston Park, Gunbar	Hay	N.S.W.
KINROSS	J. Ross, Kinross, Germanton	Hume	N.S.W.
KIRNDEEN	A. M. Bean (exors.), Kirndeen, Culcairn	Albury ...	N.S.W.
K Ж BARRABA	A. Witten, Barraba, Tamworth	Tamworth	N.S.W.
ЖM ADAMINABY	F. J. Mould, Adaminaby, Cooma	Cooma ...	N.S.W.
K MOUNT KOROITE	J. F. Kirby, Mt. Koroite, Coleraine	Wannon	VIC.
K M VELLORE	K. McLean, Vellore, Denison, Gippsland	Gippsland	VIC.
KOCKATEA C BROS	N. Fry (Manager), Kockatea, Mullewa	Mullewa	W.A.
KOOLOMURT	J. Haines, Koolomurt, Coleraine	Wannon	VIC.
KOON	Hamilton and Wilcox, Koonamore	North-Eastern District	S.A.
KOONONGWOOTONG CREEK	Mrs. F. Stanley, Koonongwootong Creek, Coleraine	Wannon	VIC.
KOONONGWOOTONG NORTH	A. Johnston (exors.), Koonongwootong North, Coleraine	Wannon	VIC.
KOORTNONG	E. McArthur, Koort-Koortnong, Camperdown ...	Western District...	VIC.
K + P	W. Parkman, Tout Calabash, Marengo	Young ...	N.S.W.
K P KILDARY	P. Kearins, Kildary, via Temora	Wagga ..	N.S.W.

K

WOOL MARKS.	WOOL GROWERS' NAMES AND ADDRESSES.	PASTORAL DISTRICT.	STATE.
K PRETTY TOWER STOCKYARD HILL	F. Rogers, Pretty Tower, Beaufort	Ripon ...	VIC.
K □ TEMPLEMORE	P. Kearins, Templemore, Marengo	Young ...	N.S.W.
KPT WARRANGEE RYLSTONE	Mrs. M. E Jamieson, Warrangee, Rylstone	Mudgee	N.S.W.
K & S GOWRIE	A. K. Cameron, Gowrie, Tenterden	Armidale	N.S.W.
K UPPINGHAM	A. Kinleside, Uppingham, Koorawatha	Young	N.S W.
K W B'DORE	Mrs. K. Walsh, Hoskin's Town, Queanbeyan	Queanbeyan	N.S.W.
K & W JONDARYAN QUEENSLAND	Jondaryan Estates Co., Jondaryan, Toowoomba	Toowoomba	Q.
KYEAMBA	A. Smith, Kyeamba, Wagga	Wagga	N.S.W.
KYLE	W. A. Ranken, Lockyersleigh, Carrick	Goulburn	N S.W.
K Y NEW ENG	A. S. Yates, Horwood, Kingstown	Armidale	N.S.W.
KYNUNA E J	E. Jowett, Kynuna, Winton..	Winton...	Q.

L

WOOL MARKS.	WOOL GROWERS' NAMES AND ADDRESSES.	PASTORAL DISTRICT.	STATE.
⟨L⟩	R. L. E. Finlay, Gundary, Goulburn ...	Goulburn	N.S.W.
L	W. Langley, Bordertown	Bordertown	S.A.
L A F BRAEMORE	L. A. Fairbairn, Braemore, Craigieburn	Central District ...	VIC.
LAIRG	W. Gunn, Lairg, Way	West Coast ...	S.A.
LAKE CORRONG	E. H. Lascelles, Lake Corrong, Hopetown	North-Western District	VIC.
LAKE COWALL	S. Wilson and Son, Lake Cowall, Marsden	Condobolin	N.S.W.
LAKE TORRENS	J. Whyte (exors.), Lake Torrens, Hergott Springs	Hergott Springs	S.A.
LAKE VICTORIA	A. Armstrong (exors.), Lake Victoria, Tareena	Wentworth	N.S.W.
LAN	R. Landale (exors.), Quiamong, Deniliquin	Deniliquin	N.S.W.
LANARK A D 7	A. Dean, Lanark, Coonabarabran	Coonabarabran	N.S.W.
LANGI KAL KAL	Campbell and Felton, Langi-Kal-Kal, Trawalla		VIC.
LANGTON	A. Menzies, Langton, Clermont	Clermont	Q.
LANGTON PEAK DOWNS	A. Menzies, Langton, Clermont	Clermont	Q.
LANSDOWNE	Lansdowne Pastoral Co., Lansdowne, Tambo	Tambo ...	Q.
LANYON	A. J. & J. Cunningham, Lanyon, Queanbeyan	Queanbeyan	N.S.W.

L

WOOL MARKS.	WOOL GROWERS' NAMES AND ADDRESSES.	PASTORAL DISTRICT.	STATE.
LANYON D N	A. J. & J. Cunningham, Lanyon, Queanbeyan	Queanbeyan	N.S.W.
LARUNDEL	A. Austin, Larundel, Cargarrie	Western District	VIC.
LAUREL PARK	H. Battenshaw, Laurel Park, Wyalong	Condobolin	N.S.W.
LAWRENNY	J. N. McArthur, Lawrenny, Caramut...	Western District...	VIC.
L B C C	L. Brown, Cope Cope, Wimmera	Wimmera	VIC.
L B EUCUMBENE	Litchfield Bros., Eucumbene, Adaminaby	Cooma ...	N.S.W.
L B KIMBOLTON	L. Brown, Kimbolton, Cope Cope, Donald	Kara-Kara	VIC.
L B M	Ledger Bros., Mullion, Yass	Yass	N.S.W.
L BROS BEULAH	Laidlow Bros., Beulah, Donald	Kara-Kara	VIC.
L & Co	Leukert and Co., Botany, Sydney		N.S.W.
L & Co ⟨A⟩	Leukert and Co., Botany, Sydney	...	N.S.W.
L & Co ⟨B⟩	Leukert and Co., Botany, Sydney	...	N.S.W.
L & Co ⟨C⟩	Leukert and Co., Botany, Sydney ...	...	N.S.W.
L & Co ⟨D⟩	Leukert and Co., Botany, Sydney		N.S.W.
L & Co ⟨E⟩	Leukert and Co., Botany, Sydney	...	N.S.W.

L

WOOL MARKS.	WOOL GROWERS' NAMES AND ADDRESSES.	PASTORAL DISTRICT.	STATE.
L & Co ◇G	Leukert and Co., Botany, Sydney	...	N.S.W.
L & Co ◇J	Leukert and Co., Botany, Sydney	...	N.S.W.
L & Co ◇JJ	Leukert and Co., Botany, Sydney	...	N.S.W.
L & Co ◇M	Leukert and Co., Botany, Sydney		N.S.W.
L & Co ◇O	Leukert and Co., Botany, Sydney		N.S.W.
L & Co ◇P	Leukert and Co., Botany, Sydney	...	N.S.W.
L & Co ◇R	Leukert and Co., Botany, Sydney	...	N.S.W.
L & Co ◇T	Leukert and Co., Botany, Sydney		N.S.W.
L & Co ◇V	Leukert and Co., Botany, Sydney		N.S.W.
L & Co ◇W	Leukert and Co., Botany, Sydney		N.S.W.
L & Co ◇X	Leukert and Co., Botany, Sydney		N.S.W.
L & Co ◇Z	Leukert and Co., Botany, Sydney		N.S.W.
L D N	H. C. White and Hunt, Londonn, Dalby	Dalby ...	Q.
L D O DARLING DOWNS	C. Cullen, Ladas Downs, Miles	Condamine	Q.

L

| --- | --- | --- | --- |
LEE	J. Lee and Co., Ltd., Larras Lake, Molong	Molong	N.S W.
L E FERNLEA	M. Pinkerton, Fernlea, Moonan	Murrurundi	N.S.W.
LEICHARDT	H. Collier, Leichardt, Clermont	St. Lawrence	Q.
L E NINGIE	L. Egan, Ningie Creek, Coonamble	Coonamble	N.S.W.
LESLIE	Leslie Bros. and Co., Lerida, Muttaburra	Muttaburra	Q.
LESLIE MANOR	L. Bell (Manager), Leslie Manor, Foxhow		VIC.
LEXINGTON	Clarke Bros., Lexington, Moyston	Wimmera	VIC.
L. E. WISEMAN ELMSWOOD	L. E. Wiseman, Elmswood, Gundy	Murrurundi	N.S.W.
LEZAYRE H K	H. C. Kelly, Lezayre, Wee Waa	Narrabri	N.S.W.
L G C DREEITE	G. Lewis, Calvert, Dreeite, Alvie		VIC.
L G FRESHWATER	Gulson Bros., Freshwater, Oxley	Balranald	N.S.W.
L H MUDGEE	L. Hawkens, Grattai, Mudgee	Mudgee	N.S.W.
LIEWAH H C K	A. T. Creswick, Liewah, Moulamein ...	Moulamein	N.S.W.
LILA	A. Tobin and Sons, Lila Springs, Ford's Bridge	Bourke...	N.S.W.
LIMESTONE J W P	J. W. Palmer, Limestone, Parkes	Forbes	N.S.W.

L

WOOL MARKS.	WOOL GROWERS' NAMES AND ADDRESSES.	PASTORAL DISTRICT.	STATE.
LINDSAY	J. M. Simpson, Lindsay, Boggabri	Narrabri ...	N.S.W.
LISSINGTON	H. D. Coward, Lissington, Enngonia	Bourke	N.S.W.
LITTLE FOREST	J. Healy, Little Forest, Gullymount	Carcoar ...	N.S.W.
L J D	L. J. Dargan, The Elms, Binalong	Young	N.S.W.
L K BUNDOLL	L. Kaufmann, Dunkeld	Wannon	VIC.
L K STEAM PLAINS	L. Kiddle, Steam Plains, Booroorban ...	Hay	N.S.W.
⟨LL⟩ KAROO	S. N. Lane, Karoo, Walmer P.O., *via* Wellington	Molong ...	N.S.W.
LLANGOLLEN	J. P. Radford, Llangollen, Cassilis	Merriwa	N.S.W.
LLANRHEIDOOL	W. Dalrymple, Llanrheidool, Winton...	Winton ..	Q.
L J EDGEFERN YOUNG	W. J. Lewis, Edgefern, Young	Young	N S.W.
L L NAMOI	Namoi Pastoral Co., Edgeroi, Narrabri	Narrabri	N.S.W.
L L NAMOI B D I	Namoi Pastoral Co., Edgeroi, Narrabri	Narrabri	N.S.W.
L L NAMOI C C	Namoi Pastoral Co., Edgeroi, Narrabri	Narrabri	N.S.W.
L L NAMOI R R	Namoi Pastoral Co., Edgeroi, Narrabri	Narrabri	N.S.W.
LLOWALONG X	A. Hamilton, Llowalong, Stratford	Gippsland	VIC.

L

WOOL MARKS.	WOOL GROWERS' NAMES AND ADDRESSES.	PASTORAL DISTRICT.	STATE.
L L V T	W. Lane, Violet Town	Central District	VIC.
L M A	L. G. McArthur, Warwarick, Camperdown	Western District...	VIC.
L M L GOWANBRAE	M. Lachlan, Boregorang, Wimmera	Wimmera	VIC.
L M N	A. Crawford, Blairmore, Boggabri	Tamworth	N.S.W.
L M NEW ENGLAND	W. Burgess, Armidale	Armidale	N.S.W.
L N O N WOODSTOCK	J. Lennon, Woodstock, Armidale	Armidale	N.S.W.
L N S BOREE	L. N. Smith, Boree, Cheeseman's Creek	Molong...	N.S.W.
L O G R	G. Loder, Abbey Green, Singleton	Singleton	N.S.W.
L O M WATERVIEW	Lloyd and Monk, Waterview, Prairie...	Hughenden	Q.
LONGARM	Wilson and Wilson, Longarm, Manilla	Tamworth	N.S.W.
LONGERENONG	H. E Bullivant, Longerenong, Murtoa	Horsham	VIC.
LONGFIELD COOMA	C. W. Pye, Longfield, Cooma	Cooma ...	N.S.W.
LONGFORD D C	A. Park (exors.), Longford, Bendemeer	Armidale	N.S.W.
LONGLANDS	A. O'Connor, Longlands, Cunnamulla	Cunnamulla ...	Q.
LONG POINT C. TEVCETTI	C. Tevcetti, Long Point, Mullion Creek	Bathurst ...	N.S.W.

L

WOOL MARKS.	WOOL GROWERS' NAMES AND ADDRESSES.	PASTORAL DISTRICT.	STATE.
LOOMBAH	G. Bruce, Loombah, Cumnock	Molong	N.S.W.
LORD'S HILL R S S	R. Stevenson, Lord's Hill, Bombala ...	Bombala	N.S.W.
LORN FIELD HD	McDoughall Bros., Lornfield, Grassdale		VIC.
LORRAINE	A.J.S. Bauk, Lorraine, Cloncurry	Cloncurry	Q.
LOUGHNAN BROS	Loughnan Bros., Kurrajong, Walgett	Walgett	N.S.W.
LOVAT DALE R F	R. Fraser (exors.), Lovatdale, Glenthompson	Western District	VIC.
LOVELY BANKS F O	F. L. Olle, Lovely Banks, Penshurst	Western District ...	VIC.
LOWE MUDGEE	C. M. Lowe, Yamble, Two Mile Flat	Mudgee	N.S.W.
LOWER I M Y 2 COOLEGONG	J. Maroney, Lower Coolegong	Young ...	N.S.W.
L P REEDY CREEK GLENTHOMPSON	W. I. Pagets, Wissen, Wickcliffe	Wimmera	VIC.
L R MULWALA	A. Sloane and Sons, Mulwala Station, Mulwala	Corowa ...	N.S.W.
⟨L⟩ ROSEDALE	J. D. Foster, Rosedale, Campbelltown	Campbelltown	TAS
L R WALLANDOOL	T. Ryan, Wallandool, Henty	Albury .	N.S.W.
L S BARRABA	S. J. and C. Lillis, Barraba, Tamworth	Tamworth	N.S.W.
L S DUNGOWAN	L. Sprague, Dungowan Station, Dungowan	Tamworth	N.S.W.

L

WOOL MARKS.	WOOL GROWERS' NAMES AND ADDRESSES.	PASTORAL DISTRICT.	STATE.
L S **F** **WELLINGROVE** **NEW ENGLAND**	Wellingrove Estate, Ltd., Wellingrove, Glen Innes	Glen Innes	N.S.W.
L & SONS **PRAIRIE**	Langmore and Sons, Prairia, Jondaryan	Hughenden	Q.
LUCKNOW	Fisken, Bunning and Co., Lucknow, Winton	Boulia	Q.
LUCKNOW **F B & Co**	Fisken, Bunning and Co., Lucknow, Winton	Boulia	Q.
LUE **MUDGEE**	V. J. Dowling (exors.), Lue, Mudgee...	Mudgee	N.S.W.
L V **YASS**	W. A. McCauley, Lucerne Vale, Coolabie	Yass	N.S.W.
L W **AIRLIE**	L. Watson, Airlie, Stratford	N. Gippsland	VIC.
L & W **BUNDARLAH**	Leighton and Ward, Bundarlah, Molong	Molong...	N.S.W.
L W **TIMOR**	L. Watson, Sunnyside, Timor	Murrurundi	N S.W.

M

WOOL MARKS.	WOOL GROWERS' NAMES AND ADDRESSES.	PASTORAL DISTRICT.	STATE.
M	J. F. Maslin, Bundaleer, Jamestown	Jamestown	S.A.
M	J. C. Manifold, Talindert, Camperdown	Western District	VIC.
M ABBOTSFORD	Melbourne Assets Co., Abbotsford, Ivanhoe	Ivanhoe	N.S.W.
M A A V	M. Abbey, Abbeyvale, Wheeo	Yass	N.S.W.
M & A B FONTENOY	M. and A. Bolger, Fontenoy, Wallendbeen	Young ...	N.S.W.
M & A B LALLA	M. and A. Bolger, Wonbobbie, Warren	Coonamble ...	N.S.W.
M A B MEILMAN	M. A. Brunet, Meilman, Euston	Balranald	N.S.W.
MACKAY BREWON	Mackay Bros., Brewon, Brewarrina	Brewarrina	N.S.W.
MACKAY CRYON	J. K. and W. H. Mackay, Cryon, Walgett	Walgett	N.S.W.
MACKAY PULLAMING	J. K. and W. H. Mackay, Pullaming, Gunnedah	Tamworth	N.S.W.
MACKAY YARRALDOOL	J. K. and W. H. Mackay, Yarraldool, Narrabri	Narrabri	N.S.W.
MACLEAN	Mrs. Maclean, Crown Station, Rylstone	Mudgee	N.S.W.
MACVILLE	D. McAlary, Millewa, via Trangie	Dubbo ...	N.S.W.
MADOWLA S	Mr. O'Shaunessy, Madowla Park, Barmah		VIC.
MADDRELL	H. F. Maddrell, Mona, Braidwood	Braidwood	N.S.W.

M

WOOL MARKS.	WOOL GROWERS' NAMES AND ADDRESSES.	PASTORAL DISTRICT.	STATE.
MAFFRA	J. C. Ryrie, Maffra, Cooma	Cooma ...	N.S.W.
MAHARATTA	M. Joseph (exors.), Maharatta, Bombala	Bombala	N.S.W.
M & A NARRAMINE	Mack and Austin, Narramine, Dubbo ..	Dubbo	N.S.W.
MANEROO	Dalgety and Co., Ltd., Maneroo, Longreach	Longreach	Q.
MANDAMAH	A. Davidson, Mandamah, West Temora	Wagga	N.S.W.
△ **MANILLA**	Barling Bros., Manilla, Upper Manilla	Tamworth ...	N.S.W.
MANUKA	A.E. & M. Co., Ltd., Manuka, Corfield	Winton	Q.
MANUS	R. McMicking, Manus, Tumberumba	Hume ...	N.S.W.
M A R	E. Mahor, Murga, Deniliquin	Deniliquin	N.S.W.
MARATHON 7 R V	Trust & Agency Co., Ltd., Marathon, Hughenden	Hughenden ...	Q.
MARDIE	Murray Squatting Co., Mardie, Onslow	Onslow ...	W.A.
MARENGO Y	W. Yeomans, Marengo Station, Marengo	Young	N.S.W.
MARILBA W S S	W. S. Suttor, Marilba, Bowning	Yass ...	N.S.W.
MARLBONE	P. O'Mullane, Marlbone, Pilliga	Pilliga	N.S.W.
MARMADILLA	Malvern Hills Pastoral Co., Marmadilla, Springsure	Springsure ...	Q.

M

WOOL MARKS.	WOOL GROWERS' NAMES AND ADDRESSES.	PASTORAL DISTRICT.	STATE.
M A R MYRTLE PARK	C. McAlister, Myrtle Park, Finley	Jerilderie	N.S.W.
MARNOO	Skene Bros., Marnoo		VIC.
MARTINDALE	W. T. Mortlock, Martindale, Mintaro	Mintaro	S.A.
MARTINDALE M F	M. Freudenstein, Martindale, Monteagle	Young ...	N.S.W.
MARRA	Hay, Graves and Paxton, Marra, Wilcannia	Wilcannia	N.S.W.
MARRAMOOK B	A. Bostock, Marramook, Woolsthorpe	Warrnambool	VIC.
MARYVALE	R. G. Maiden, Maryvale, Nyngan	Canonbar	N.S.W
M A TALMO	M. Armour, Talmo, Bookham	Young	N.S.W.
MATHONG	S. Litchfield, Mathong, Dalgety	Cooma ...	N.S.W.
MATHOURA	Goldsbrough, Mort and Co., Mathoura Station, Mathoura	Deniliquin	N.S.W.
MAWALLOCK	G. Lewis (Manager), Mawallock, Beaufort	Ripon	VIC.
MAYFIELD	J. R. E. Roberts, Mayfield, Boro	Braidwood	N.S.W.
MAYO	G. Gray, Mount Mayo, Woodhouselea...	Goulburn	N.S.W.
MAXWELTON C C M	Chave, Chave and Merson, Maxwelton, Richmond	Hughenden	Q.
M BEERBONG	A. Maguire, Beerbong, Gilgandra	Coonabarabran	N.S.W.

WOOL MARKS.	WOOL GROWERS' NAMES AND ADDRESSES.	PASTORAL DISTRICT.	STATE.
M BINNEGUY	Manche Bros., Binneguy Station, Binneguy	Moree ...	N S W.
M B KATANDRA	M. Breen, Katandra, Shepparton	Euroa	VIC.
M B LENY BRAES	Mrs. M Buchanan, Leny Braes, Clementston	Talbot ...	VIC.
M B L FIVE MILE	M. Ball, Five Mile, Gundagai	Gundagai	N.S.W.
M B MOUNT PETER	M. Byrnes, Mt. Peter, Wagga	Wagga...	N.S.W.
M BOLAC	J. Moffatt, Lake Bolac	Western District	VIC.
M BROOKFIELD	McGregor Bros., Brookfield, Cooma	Cooma ...	N.S W.
M BROS BREWON	J. K. & W. H. Mackay, Brewon, Brewarrina	Brewarrina	N.S.W.
M B WALCHA	W. M. Borthwick, Walcha, Armidale	Armidale	N.S.W.
M B WEEUMBAH	Milburn Bros , Weeumbah, Longreach	Longreach	Q.
M CARLISLE	W. C. W. Milne, Carlisle, Fiefield	Condobolin ...	N.S.W.
M CANONBAR	Goldsbrough, Mort and Co., Canonbar, Nyngan	Canonbar ...	N.S.W.
McB & Co MOUNT POOLE	M. Lang and Co., Mount Poole, Milparinka	Milparinka ...	N.S.W.
M C BRUE PLAINS	M. Coalston, Brue Plains, Parkes	Forbes ...	N.S.W.
McC HILLSIDE	J. McCarry, Hillside, Coonamble	Coonamble ...	N.S.W.

M

M

WOOL MARKS.	WOOL GROWERS' NAMES AND ADDRESSES.	PASTORAL DISTRICT.	STATE.
M C L HARDWICKE YASS	M. C. Langtree, Hardwicke, Yass	Yass	N.S.W.
McL THORNTON	G. W. McLeish, Thornton, Nevertire	Dubbo	N.S.W.
M C L YASS PLAINS YASS	M. C. Langtree, Yass Plains, Yass	Yass	N.S.W.
McM BROS KELSO	J. Macfarlane and Co., Rockhampton...	Rockhampton	Q.
McM CROPPA	I. MacMaster, Croppa, Warialda	Warialda	N.S.W.
M C MERRILL	M. Clancy, Merrill, Gunning	Yass	N.S.W.
McM KELSO	McMaster Bros., Rockhampton	Rockhampton	Q.
⬦M⬦ **COMUNG**	D. McDonald, Comung, Kingston	Kingston	S.A.
McR MOUNT PLEASANT	A. G. McRobert, Mt. Pleasant, Toollern	Central District ...	VIC.
M C TERANG	J. McCall, Terang ...	Western District ..	VIC.
McW RODNEY DS	T. McWhannell (exors.), Rodney Downs, Ilfracombe	Barcaldine	Q.
M D	Campbell and Felton, Swan Hill	Northern District	VIC.
M DANDALOO	J. Martell, Dandaloo, Dandaloo	Dubbo ...	N.S.W.
⬚MDB⬚ **OAK HILLS**	D. W. McDonald, Oak Hills, Kellalac...	Borung...	VIC.
M D & Co EURELLA FITZROY DOWNS	F. Dunsmuir, Eurella, Roma...	Mitchell ...	Q.

WOOL MARKS.	WOOL GROWERS' NAMES AND ADDRESSES.	PASTORAL DISTRICT.	STATE.
M D & Co **MT WOOD**	Moore, Dorward and Palmer, Mt. Wood, Tiboo-burra	Milparinka	N.S.W.
M D **ELGIN**	A. McDonald, Elgin, Condah	Normanby	VIC.
M & D **GLENGALLAN**	Marshall and Slade, Glengallan, Warwick	Warwick	Q.
M D **SEBASTOPOL**	A. McLennon, Sebastopol, Booligal	Balranald	N.S.W.
M D **TUNGATTO**	E. McDonald, Tungatto, Way	Way	S.A.
MEADOWS **C C**	C. Carr, The Meadows, Obley	Molong...	N.S.W.
MEADOWS **H B W**	H. B. Welsh, The Meadows, Cobar	Cobar	N.S.W.
MEALE BROS **BRAWLIN**	Meale Bros., Brawlin	...	N.S.W
ME **BRAE SPRINGS**	T. H. Mate and Co., Brae Springs, Albury	Albury ...	N.S.W.
M **EDEOWIE**	V. H. Mogg, Edeowie	Northern District	S.A.
MELLERSTAIN	W. Douglass, Mellerstain, Mansfield	Mansfield	VIC.
MELOOL	A.L. & F. Co., Ltd., Melool, Moulamein	Moulamein	N.S.W.
MELROSE PLAINS	T. James and Co., Melrose Plains, Condobolin ...	Condobolin	N.S.W.
MELYRA	Union Bank of Australia, Melyra, Grenfell	Forbes ...	N.S.W.
MEMAGONG	Browne Bros., Memagong, Young	Young	N.S.W.

WOOL MARKS.	WOOL GROWERS' NAMES AND ADDRESSES.	PASTORAL DISTRICT.	STATE.
⌒ M EMU HILL	Mrs. A. Lewis, Emu Hill, Linton	Grenville	VIC.
MENINGOORT	J. N. McArthur, Meningoort, Camperdown	Camperdown	VIC.
MERCADOOL	Firebrace and Co., Mercadool, Walgett	Walgett	N.S.W.
MERRANG	R. Rood, Merrang, Hexham...	Western District	VIC.
MERRIJIG	G. C. Noble, Merrijig, Pettavel	... ...	VIC.
MERRI MERRIGAL	J. Sanderson and Co., Merri Merrigal, Hillston	Hillston	N.S.W.
MEROTHERIE ◇ J H B	Bowman Bros., Merotherie, Gulgong ...	Mudgee ...	N.S.W.
MERRYANBONE	W. Hay, Merryanbone, Canonbar	Canonbar ...	N.S.W.
MERUNGLE	W. Tully, Merungle, Booligal	Hillston	N.S.W.
MERYULA	Goldsbrough, Mort and Co., Meryula, Cobar	Cobar ...	N.S.W.
M F CLAVERTON	F. Fallen, Claverton, Balladoran	Dubbo	N.S.W.
M F OAKVIEW	M. Flinn, Oakview, The Rock	Wagga...	N.S.W.
M G CLIFTON	S. Gall, Clifton, Moree	Moree	N.S.W.
M G G	K. Murchison, Strathearn, Girilambone	Canonbar	N.S.W.
M GOOD WEANERS CAMP	M. Good, sen., Weaners' Camp, Bourke	Bourke... ...	N.S.W.

M

WOOL MARKS.	WOOL GROWERS' NAMES AND ADDRESSES.	PASTORAL DISTRICT.	STATE.
M G PEAKE	McGrath Bros., Peake, Onslow	Onslow	W.A.
M H ROSE VALE ILLABO	R. Hamilton, Rosevale, Illabo	Gundagai	N.S.W.
MIDKIN	Robertson and Son, Midkin and Telleraga, Moree	Moree	N.S.W.
MILANGIL	W. L. Manifold, Milangil, Camperdown	Camperdown ...	VIC.
MILBANK ⬥PH⬥ **JUNEE**	P. Hefferman, Millbank and Clear Hills, Junee...	Wagga... ...	N.S.W.
MILDURA	B. Chaffey, Mildura	River Murray ...	VIC.
MILEURA	Walsh and Son, Mileura, Murgoo	Murgoo ...	W.A.
MILFORD	A. B. McKenzie, Milford, O'Connell ...	Bathurst ...	N.S.W.
MILLEAR WANGANELLA ESTATE	T. Millear (exors.), Wanganella Estate, Deniliquin	Deniliquin	N.S.W.
MILLERS CREEK W J R	W. J Reid (exors.), Miller's Creek, Willow Tree	Tamworth	N.S.W.
MILLSTREAM	C. Elliott (Manager), Millstream, Roebourne	Roebourne	W.A.
MILO	J. Mooney, Milo, Moree	Moree	N.S.W.
MILO E	J. Mooney, Milo, Moree	Moree ...	N.S.W.
MINDEROO	F. Burt and Co., Minderoo, Onslow	Onslow	W.A.
MINEMBAH S B	S. Brown, Minembah, Whittingham	Singleton	N.S.W.

WOOL MARKS.	WOOL GROWERS' NAMES AND ADDRESSES.	PASTORAL DISTRICT.	STATE.
MINIMI	Paltridge Bros., Minimi, St. George	St. George ...	Q.
MINJAH	S. F. Mann, Minjah, Warrnambool	Warrnambool ...	VIC.
MINTO	J. Rutherford, Minto, Bibbenluke	Bombala	N.S.W.
MIRILBA	W. G. Hayes, Mirilba, Uralla	Armidale	N.S.W.
MIRRANATWA BEV	J. Fox, Mirranatwa, Victoria Valley ...	... ...	VIC.
MIT	G. Mitchell, Yerong Creek, Urana	Urana ...	N.S.W.
MITCHELL DOWNS	West Queensland Pastoral Co., Mitchell Downs, Mitchell	Mitchell ...	Q.
MITTAGONG	J. S. Edmondson and Co., Mittagong, Yerong Creek	Wagga ...	N.S.W.
M J B THE ROOKERY	M. J. Brown, The Rookery, Cobar	Cobar ...	N.S.W.
M J H	M. Hobbins, Oldcastle, Leadville	Mudgee ...	N.S.W.
M J L BALDHILL CK	W. Firman (Manager), Bald Hill Creek, Kalkallo	Central District ...	VIC.
MK	W. S. Macke and Co., Moffatt	North-Western District	VIC.
M K K	A. Drew, Macarthur	Western District...	VIC.
MK MUDGEE	Mattrick and Sutter, Forest Lodge, Hargraves	Mudgee ...	N.S.W.
3 K TULLICK NEW ENG	A. Mackay (exors.), Tullick, Armidale	Armidale ...	N.S.W.

M

WOOL MARKS.	WOOL GROWERS' NAMES AND ADDRESSES.	PASTORAL DISTRICT.	STATE.
M K Y **BREWON**	Mackay Bros., Brewon, Brewarrina	Brewarrina	N.S.W.
M & L **CORONA**	Mair and Learmouth, Corona Downs, Longreach	Longreach	Q.
ML **MINILYA**	D. N. McLeod, Manilya, Carnarvon	Carnarvon	W.A.
M M	A.E.M. Co., Ltd., Mt. Margaret, Thargomindah	Thargomindah	Q.
M M **BINDI**	E. E. Margetts, Bindi	... ...	VIC.
M M **BLAKNEY**	M. Moore, Big Flat, Dalton ...	Yass ...	N.S.W.
M — M **B** **NEW** **ENGLAND**	Marsh Estate, Booroobong, Armidale...	Armidale ...	N.S.W.
M M **C**	Mrs. McClean, Crown, Glen Alice	Mudgee ...	N.S.W.
M — M **S** **NEW ENG**	Marsh Estate, Salisbury Court, Uralla	Armidale	N.S.W.
M N **A**	J. Macnamara, Spring Creek, Maryvale	...	N.S.W.
M N **LAKE VIEW**	M. O'Neill, Lake View, Adaminaby ...	Cooma ...	N.S.W.
M N **NOONDAH**	Gurner and Co., Noondah, Warren	Coonamble	N.S.W.
M N **REDBANK**	E. Francis, Redbank, Stratford	N. Gippsland	VIC.
MOB **IRONBONG**	M. O'Brien, Ironbong, Bethungra	Wagga	N.S.W.
MOFFAT **BERRAMBOOL**	W. Moffatt, Berrambool, Wickliffe	Wimmera	VIC.

M

WOOL MARKS.	WOOL GROWERS' NAMES AND ADDRESSES.	PASTORAL DISTRICT.	STATE.
MOGONG	J. Carter, Mogong, Canowindra	Molong... ...	N.S.W.
MOIRA VALE	A. Lindsay and Sons, Moira Vale, Lansdale	Condobolin	N.S.W.
MOKANGER	R. Black (Manager), Mokanger, Cavendish	Wannon ...	VIC.
MOLLEE	McGill and Co., Mollee, Narrabri	Narrabri ...	N.S.W.
MOMALONG	Horsfall and Carrington, Momalong, Berrigan ...	Jerilderie	N.SW.
MOMBA	Momba Pastoral Co., Ltd., Momba, Wilcannia ..	Wilcannia	N.S.W.
MOONGULLA	C. Sinclair, Moongulla, via Collarendabri	Walgett	N.S.W.
MOOCULTA	Mrs. J. Barton, Mooculta, Bourke	Bourke...	N.S.W.
MOOLBONG	W. Murray, Moolbong, Booligal	Hillston	N.S.W.
MOOLOOLOO	W. A. Ferguson (Manager), Moolooloo, Parachilno	Parachilno	S.A.
MOOLERIC	Ramsey Bros., Mooleric, Birregurra ...	Western District...	VIC.
MOOLPA	P. Mein, Moolpa, Moulamein ...	Moulamein	N.S.W.
MOONGAREE T J E	T. J. Elliott, Moongaree, Cunnamulla ..	Cunnamulla ...	Q.
MORANGORELL U B	Union Bank of Australia, Morangorell Station, Morangorell	Young	N.S.W.
MOORAK	P. J. Browne, Moorak, Mt. Gambier ...	Mt. Gambier ...	S.A.

M

WOOL MARKS.	WOOL GROWERS' NAMES AND ADDRESSES.	PASTORAL DISTRICT.	STATE.
MOORARA	Bank of Adelaide, Moorara, Pooncaira	Wentworth	N.S.W
MOORARA S	Barrett and Wreford, Moorara, Pooncaira	Wentworth	N.S.W.
MOORILLA	A. Sloane and Sons, Moorilla, Young...	Young	N.S.W.
MOORLANDS	Moore Bros., Moorlands, Moree	Moree ...	N.S.W.
MOORNA (W)	W. Crozier, Moorna, Wentworth	Wentworth	N.S.W.
MOOTHUMBIL	A.E. & M. Co., Ltd., Moothumbil, Nymagee	Hillston	N.S.W.
MORDIALLOC FOY	H. V. Foy, Mordialloc, Trundle	Forbes ...	N.S.W.
MOREDUVAL	K. J. P. Simson, Moreduval, Quirindi..	Tamworth	N.S.W.
MORELLA	Champion Bros., Morella, Walgett	Walgett	N.S.W.
MORENDAH	Pedley and Garland, Morendah, Walgett	Walgett	N.S.W.
MORGIANA	Mrs. J. Trangmar, Morgiana, Wannon	Wannon	VIC.
MOROCO E	A. J. McLaurin, Moroco, Deniliquin ...	Deniliquin	N.S.W.
MOROCO WEST	R. W. McLaurin, Moroco West, Deniliquin	Deniliquin	N.S.W.
MORTON PLAINS	Trust and Agency Co., Morton Plains, Eungonia	Bourke...	N.S.W.
MOUNT C P D CAMEL	C. P. Davis, Heathcote	Central District	VIC.

WOOL MARKS.	WOOL GROWERS' NAMES AND ADDRESSES.	PASTORAL DISTRICT.	STATE.
MOUNT EVANS	W. B. Cummings, Mount Evans, Darlington	Western District	VIC.
MOUNT GRENFELL	S. F. Hervey, Mount Grenfell, Cobar...	Cobar	N.S.W.
MOUNT MELVILLE	Doyle Bros., Mount Melville, Cavendish	Wannon	VIC.
MOUNT STONE	W. Young, Mount Stone, Dunkeld	Wannon	VIC.
MOUNT VIOLET **Q O**	J. Cumming, Mount Violet, Camperdown	Camperdown	VIC.
MOUTAJUP J W	J. White, Moutajup	Wannon	VIC.
MOYNE FALLS	T. Robertson, Moyne Falls, Macarthur	Western District...	VIC.
M P G	Mitchell and Sons, Pelican, Braidwood Road	Goulburn	N.S.W.
MP GRANGE	P. Mitchell-Hill, Grange, Moira	Deniliquin	N.S.W.
M Q ERLSIDE	M. Quigley, Erlside, Warren	Coonamble	N.S.W.
M R A	E. S. N. R. A. Anthill, Girilambone, Canonbar...	Canonbar	N.S.W.
M R BOBBERA	Mary Ryan, Bobbera, Binalong	Young	N.S.W.
M R COOTABINYA	M. Ryan, Cootabinya, Blackall	Blackall	Q.
M R GREENE	M. R. Greene, Greystone, Rowsley	Central District...	VIC.
M ROCK FLAT	J. Mooney, Rock Flat, Cooma	Cooma ...	N.S.W.

M

WOOL MARKS.	WOOL GROWERS' NAMES AND ADDRESSES.	PASTORAL DISTRICT.	STATE.
M R O GLEN WILLAN	F. McRae, Wallup, via Warracknabeal	Northern District	VIC.
M RUTHERGLEN	A. Mitchell, Rutherglen, Woolbrook ...	Armidale	N.S.W.
M R WESTBROOK	M. Ryan, Westbrook, Avenil	Central District ...	VIC.
M. RYAN CARRAWA	M. Ryan, Carrawa, Trunkey	Carcoar ...	N.S.W.
M S BYALLA	S. McCaughey, Byalla, Gunning	Yass	N.S.W
M S CADDIGAT	M. Shanley, Caddigat, Adaminaby	Cooma ...	N.S.W.
M S EULOMO	M. Sawyer, jun., Eulomo, Bethungra ...	Gundagai	N.S.W.
M & S OLIVES	Mitchell and Sons, The Olives, Howlong	Albury ...	N.S.W.
M SOUTH BRIGHTON	R. Lindsay (Manager), South Brighton, Horsham	Horsham	VIC.
M & S T	Mitchell and Sons, The Olives, Howlong	Albury ...	N.S.W.
MT ABUNDANCE	S. A. Investment Co., Ltd., Mount Abundance, Roma	Roma ...	Q.
MT ALFRED	M. Good, Mount Alfred, Charleville	Charleville	Q.
MT BRYAN	C. W. Bowman, Mount Bryan, Hallett	Hallett ...	S.A.
MT BUNDY	Morse and Tourle, Bundy, Coonamble	Coonamble	N.S.W.
MT ELEPHANT	H. A. Currie, Mount Elephant, Derrinallum	Western District	VIC.

M

WOOL MARKS.	WOOL GROWERS' NAMES AND ADDRESSES.	PASTORAL DISTRICT.	STATE.
M TERANGAVILLE	M. Stowell, Terangaville, Kerrisdale ...		VIC.
MT HESSE	J. L. Kininmouth, Mount Hesse, Ombersley		VIC.
MT MARGARET M D I & Co	A.E. & M. Co., Ltd., Mount Margaret, Thargomindah ...	Thargomindah	Q.
MT MERCER	L. Bell, Mount Mercer Station, Mount Mercer	Grenville	VIC.
MT MITCHELL	Robertson Bros., Mount Mitchell, Waubra	Talbot ...	VIC.
MT MORIAC	R. Fletcher, Mount Moriac, Mount Moriac	Western District	VIC.
MT MYRTOON	J. Thornton, Mount Myrntoon, Kariah		VIC.
MT PLEASANT J C	J. Collett, Mount Pleasant, Gunning ...	Yass	N.S.W.
MT REMARKABLE	D. Sinclair (Manager), Mount Remarkable, Melrose ...	Melrose...	S.A.
MT SCHANCK	W. J. O. Clarke, Mount Schanck, Mount Gambier	Mount Gambier	S.A.
MT SHADWELL G F	G. S. Fitzgerald, Mount Shadwell, Mortlake	Western District	VIC.
MT STEPHEN	W. Coombe, Mount Stephen, Gordon ..	Gordon...	S.A.
M T ◇ URALLA	Burrow Bros., Toryburn, Uralla	Armidale	N.S.W.
MT WIDDERIN F S AUSTIN	F. S. Austin, Mount Widderin, Skipton	Ripon	VIC.
MUBRUMBAH	W. McDowell, Mubrumbah, Coonamble	Coonamble	N.S.W.

M

WOOL MARKS.	WOOL GROWERS' NAMES AND ADDRESSES.	PASTORAL DISTRICT.	STATE.
MUCCAN	Ball Bros., Muccan, Condon	Condon	W.A.
MULGUNNIA	T. A. Smith, Mulgunnia, Trunkey	Carcoar	N.S.W.
MULLAGH	G. Fitzgerald, Mullagh, Harrow	Dundas ..	VIC
MULLER BROS BILLIAN	Muller Bros., Billian, Yea	Anglesey	VIC.
MULURULU	Bright, Keating and Co., Mulurulu, Balranald	Ivanhoe	N.S.W.
MULWALA	A. Sloane and Sons, Mulwala, Mulwala	Corowa...	N.S.W.
MUM	Kater Bros., Mumblebone, Warren	Coonamble	N.S.W.
MUMBLEDOOL	Sanderson and Co., Mumbledool, Narrandera	Narrandera	N.S.W.
MUNARDO	J. Hannan, Munardo, Winnowie	Winnowie	S.A.
MUNDADOO	J. Green, Mundadoo, Brewarrina	Brewarrina	N.S.W.
MUNDI MUNDI	C. R. Murphy, Mundi Mundi, Silverton	Menindie	N.S.W.
MUNDOWDNA	J. Whyte (exors.), Mundowdna, Hergott Springs	Hergott Springs	S.A.
MUNGERIBAR T & A B	T. H. Bragg, Mungeribar	Dubbo ...	N.S.W.
MUNGERY S S	Strahorn Bros., Mungery, Tomingley...	Dubbo ...	N.S W.
MUNGIE BUNDIE	J. McDonald, Mungie Bundie, Moree...	Moree ...	N.S.W.

WOOL MARKS.	WOOL GROWERS' NAMES AND ADDRESSES.	PASTORAL DISTRICT.	STATE.
MUNTHAM H M	H. M. Mackinnon, Muntham, Casterton	Western District	VIC.
M URILA	R. Moore, Urila, via Queanbeyan	Queanbeyan	N.S.W.
MURRABINNA F BROS	Fraser Bros., Murrabinna, Kingston	Kingston	S.A.
MURRAWOMBIE	A.J.S. Bank, Murrawombie, Canonbar	Canonbar	N.S.W.
MURRAY BROS MALLINA	Murray Bros., Mallina, Roeburne	Roeburne	W.A.
MURRAY DAWSON WIRRA WIRRA	M. Dawson, Wirra Wirra, Mount Crawford		S.A.
MURRULEBALE ☆ G McD	Scottish, Australian Investment Co., Ltd., Murrulebale, Old Junee	Wagga	N.S.W.
MURRUMBOGIE	E. Curr, Murrumbogie, Trundle	Condobolin	N.S.W.
MUTOOROO	Elder and Waite, Mutooroo, Cockburn	Cockburn	S.A.
M V Y TARRABANDRA	J. and T. McEvoy, Tarrabandra, Gundagai	Gundagai	N.S.W.
M WALLABADAH	J. M. L. MacDonald, Wallabadah	Tamworth	N.S.W.
M W HOLLYWOOD	M. Watson, Hollywood, Narrawa	Yass	N.S.W.
M W L MIDDLEFIELD	W. W. Lee, Middlefield, Dandaloo	Dubbo	N.S.W.
M W P GLENORCHY	J. McNicol (Manager), Glenorchy Station, Merino	Western District	VIC.
MYALL CREEK	Young Bros. and Co., Myall Creek, Ivanhoe	Ivanhoe	N.S.W.

M

WOOL MARKS.	WOOL GROWERS' NAMES AND ADDRESSES.	PASTORAL DISTRICT.	STATE.
MYALL CREEK NEW ENGLAND	Young Bros. and Co., Myall Creek, Inverell	Warialda	N.S.W.
MYALL MUNDI X	Horrigan Bros., Myall Mundi, Trangie	Dubbo ...	N.S.W.
MYALL PARK J P	J. Patrick, Myall Park, Gilgandra	Coonamble	N S.W.
MYALL PLAINS	H. Campbell, Myall Plains, St. George	St. George	Q.
M YALLUM	J. Riddock (exors.), Yallum, Penola ...	Penola ...	S.A.
MYRNGRONG	A. B. & G. F. Cumming, Myrngrong, Camperdown	Camperdown	VIC.

WOOL MARKS.	WOOL GROWERS' NAMES AND ADDRESSES.	PASTORAL DISTRICT.	STATE.
N 3	Mundaroo Estate, Glenroy, Tumberumba	Home ...	N.S.W.
NAG & Co BURRA BURRA	N. A. Gatenby and Co., Burra Burra, Trundle	Condobolin	N.S.W.
NAG & Co JEMALONG	N. A. Gatenby and Co., Jemalong, Forbes	Forbes	N.S.W.
NAG & Co RABY	N. A. Gatenby and Co., Raby, Warren	Coonamble	N.S.W.
NALPA	Hon. J. L. Stirling, Nalpa, Strathalbyn	Strathalbyn	S.A.
NALPA E C S	Hon. J. L. Stirling, Nalpa, Strathalbyn	Strathalbyn	S.A.
NALYAPPA	H. R. Hancock, Nalyappa, Moonta	Moonta...	S.A.
NAMBROK	T. S. Armstrong, Nambrok, Rosedale	Gippsland	VIC.
NANENA	J. B. Dulhunty and Co., Nanena, Bathurst	Bathurst	N.S.W.
NANGERIBONE	A.M. & A. Co., Ltd., Nangeribone, Nymagee	Condobolin	N.S.W.
NANGUNIA	E. J. Gorman, Nangunia, Berrigan	Condobolin	N.S.W.
NANGUS M	J. & J. W. McKinney, Nangus	Gundagai	N.S.W.
NANGWARRY	A. Gardiner, Nangwarry, Lake Mundi	...	VIC.
NANIMA	C. H. Barton, Nanima, Wellington	Molong	N.S.W.
NANIMA LACHLAN	P. Wenz, Nanima, Cowra	Carcoar ...	N.S.W.

N

WOOL MARKS.	WOOL GROWERS' NAMES AND ADDRESSES.	PASTORAL DISTRICT.	STATE.
NANUTARRA	W. G. Learmouth (Manager), Nanutarra, Onslow	Onslow ...	W.A.
NANYAH	W. C. H. Elliott, Nanyah, Cunnamulla	Cunnamulla	Q.
NAP NAP	R. B. Ronald and Sons, Nap Nap, Maude	Hay	N.S.W.
NARADA DOWNS	Browne Bros., Narada Downs, Tambo	Tambo ...	Q.
NAREEN	C. Elliott, Nareen, Nareen ...	...	VIC.
NARINGAL	W. T. Rowe, Glenfine, Hollybush		VIC.
NARMBOOL	H. A. Austin, Narmbool, Elaine	Grenville	VIC.
NARRABUNDA P S	P. J. Sheedy, Narrabunda, Queanbeyan	Queanbeyan	N.S.W.
NARRAPUMELAP	G. N. Buckley, Narrapumelap, Wickliffe	Wimmera	VIC.
NARRINGA	J. Gibson and Sons, Narringa, Gunbar	Hay	N.S.W.
NARRUNG	P. Charley, Narrung, McLeay	...	S.A.
N C MINGBOOL	J. F. Kirby, Mingbool, Coleraine	Western District...	VIC.
N C WOODFORD	M. E. Campbell, Woodford Island, Brushgrove...	Grafton	N.S.W.
NE	E. Noonan, Crowlands	Western District...	VIC.
NEBEA	E. Whitney and Co., Neben, Coonamble	Coonamble	N.S.W.

WOOL MARKS.	WOOL GROWERS' NAMES AND ADDRESSES.	PASTORAL DISTRICT.	STATE.
NEKARBO	Walker Bros., Nekarbo, Cobar	Cobar ...	N.S.W.
N ELLERSLIE	E. R. Turner, Ellerslie, Tomingley	Dubbo	N.S.W.
NEL	N. E. Lane, Majuba, Dubbo...	Dubbo	N.S.W.
NELUNGALOO	Commercial Bank of Australia, Nelungaloo, Parkes	Forbes ...	N.S.W.
NEPTUNE R 5	Mrs C. A. Ripper, Echuca ...	Northern District	VIC.
NETALLIE	A.M. & A. Co., Ltd., Netallie, Wilcannia	Wilcannia	N.S.W.
NEW ARMATREE R V	Mrs. J. Harvey, New Armatree, Armatree	Coonamble	N.S.W.
NEWCOMEN ANGLEDOOL	A. M. L. & F. Co., Ltd., Angledool, Walgett	Walgett	N.S.W.
NEW COREEN	F. Dunn, New Coreen, Middledale	Corowa ...	N.S.W.
NEW GULARGAMBONE M R	Mrs. M. Marshall, New Gulargambone	Coonamble	N.S.W.
NEW HOPE PARK W B	W. J. Bissett, New Hope Park, Serpentine	Northern District	VIC.
NEWINGA	Chapman, Higgins and Co., Newinga, Mungindi	St. George	Q.
N G WOODFORD	N. Graham, Woodford, Numby	Young ...	N.S.W.
NICHOL	J. Nichol, Yarram Yarram	Gippsland ...	VIC.
NICKAVILLA	Union Bank of Australia, Nickavilla, Adavale ...	Adavale	Q.

WOOL MARKS.	WOOL GROWERS' NAMES AND ADDRESSES.	PASTORAL DISTRICT.	STATE.
NILLERA BROWN	E. Brown (exors.), Nillera, Cobar	Cobar	N.S.W.
NILMA	W. R. McCulloch (exors.), Nilma, Come-by-Chance	Walgett	N.S.W.
NIMBY	W. Cummings, Nimby, Reid's Flat	Young ...	N.S.W.
(NIVE DOWNS mark)	Scottish-Australian Investment Co., Nive Downs, Augathella	Augathella	Q.
N 3 **MUNDAROO**	W. Elliott, Mundaroo, Tumberumba ...	Hume ...	N.S.W.
N N A C D	E. Newnham, Nagambie	Northern District	VIC.
NOORENDOO	J. White, Devon Park, Dunkeld	Wannon	VIC.
NOORONG	T. Armstrong (exors.), Noorong, Moulamein	Moulamein	N.S.W.
NORTH BOOBOOROWIE	J. Lowden, North Booboorowie, Kooringa	Kooringa	S.A.
NORTH GOGELDRIE	A. M. & A. Co., Ltd., North Gogeldrie, Whitton	Narrandera ...	N.S.W.
NORTH STATION	W. T. Mainfold, North Station, Mortlake ...	Western District...	VIC.
NORTH TOOLBURRA D DOWNS	Mrs. E. Swinburn, North Toolburra ...	Warwick	Q.
NORTH YANCO	S. J. McCaughey, North Yanco, Yanco Siding...	Narrandera ...	N.S.W.
N P A	R. J. Matheson, Nilpena, via Port Augusta ...	Port Augusta ...	S.A.
N P B	H. C. White, Havilah, Mudgee	Mudgee ...	N.S.W.

N

WOOL MARKS.	WOOL GROWERS' NAMES AND ADDRESSES.	PASTORAL DISTRICT.	STATE.
N P I O	W. Porter, New Park, Forbes	Forbes	N.S.W.
N S	N. Stephens, Lower Broughton	Broughton	S.A.
N S	McInnes Bros., Broadford	Central District	VIC.
Nth WAKOOL	Sir R. T. H. Clarke, North Wakool, Deniliquin	Deniliquin	N S W.
NULLAWA	T. J. Sherwin, Nullawa, Brewarrina ...	Brewarrina	N.S.W.
NUNTHERUNGIE W & E K	A. M. & A. Co., Ltd., Nuntherungie, Wilcannia	Wilcannia	N.S.W.
N WENTWORTH	G. Moran, Wentworth, Coonamble	Coonamble	N.S.W.
N W NORADJUHA	N. Wilson, Noradjuha	Horsham	VIC.
NZ & A LAND Co BANGATE	N.Z. & A. Land Co., Ltd., Bangate, Walgett	Walgett	N.S.W.
NZ & A LAND Co BUNDURE	N.Z. & A. Land Co., Ltd., Bundure, Jerilderie ..	Jerilderie	N.S.W.
NZ & A LAND Co EDDINGTON	N.Z. & A. Land Co., Ltd., Eddington, Richmond	Hughenden	Q.
NZ & A LAND Co GOONDOOBLUIE	N.Z. & A. Land Co., Ltd., Goondoobluie, Walgett	Walgett	N.S.W.
NZ & A LAND Co ORANDUMBIE	N.Z. & A. Land Co., Ltd., Orandumbie, Walcha	Armidale	N.S.W.
NZ & A LAND Co TILL TILL	N.Z. & A. Land Co., Ltd., Till Till, Balranald ...	Balranald ...	N.S.W.
NZ & A LAND Co WALHALLOW	N.Z. & A. Land Co., Ltd., Walhallow, Quirindi	Tamworth	N.S.W.
NZ & A LAND Co WALHALLOW COLLINGWOOD	N.Z. & A. Land Co., Ltd., Walhallow, Quirindi	Tamworth	N.S.W.
NZ & A LAND Co WELLSHOT	N.Z. & A. Land Co., Ltd., Wellshot, Ilfracombe	Longreach	Q.

O

WOOL MARKS.	WOOL GROWERS' NAMES AND ADDRESSES.	PASTORAL DISTRICT.	STATE.
◇	W. Officer, Balmoral	Western District ..	VIC.
OAKABELLA	L. C. Burges, Oakabella, Northampton	Northampton	W.A.
OAKBANK J D G	E. Daffett, Oakbank, Heywood	Western District...	VIC.
OAKDENE	The A.L. & F. Co. of Australia, Oakdene, Kilfera (Head Office—William Street, Melbourne)	Ivanhoe	N.S.W.
OAKDEN HILLS	B. Ives and Co., Oakden Hills, Port Augusta	Port Augusta	S.A.
OAKHURST	Mrs. M. Ffrench, Oakhurst, Wyalong	Forbes ...	N.S.W.
OAKLANDS D R M	D. R. Myers, Oaklands, via Port Lincoln	Port Lincoln	S.A.
OAKVALE 2 F YASS	G. Franklin, Yeumburra, Yass	Yass	N.S.W.
OAK VALE R M	Mitchell Bros., Oak Vale, Karnak		VIC.
OBAN	D. McMaster, Oban, Coolah...	Merriwa	N.S.W.
OBERNE B X	Goldsbrough, Mort and Co., Oberne, Tarcutta	Gundagai	N.S.W.
O B GREEN ARM	Mrs B. O'Brien, Green Arm, Merriwa	Merriwa	N.S.W.
O B LERIDA	Oakden and Brown, Lerida, Cobar	Cobar	N.S.W.
O BROS KILFERA	Osborne Bros., Kilfera, Ivanhoe	Ivanhoe	N.S.W.
O B SPRINGVALE	J. F. O'Beirne, Springvale, Horsham	Wimmera	VIC.

O

WOOL MARKS.	WOOL GROWERS' NAMES AND ADDRESSES.	PASTORAL DISTRICT.	STATE.
O B SWIFTS CREEK	J. O'Brien, Swift's Creek, Gippsland	Gippsland ...	VIC.
O B X DUNUMBRAL	The A. M. L. & F. Co., Ltd., Dunumbral, Collarendabri	Walgett ...	N.S.W.
O B X RANGERS VALLEY	Campbell Bros., Rangers' Valley, Dundee Railway Station	Glen Innes ...	N.S.W.
O'C	Daly Bros., Mullengandera, Albury ...	Albury ...	N.S.W.
O'CONNELL BROS MUDGEE GOODIMAN	O'Connell Bros., Goodiman, Gulgong	Mudgee	N.S.W.
O. COX GRUBBEN	O. Cox (exors.), Grubben, Yerong Creek	Wagga ...	N.S.W.
[O D	Daly Bros., Mullengandera, Albury ...	Albury	N.S.W.
O E	W. E. A. Edwick, Albert Park, Serpentine	Northern District	VIC.
O E D	W. E. A. Edwick, Glengarry, Gippsland	Gippsland ...	VIC.
OFFHAM	T. W. Palmer & Co., Offham Siding, Cunnamulla	Cunnamulla ...	Q.
OGILVIE ILPARRAN	W. F. Ogilvie, Ilparran, Matheson ...	Glen Innes ...	N.S.W.
O I O BENAMBRA	C. L. Griffith, Benambra, Culcairn	Hume	N.S.W.
O I SPRING MOUNT	C. Mott, Spring Mount, Black Mountain	Armidale ...	N.S.W.
OKILTABIE	A. and F. Robinson, Okiltabie, Talia	Talia	S.A.
Ⓘ OLD CARABOBOLA	Morrice and Thompson, Old Carabobola, Germanton	Hume	N.S.W.

WOOL MARKS.	WOOL GROWERS' NAMES AND ADDRESSES.	PASTORAL DISTRICT.	STATE.
OLIVE DOWNS	Price and Johnson, Olive Downs, Tibooburra	Milparinka	N.S.W.
OLIVE GROVE W H	J. Hay, Olive Grove, Bordertown	Bordertown	S.A.
O O O	H. W. & G. A. Brown, Ross...	Ross	TAS.
O P	J. & G. R. Hope, Darriwell, Moorabool	Geelong	VIC.
OPOSSUM PLAIN J C	J. Chenery, jun., Opossum Plain, Humula	Hume	N.S.W.
OPOSSUM PLAIN S M	J. Chenery, jun., Opossum Plain, Humula	Hume	N.S.W.
O R M QUEENSLAND	T. Alford, Woolscourers, Brisbane		Q.
OSBORNE ◇O◇	J. Clee, Osborne, Eglinton	Bathurst	N.S.W.
O S GLENWOOD	T. O'Sheara, Glenwood, German Hill...	Molong...	N.S.W.
O S HYNAM	O. Smith and Co., Hynam, Narracoorte	Narracoorte	S.A.
OTTERBOURNE A B T	A. B. Triggs, Otterbourne, Yass	Yass	N.S.W.
O T W PARADISE	O. T. Wills, Paradise, Borung	North-Western District	VIC.
OURNIE	J. & P. J. McMeekin, Ournie Station, Ournie	Hume	N.S.W.
OVERFLOW	J. Mackay, Overflow, Warren	Coonamble	N.S.W.
OVERNEWTON	W. Taylor, Overnewton, Sydenham		VIC.
OVERTON	W. Munt, Overton, Rupanyup	Wimmera ...	VIC.
O V V GREEN HILLS	J. & W. Crombie, Green Hills, Muttaburra	Muttaburra	Q.

WOOL MARKS.	WOOL GROWERS' NAMES AND ADDRESSES.	PASTORAL DISTRICT.	STATE.
P	Mark, Sprot and Co., Hokitika	Hokitika ...	N.Z.
P (diamond)	River Don Trading Co., Westernport...	Westernport	TAS.
PADDINGTON	A. M. L. & F. Co., Ltd., Paddington, Mossgiel...	Ivanhoe ...	N.S.W.
PAIKA	P. McPherson, Paika, Balranald	Balranald	N.S.W.
PAN	McGill and Co., Mollee, Narrabri ...	Narrabri ...	N.S.W.
PALLAL	Mack and Austin, Pallal, Bingera	Moree ...	N.S.W.
PANYYABYR McN	McNeill Bros., Panyyabyr	Western District...	VIC.
PARATOO	H. P. McLachlan, Paratoo Station, Paratoo		S.A.
PARDO	T. Metcalf and Co., Pardo, Condon ...	Condon...	W.A.
PARKSIDE	J. Nicol, Parkside, Tarraville	Gippsland	VIC.
PARKVILLE P X P	W. Parkman, Parkville, Marengo	Young ...	N.S.W.
PARWAN	L. J. Stanghton, Parwan	...	VIC.
PATCH J S	J. Sinclair, Green Patch, Port Lincoln	Port Lincoln ...	S.A.
PATTERDALE	E. Cameron, Patterdale, Lagunta		TAS.
P B	P. Brassington, Stockport, Bombala ...	Bombala	N.S.W.

P

WOOL MARKS.	WOOL GROWERS' NAMES AND ADDRESSES.	PASTORAL DISTRICT.	STATE.
P & B **CORELLA**	Scottish-Australian Investment Co., Corella, Bourke	Bourke...	N.S.W.
P B E **EDDY PARK**	P. B. Eddy, Eddy Park, Inverell	Glen Innes	N.S.W.
P B **GREEN BANK**	Prowse Bros., Greenbank, Adelong	Gundagai	N.S.W.
PBS **BALLADONIA**	Ponton Bros. and Sharp, Point Malcolm, Eucla	Eucla	W.A
P B **SILENT** **VALE**	P. Brennan, Silent Vale, Mundooran ...	Coonabarabran	N.S.W.
P T **TARCUTTA**	P. Burt, Fairview, Tarcutta ...	Wagga ...	N.S.W.
P C **BURREN BURREN**	P. Commins, Burren Burren, Mogil	Walgett	N.S.W.
P C C **INVERELL**	P. C. & J. Campbell, Pindari, Inverell	Glen Innes	N.S W.
P C **PEECHELBA**	Hogan Bros., Peechelba, Bundalong South	Moira	VIC.
P C **WERRIBEE**	F. C. Rowlands, Werribee, Waugoola...	Carcoar	N.S.W.
P C **YETMAN**	P. Callacher, Yetman, Warialda	Warialda	N.S.W.
P & D **TOOGIMBIE**	L. Parsons, Toogimbie, Hay...	Hay	N.S.W.
PENOLA	R Rymill, Penola Station, Penola	Penola ...	S.A.
PERRICOOTA	F. O. Falkner and Sons, Ltd., Perricoota, Moama	Deniliquin	N.S.W.
PEVENSEY	A. & A. Tyson, Pevensey, Hay	Hay	N.S.W.

P

WOOL MARKS.	WOOL GROWERS' NAMES AND ADDRESSES.	PASTORAL DISTRICT.	STATE.
P F	H. J. Barber and Co., Cooradigbee, Yass	Yass	N.S.W.
P F **DROMONA**	R. Forrest, Dromona, Bullarah	Moree ...	N.S.W.
P F **G**	P. Ferguson, Gulargambone, Coonamble	Coonamble	N.S.W.
P F Y **SPRING FARM**	P. Foley, Spring Farm, Bongongolong	Gundagai	N.S.W.
P H **BANKSIDE**	J. P. Hartnett, Bankside, Morundah ...	Urana	N.S.W.
PH **CLEAR HILLS** **JUNEE**	P. Heffernan, Clear Hills, Junee	Wagga ...	N.S.W.
P H O **BOWYLIE**	P. H. Osborne (exors.), Bowylie, Gundaroo	Queanbeyan	N.S.W.
P H O **CONAPAIRA**	P. H Osborne (exors.), Conapaira, Whitton	Narrandera	N.S.W.
P H O **CURRANDOOLEY**	P. H. Osborne (exors.), Currandooley, Bungendore ...	Queanbeyan	N.S.W
P H O **DOURO**	P. H. Osborne (exors.), Douro, Yass ...	Yass	N.S.W.
P H O **ORANGE PLAINS**	P. H. Osborne (exors.), Orange Plains, Dandaloo	Condobolin	N.S.W.
P H O **THORNDALE**	P. H. Osborne (exors.), Thorndale, Nyngan	Canonbar	N.S.W.
P I	I. O. Inglis, Bacchus Marsh ...	Central District ...	VIC.
PIANGOBLA	A. E & M. Co., Ltd., Piangobla, Collarendabri	Walgett	N.S.W.
PIETZ **N**	C. Nagoreka, Hoch Kirch	Western District...	VIC.

P

WOOL MARKS.	WOOL GROWERS' NAMES AND ADDRESSES.	PASTORAL DISTRICT.	STATE.
PIKEDALE	C. F. White, Pikedale, Stanthorpe	Stanthorpe	Q.
PILTON DARLING DOWNS	W. J. Wilson and Co., Pilton, Clifton	Allora	Q.
PINE PLAINS	F. LaCouteure (Manager), Pine Plains, Hopetoun	Lake Korrong	VIC.
PINE RIDGE	J. H. Buckland, Pine Ridge, Gulgong ..	Coonabarabran	N.S.W.
PINE VALLEY R S M	A. Haine, Pine Valley, Cooma	Cooma ...	N.S.W.
P I P DARLING DOWNS	W. Pierce, Lemon Tree, Yandilla	Toowoomba	Q.
PITCAIRN	A. D. Sawyer, Pitcairn, Nackara	Nackara	S.A.
P J C	J. Creed, Borhoney Ghurk, Morrison's, Rokewood	Western District...	VIC.
P L	P. Larney, Currajong, Coonamble	Coonamble	N.S.W.
PLAINS	J. Russell, Bornmah Plains ...	Western District...	VIC.
PLUMTHORPE	Wilson Bros., Plumthorpe, Barraba ...	Tamworth	N.S.W.
P & M DINTON VALE	Palmer and McColl, Dinton Vale, Inverell	Glen Innes	N.S.W.
Ʊ M FOREST LODGE	P. Malloy, Forest Lodge, Forbes	Forbes ...	N.S.W.
P M I ROSS	P. McIntyre, Ross, Robe	Robe	S.A.
P M L CHIPDALE	P. L. McLoughlan, Chippendale Creek, Moonan Flat	Murrurundi	N.S.W.

P

WOOL MARKS.	WOOL GROWERS' NAMES AND ADDRESSES.	PASTORAL DISTRICT.	STATE.
P N	P. Nohelly, Polly Boorme, Baradine	Coonamble	N.S.W.
P NO GO	J. H. Peters, Nogo, Longreach	Longreach	Q.
P O D NEW PARK	W. Porter, New Park, Forbes	Forbes ...	N.S.W.
P O H B	P O'Halloran, Dorinoreve, Balranald	Balranald	N.S.W.
POINTVALE R	D. Robertson, Point Vale, Dunkeld, Hamilton ...	Western District	VIC.
POLLOCK	A. Cameron, Pollock, Nagambie	North-Eastern District	VIC.
POLLY BREWON	Barton and Taylor, Polly Brewon, Walgett	Walgett	N.S.W.
POLTALLOCH K D B	K. D. Bowman, Poltalloch, Meningie ...	Meningie	S.A.
POMINGALARNA ✸	McKay and Copland, Pomingalarna. Wagga	Wagga	N.S.W.
POPLAR GROVE R H	Mrs. R. Hunt. Poplar Grove, Pettavel Railway Station ...	Western District...	VIC.
P ORANGE GROVE	J. J. Perrett, Orange Grove, Manilla ...	Tamworth	N.S.W.
PORTLAND	Portland Downs Pastoral Co., Portland Downs, Ilfracombe	Barcaldine	Q.
PORTREE	Craig and Roberts, Portree, Port Headland	Port Headland	W.A.
POWELLA	Clarke and Tait, Powella, Aramac	Aramac...	Q.
POOLAMACCA	J. W. Brougham, Poolamacca, Broken Hill	Menindie	N.S.W.

P

WOOL MARKS.	WOOL GROWERS' NAMES AND ADDRESSES.	PASTORAL DISTRICT.	STATE.
POON BOON	A. M. L. & F. Co., Ltd., Poon Boon, Stoney Crossing	Moulamein	N.S.W.
P & P	J. Parker, Wychproof	North-Western District	VIC.
⬦P⬦ PARADISE	T. E. Pennington, Paradise, St. Arnaud	Kara Kara	VIC.
PRAIRIE PARK	J. Hewlett, Prairie Park, Deniliquin	Deniliquin	N.S.W
P R JONES CREEK	P. Reardon, Jones Creek, Gundagai	Gundagai	N.S.W.
P. RYAN CASHEL	P. Ryan, Cashel, Pilliga	Pilliga ...	N.S.W.
P S COOLAC	Sullivan Bros., Coolac, Gundagai	Gundagai	N.S.W.
P S ELGIN	P. Sutherland, Elgin, Turner	Turner ...	S.A.
P S ELLERSLIE	Peterson and Sargood, Ellerslie, Adelong	Gundagai	N.S.W.
P & S JERILDERIE	Peterson and Sargood, Wunnamurra, Jerilderie	Jerilderie	N.S.W.
P SMITH BARWON BANK GEELONG	P. Smith, Barwon Bank, South Geelong	Geelong	VIC.
P S YARRA	P. Squire, Yarra, Cowra	Young	N.S.W.
P T BYALLA	J. Tully, Byalla, Gunning	Yass	N.S.W.
P T GLENVIEW	Blazley Bros., Glenview, Woodstock	Carcoar	N.S.W.
P TYSON LAKE BOLAC	P. Tyson, Lake Bolac, Wickliff Road...	Ararat ...	VIC.
P W DENISTOUN	J. D. Wood, Denistoun, Bothwell	Bothwell	TAS.
P W KIKIAMAH	Bank of N.S.W., Kikiamah, Young	Young ...	N.S.W.

Q

WOOL MARKS.	WOOL GROWERS' NAMES AND ADDRESSES.	PASTORAL DISTRICT.	STATE.
Q COOMA	M. J. McGuffieke, Mowenbah, Jindabyne	Cooma	N.S.W.
Q M E & A Co LTD	Queensland Meat Export and Agency Co., Ltd., Magowra and Miranda Downs, Croydon ..	Norman	Q.
Q N TARELLA	E. Quinn and Co., Tarella, Wilcannia...	Wilcannia ...	N.S.W.
Q PINE CREEK	Thomas and Gare, Glen View, Hallett	Hallett	S.A.
QUABOTHO T	G. E. Traquair, Quabotho, via Quambone	Coonamble	N.S.W.
QUAMBY	J. & W. Lindsay, Quamby, Woolsthorpe	Warrnambool ...	VIC.
QUANTAMBONE	R. H. Meares and Co., Quantambone, Brewarrina	Brewarrina	N.S W.
QUEENSLAND Z ROCKLANDS	A. F. Evans, Rocklands, Dalveen	Warwick ...	Q.
QUIAMONG	R. Landale, Quiamong, Conargo	Deniliquin ...	N.S.W.
QUILBONE V	Veech Bros., Quilbone, Quambone	Coonamble ...	N.S.W.
QUILBONE VEECH	Veech Bros, Quilbone, Quambone	Coonamble ...	N.S.W.
QUIRINDI M WALLABADAH	J. M. L. McDonald, Wallabadah, Tamworth	Tamworth ...	N.S.W.

R

| --- | --- | --- | --- |
R (in circle)	J. I. Ryan, Rockwell, Gilgandra	Coonabarabran	N.S.W.
R ✳	W. Robertson, Balmoral	Western District	VIC.
R & A ADELONG	Roche and Awagon, Condoblinga, Adelong	Gundagai	N.S.W.
RABY	G. A. Church, The Retreat, Bringelly	Picton	N.S.W.
RAINSCOURT	Cameron and Harrison, Rainscourt, Hughenden	Hughenden	Q.
R A M (triangle)	R. J. Rankin, Mooroodue	South-Eastern District	VIC.
R A NOYEAU	W. Tucker, Noyeau, Woodstock	Carcoar	N.S.W.
RAPID BAY W G	H. Gerrard (exors.), Old Yoho, Delamere		S.A.
RAR MUDGEE	A. Robe, Pianbong, Mudgee	Mudgee	N.S.W.
RAVENSFIELD	Wilson Bros., Ravensfield, Booligal	Hay	N.S.W.
RAVENSWORTH	W. H. Mackay, Anambah, West Maitland	Maitland	N.S.W.
R A W CLERKNESS	R. A. Wiseman, Clerkness, Bundarra...	Armidale	N.S.W.
R A W & Co NEW ENG	R. A. & A. Wauch, Branga Park, Glen Morrison	Armidale	N.S.W.
R BANDA NEW ENG	M. Hayne, Rimbanda, Kentucky	Armidale	N.S.W.
R B BROUGHTON	E. Broughton, Brimboal	...	VIC.

R

WOOL MARKS.	WOOL GROWERS' NAMES AND ADDRESSES.	PASTORAL DISTRICT.	STATE.
R B G MUDGEE GRATTAI	Reeves Bros., Grattai, Mudgee	Mudgee	N.S.W.
R B H OONDOOROO	Ramsay Bros. and Hodgson, Oondooroo, Winton	Winton...	Q.
R BIRAGANBIL MUDGEE	R. Rouse, jun., Biraganbil, Gulgong	Mudgee	N.S.W.
R BROS EMU FLAT	F. W. Reynolds, Emu Flat, Binalong...	Young	N.S.W.
R BROS MUDGEE	J. J. Ryan, Goolma, Yamble ..	Mudgee	N.S.W.
R. BRUCE	R. Bruce, Coondambo, *via* Port Augusta	Port Augusta	S.A.
R B WHYDOWN	R. Bailey, Whydown, Nackara	Nackara	S.A.
R C	R. Curnon, Wattle Mountain, Portland	Bathurst	N.S.W.
R CARNGHAM	J. Russell, Carngham	Western District...	VIC.
R C C CLYDE	Reardon Bros., Clyde, Bullarah	Moree ...	N.S.W.
R C H NARRAWA	R. Collins, Narrawa, Coonamble	Coonamble	N.S.W.
R C L V W	R. Cootes, Boort	North-Western District	VIC.
R COX MARRAR	H. T. Dawson (exors.), Marrar	Wagga	N.S.W.
R COX WOODPARK	H. T. Dawson (exors.), Wood Park, Armidale ...	Armidale	N.S.W.
R C RAGLAN	R. J. Christian, Lock Avine, Raglan ...	Bathurst	N.S.W.

R

WOOL MARKS.	WOOL GROWERS' NAMES AND ADDRESSES.	PASTORAL DISTRICT.	STATE.
℟	Mrs. J. Davidson, Illawong, Jugiong ...	Gundagai	N.S.W.
R D A NORTH CUERINDI	R. D. Allen (exors.), Cuerindi, Manilla	Tamworth	N.S.W.
R D B BURREN	R. D. Barton, Burren, Narrabri	Pilliga ...	N.S.W.
R D BREAKFAST CREEK	Richard Dwyer, Breakfast Creek, Burrowa	Young ...	N.S.W.
R D LOLLEEP	R. Dugan, Lolleep, Walgett...	Walgett	N S.W.
R D S	W. M. K. Shaw, Rifle Farms, Digby ...	Western District...	VIC.
R E	J. Ryan, Edenhope Station, Edenhope	Western District...	VIC.
REDBANK	E. Francis, Redbank, Stratford	N. Gippsland	VIC.
R W GEURIE	G. Rowe, Spicer's Creek, Wellington ...	Molong...	N.S.W.
R E J CLONARD	R. E. Jakins, Clonard, Mungindi	Moree ...	N.S.W.
R E R & Co WALLA WALLA	R. E. Rawlins and Co., Walla Walla, Forbes	Forbes ...	N.S.W.
RESTDOWN	M. & E. J. Burgess, Restdown, Cobar	Cobar ...	N.S.W.
RETREAT	Youngman Bros., Retreat, Casterton ...	Western District...	VIC.
R F	R. Fitzgerald, Dabee, Rylstone	Mudgee	N.S.W.
R F D	E. F. Doyle, Purlewah, Werris Creek	Narrabri	N.S.W.

R

WOOL MARKS.	WOOL GROWERS' NAMES AND ADDRESSES.	PASTORAL DISTRICT.	STATE.
R F EASTWOOD	J. Faulks, Eastwood, Cullinga	Young ...	N.S.W.
R F H J D	R. M. Fitzgerald, Dabee, Rylstone	Mudgee	N.S.W.
R F H YABTREE	R. F. L. Horsley, Yabtree, Mundarlo ...	Gundagai	N.S.W.
R F M E GLENROY	R. F. M. Eckford, Glenroy and Terala, Moree ...	Moree	N.S.W.
R G BANK VALE	R. Guest, Bank Vale, Boree Creek	Urana ...	N.S.W.
R G BICTON	R. Gibson, Bicton, Cressy	Cressy	TAS.
R G BUNDIDGERIE	R. Guest, Bundidgerie, Narrandera	Narrandera	N.S.W.
R G BUSHY PARK	B. T. Bennett (Manager), Bushy Park, Brigalong	N. Gippsland	VIC.
R G G DAVYS PLAIN	R. G. Glasson, Davy's Plain, Cudal	Molong	N.S W.
R G H K	R. G. Higgins, Kickerbit, Quirindi	Tamworth ...	N.S.W.
⬦RG⬦ M P	R. Godfree, Mount Pleasant...	Mt. Pleasant ...	S.A.
R GOREE	D. & J. Robertson, Goree, Narrandera	Narrandera ...	N.S.W.
R G ROSEWOOD	R. Gibson, Rosewood, Condobolin	Condobolin	N.S.W.
R G T MALAHIDE	Mrs. Talbot, Malahide, Fingal	Fingal ...	TAS.
R H EDENMORE	F. Holcombe, Edenmore, Pilliga	Pilliga ...	N.S.W.

R

WOOL MARKS.	WOOL GROWERS' NAMES AND ADDRESSES.	PASTORAL DISTRICT.	STATE.
RHEINHOLD JENDE LAHARUM	R. Jende, Laharum, Horsham	Horsham	VIC.
R H GOBABLA	R. Humphries, sen., Gobabla, Dubbo	Dubbo ...	N.S.W.
R H H URALLA	R. Hudson, Balala, Uralla ...	Armidale	N.S.W.
R H KULKI	R. Hargrave, Kulki, Inverell	Glen Innes	N.S.W.
R H L EURIMBLA	R. H. Lord, Eurimbla, Narrabri	Narrabri	N.S.W.
R H R IRVINGDALE	W. M. Irving, Irvingdale, Barcaldine...	Barcaldine	Q.
R H R MINNIE DOWNS	W. M. Irving and Co., Minnie Downs, Tambo	Tambo ...	Q.
R I BENTLY	H. J. Biggs, Bently, Gawler	Gawler ...	S.A.
RICHMOND C	H. N. Conn, Richmond, Bland	Young ...	N.S.W.
R I MULLABY	J. A. Riggs, Mullaby, Kooringa	Kooringa	S.A.
RIPPLE VALE	O. Armitage, Ripple Vale, Birregurra	Winchelsea	VIC.
RIPPON HURST S J	Sargood and Jenner, Rippon Hurst, Macarthur	Normanby	VIC.
R J BOLAC PLAINS	R. Jamieson, Bolac Plains, Darlington	Camperdown	VIC.
R J JEIR	Johnson Estate, Jeir, Yass	Yass	N.S.W.
R J MUNDOONAN	Johnson Bros., Mundoonan, Yass	Yass	N.S.W.

R

WOOL MARKS.	WOOL GROWERS' NAMES AND ADDRESSES.	PASTORAL DISTRICT.	STATE.
R J P **BOXVALE**	R. J. Porter, Boxvale, Quirindi	Tamworth	N.S.W.
R J P H **NAMOI PARK**	R. J. P. Higgins, Namoi Park, Manilla	Tamworth ...	N.S.W.
R J **STONY POINT**	R. Jamieson, Stony Point, Darlington	Camperdown	VIC.
R J **TAEMAS**	Jones Bros., Taemas, Yass ...	Yass ...	N.S.W.
R. LACK **GOOLRING**	R. Lack, Goolring, Enngonia	Bourke... ...	N.S.W.
R **LANGI WILLI**	G. Russell, Langi Willi, Linton	Ballarat ...	VIC.
R **LAWALUK**	H. Read, Lawaluk, Mt. Mercer	Grenville ...	VIC.
R L F	G. E. Faithful, Inveralochy, Lake Bathurst	Goulburn	N.S.W.
R L G **HILLSIDE**	J. Roberts, Hillside, Cootamundra	Young	N.S.W.
R L **HOWLONG**	A. Macvean, Howlong	Albury	N.S.W.
R L J **CALLANDOON**	R. S. Jenkins, Callandoon, Goondiwindi	Goondiwindi ...	Q.
R L P	R. L. Post, Pullitop, Wagga	Wagga... ...	N.S.W.
⬦**R**⬦ **PADTHAWAY**	R. Lawson, Padthaway, Narracoorte ...	Narracoorte ...	S.A.
R L **S P**	A. B. Ryall, Spring Plain, Cooma	Cooma	N.S.W.
R M F	R. M. Fitzgerald, Tongy, Cassilis	Merriwa ...	N.S.W.

R

WOOL MARKS.	WOOL GROWERS' NAMES AND ADDRESSES.	PASTORAL DISTRICT.	STATE.
◇ **R** **MIMOSA**	Robertson Bros., Mimosa, Temora	Wagga...	N.S.W.
R M **KINTYRE**	R. Matheson, Kintyre, Casterton	Western District.	VIC.
R M L **ARDLE GULLY**	McLennon Bros., Ardle Gully, Armidale	Armidale	N.S.W.
R M L **KILCOY** **NEW ENG**	McLennon Bros., Kilcoy, Armidale	Armidale	N.S.W.
R M U **H** **N E**	R. Mulligan, Hillsboro, Boorolong	Armidale	N.S.W.
R **NARROW PLAINS**	J. & W. S. Ramsey, Narrow Plains, Corowa	Corowa...	N.S.W.
R ◇ **NEW ENGLAND**	R. Bell, Merryworth, Black Mountain	Armidale ...	N.S.W.
ROACHDALE **D R**	Roach Bros., Roachdale, Ralvona	Hume ...	N.S.W.
ROCHESTER PARK **P D**	P. Doheuty, Rochester Park, Rochester	Northern District	VIC.
ROCK BROOK **J & T G** **BUNG BONG**	Gordon Bros., Rock Brook, Bung Bong Railway Station	Talbot	VIC.
🐴	W. D. Crozier, Rockbrook, Kapunda ...	Kapunda ...	S.A.
ROCKLYNNE	Mrs. S. Bates, Rocklynne, Cheeseman's Creek ...	Molong...	N.S.W.
ROCKVIEW **J W**	J. Waters, Rockview, Narcen	... ...	VIC.
ROCKWOOD	Stuart Bros. and McCaughey, Rockwood, Muttaburra	Muttaburra	Q.
ROMA **NARRABRI**	J. Lehane, jun., Roma, Woodstock	Narrabri	N.S.W.

R

WOOL MARKS.	WOOL GROWERS' NAMES AND ADDRESSES.	PASTORAL DISTRICT.	STATE.
ROMAWI	Michaelis, Hallenstein and Co., Paynesville, Gippsland	Gippsland	VIC.
ROSEBROOK	M. Harnett (exors.), Rosebrook, Cooma	Cooma ...	N.S.W.
ROSEHILL E McG	D. & J. McGledge, Rosehill, Wantabadgery	Gundagai ...	N.S.W.
ROSENEATH	C. Simson, Roseneath, Casterton	Glenelg... ...	VIC.
ROSEVALE A D	A Dalzeil, Rosevale, Louther	Bathurst ...	N.S.W.
ROSEVALE R G M	R. G. Martin, Rosevale, Uranquinty	Wagga... ...	N.S.W.
ROSLYN	A. J. McInnes, Roslyn, Goulburn	Goulburn ...	N.S.W.
ROSS BALAKLAVA	A. F. Ross, Balaklava, Matheson	Glen Innes	N.S.W.
ROSSLYN T	A J. McInnes, Roslyn, Goulburn	Goulburn ...	N.S.W.
ROSSMORE (H)	W. Hocking, Rossmore, Wee Waa	Pilliga	N.S.W.
ROUNDHILL	J. Balfour and Sons, Round Hill, Culcairn	Albury... ...	N.S.W.
ROXBY W F V	W. Volum, Roxby, Gnarwarre and Murgheboluc	Mt. Moriac ...	VIC.
R P BECTIVE	J. S. Vickery, Bective, Tamworth	Tamworth ...	N.S.W.
R P C PYALONG	J. Scott, jun., Pyalong, High Camp Plain	... ...	VIC.
ℛℛ BOLOCO	R. W. Rose, Boloco, Boloco . .	Cooma ...	N.S.W.

R

WOOL MARKS.	WOOL GROWERS' NAMES AND ADDRESSES.	PASTORAL DISTRICT.	STATE.
R R **BOONALDOON**	R. Richards, Boonaldoon, Moree	Moree ...	N.S.W.
ꓤR **CLIFTON**	Hon. R. H. Roberts, Clifton, Young ...	Young ...	N.S.W.
ꓤR **ELI-ELWAH**	J. Russell, Eli-Elwah, Hay ...	Hay	N.S.W.
R R **HARROW**	Ramsay Bros., Harrow, Cambooya ...	Toowoomba	Q.
R **ꓤ** **NARWONAH**	C. Rice, Narwonah, Narramine	Dubbo ...	N.S.W.
ꓤR **TIVERTON**	R. H. Roberts, Tiverton, Barwang	Young ...	N.S.W.
R R **W V** **WELLINGTON** **VALE**	Robertson and Co., Wellington Vale, Deepwater	Tenterfield	N S.W.
R R **W V**	Robertson and Co., Wellington Vale, Deepwater	Tenterfield	N.S.W.
R S **BELALIE**	A. & N. Z. M. Co., Ltd., Belalie, Enugonia	Bourke ...	N.S.W.
R S **BOOLCOOMATTA**	R. Salmon, Boolcoomatta, Olary	Olary	S.A.
R T	J. Taylor, Waiwera, Millie	Narrabri	N.S.W.
R **TOCAL**	J. Rhodes, Tocal, Longreach	Longreach	Q.
R ꓤ **ROSEWIN**	D. Taskis, Rosewin, Mullengandra	Albury ...	N.S W.
♛ **R U D**	J. Rudd, Colombo Plains, Urana	Urana	N.S.W.
RUSL. PARK	J. Taylor, Russell Park, Surat	Surat ...	Q.

R

WOOL MARKS.	WOOL GROWERS' NAMES AND ADDRESSES.	PASTORAL DISTRICT.	STATE.
RUSSELL	J. Day, Russell, Wycheproof ...	Kara Kara ...	VIC.
RUTHVEN	Bank of Victoria, Ruthven, Isisford ...	Isisford... ...	Q.
RUTLAND	Good Bros., Rutland, Grenfell ...	Forbes	N.S.W.
RVL	Col. W. V. Legge, Hobart	...	TAS.
R W & Co RESTDOWN	M. & E. J. Burgess, Restdown, Cobar	Cobar	N.S.W.
R W F HILLSIDE	R. W. Feltus, Hillside, Way	Way ...	S.A.
R. W. HINKSON BROUGHTON	R. W. Hinkson, Broughton, Lillimur ...	Dimboola	VIC.
R W P H	R. W. Rodger, Home Chase, Colac ...	Western District...	VIC.
R Y	L. Ryder, Yarrambee, Calga ...	Coonamble ...	N.S.W.
R YARIMA	J. Nelson (Manager), Yarima, Cressy...	Western District...	VIC.
R Y MICALAGO	A. Ryrie, Michelago, Cooma...	Cooma	N.S.W.

S

WOOL MARKS.	WOOL GROWERS' NAMES AND ADDRESSES.	PASTORAL DISTRICT.	STATE.
S	M. Sellors, Mumbil, Molong...	Molong...	N.S.W.
S	A. Kelly, Wycheproof	Kara Kara	VIC.
S	L. Spehr, Millicent	Millicent	S.A.
S	P. Sinclair, Selma, Mathoura	Deniliquin	N.S.W.
S	P. Sinclair, Millicent	Millicent	S.A.
SALT CREEK	P. McIntyre, Salt Creek Salt Works ...	Western District...	VIC.
SANDY CAMP	J. McLeish, Sandy Camp, Bullagreen...	Coonamble	N.S.W.
SANT WOODLAND	Z. Santilla, Woodland, Womboota	Deniliquin	N.S.W.
SAUMAREZ	White Bros., Saumarez, Armidale	Armidale	N.S.W.
S A W	S. A. Witts, Berrebangle, Gunning ...	Yass	N.S.W.
S B	Sullivan Bros., Turkey Creek, Mount Morgan ...	Mt. Morgan	Q.
S + B ANNANDAYLE	S. P. Bowler (exors.), Annandale, Germanton ...	Hume ...	N.S.W.
S B BOLONG	Savage Bros., Bolong, Frogmore	Young ...	N.S.W.
S B MULLAH	S. Beveridge, Mullah, Trangie	Dubbo ...	N.S.W.
S. BROS NUBBA	Sawyer Bros., Nubba, Wallendbeen ...	Young ...	N.S.W.

WOOL MARKS.	WOOL GROWERS' NAMES AND ADDRESSES.	PASTORAL DISTRICT.	STATE.
S. BROS & T	Singleton Bros., Louth, Bourke	Bourke...	N.S.W.
S B **T** **INGLESIDE**	S. Best, Ingleside, Tangmangaroo	Yass	N.S.W.
S B **∧** **WAMBIANA**	S. Beveridge, Wambiana, Trangie	Dubbo	N.S.W.
S C **B**	S. Carter (exors.), Pine Hills Estate, Binalong...	Young	N.S.W.
S C **CLEA HILL**	S. Calvert, Clea Hill, Maroona	Ripon ...	VIC.
S C C **ROSEBROOK**	M. Harnett (exors.), Rosebrook, Cooma	Cooma...	N.S.W.
S C **DELEGATE**	A. H. Jeffrey, Delegate, Bombala	Bombala	N.S.W.
S C **McL** **BELFORD**	Scott, Cameron and McLean, Belford, Richmond	Hughenden	Q.
S C M **VALEBEDER** **YASS**	S. C. Maddrell, Vale Beder, Bowning ..	Yass	N.S.W.
S & D **BURROWA**	J. B. Dunlop, Goba Creek, Burrowa	Young ...	N.S.W.
S D **COOMA**	S. Dempsey, Cooma, Narrabri	Narrabri	N.S.W.
S & D **GOBA CREEK**	J. B. Dunlop, Goba Creek, Burrowa ...	Young ...	N.S.W.
S͡E	D. McKinnon (exors.), Marida, Yallock, Boorcan	Camperdown	VIC.
S **ELCHO**	H. M. Sutherland, Elcho Lara, Geelong	Geelong	VIC.
SERPENTINE	Hugh Ross, Serpentine, Inglewood	Northern District	VIC.

WOOL MARKS.	WOOL GROWERS' NAMES AND ADDRESSES.	PASTORAL DISTRICT.	STATE.
SESBANIA	Manifold, Bostock and Co., Sesbania, Corfield ...	Winton	Q.
SEVERNE CARWELL	Severne Bros., Carwell, Gulargambone	Coonamble	N.S W.
S F WOLKARA	Fennell Bros., Wolkara, Brewarrina	Brewarrina	N S.W.
S G CLIFTON	S. Gall, Clifton, Moree	Moree	N.S.W.
S G NULLAMANNA	S. Gall, Nullamanna, Inverell	Glen Innes	N.S.W.
S GOONAMBILL WW	W. Wilson (exors.), Goonambill, Daysdale	Corowa...	N.S.W.
S GRANGE	C. I. Sutherland, Maroona	Western District...	VIC.
S G R SUNNYSIDE HALLS CREEK	S. G. Roberts, Sunnyside, Hall's Creek	Tamworth	N.S.W.
S G S EUMERALLA	S. G. Staughton, Eumeralla, Macarthur	Western District...	VIC.
S. G. SMITH UPPER BALABLA	S. G. Smith, Upper Balabla, Tubbal ...	Young ...	N.S.W.
S GUNBOWER	Stirling and Gerrand, Gunbower, Pittsworth	Toowoomba	Q.
S H	S. Hazlett, Craigmore, Walgett	Walgett	N.S.W.
SHANNON KAPUNDA	A. Shannon, Kapunda	Kapunda ...	S.A.
S H B	S. H. Blenkley, Horsham	Horsham	VIC.
S & H BADEN PARK	Bank of N.S.W., Baden Park, Cobar ...	Cobar ...	N S.W.

WOOL MARKS.	WOOL GROWERS' NAMES AND ADDRESSES.	PASTORAL DISTRICT.	STATE.
S H **CRAIGMORE**	S. Hazlett, Craigmore, Walgett	Walgett	N.S.W.
SHERWOOD **J. BAKER**	J. Baker, Sherwood, Temora	Wagga...	N.S.W.
S & H **MIMOSA WEST**	Bank of N.S.W., Mimosa West, *via* Coolamon ...	Wagga...	N.S.W.
S H **SOMERCOTES**	T. Riggall, Somercotes, Ross	Ross	TAS.
SIAM	J. Brennan, Siam, Port Augusta	Port Augusta	S.A.
S I **B** **BUNDA BURRA**	Mrs. M. A. Strickland, Barreenong, Forbes	Forbes ...	N.S.W.
S J B **ALLOWAY**	S. J. Barden, Alloway, Gilgandra	Dubbo ...	N.S.W.
S **J G**	E. T. & N. H. Gibbs, Mt. Campbell, Queanbeyan	Queanbeyan	N.S.W.
S J P **OAKLEIGH**	S. J. Perfrement, Oakleigh, Currabubula	Tamworth	N.S.W.
SKENE	J. Robertson, Skene, Hamilton	Hamilton	VIC.
S **KINDRA**	J. Stinson (exors.), Kindra, Coolamon...	Wagga...	N.S.W.
S K S	R. Futter, Cunningham Plains, Cunningham	Young ...	N.S.W.
S L O **ROSLYN**	J. Sloane, Roslyn, Stuart Town	Molong...	N.S.W.
S L **SOHO**	Mrs. M. Lees, Soho, Drysdale	Western District...	VIC.
S L **TYNEDALE**	S. Latherne, Tynedale, Cooma	Cooma ...	N.S.W.

S

WOOL MARKS.	WOOL GROWERS' NAMES AND ADDRESSES.	PASTORAL DISTRICT.	STATE.
S & Mc G W	Stewart and McGee, Wooloondool, Hay	Hay	N.S.W.
S & M CURRAH	Scott and McMillan, Currah, Moree	Moree ...	N.S.W.
S N BUDGEREE	S. Nell, Budgeree, via Talmoi	Moree ...	N.S.W.
SOGLIO	G. F. DeSalis, Soglio, Michelago	Cooma ...	N.S.W.
S O RYLSTONE	W. McQuiggin, Craigmore, Rylstone ...	Mudgee	N.S.W.
S O SUNNYSIDE NEW ENGLAND	J. Whitten, Summerville, Kentucky	Armidale	N.S.W.
SOUTH CARAMUT	E. R. DeLittle, South Caramut, Caramut	Warrnambool	VIC.
SOUTH KONONGWOOTONG	A. Johnson (exors.), South Konongwootong, Coleraine	Western District...	VIC.
S P	S. Perrett, Frogmore Park, Gunnedah	Tamworth	N.S.W.
SPES BONA	J. H. Fisher, Bona, Warren...	Coonamble	N.S.W.
SPRINGBANK	W. Sullivan, Springbank, Queanbeyan	Queanbeyan	N.S.W.
SPRINGFIELD BURROWA	V. Osborne, Spring Field, Burrowa	Young ...	N.S.W.
SPRINGFIELD H	J. H. Hart, Springfield, Blackall	Blackall	Q.
SPRINGFIELD U	J. McAuliffe, Springfield, Jeir	Yass	N.S.W.
SPRINGFIELD WEBB	Springfield Pastoral and Estates Co., Ltd., Springfield, Byng	Bathurst	N.S.W.

WOOL MARKS.	WOOL GROWERS' NAMES AND ADDRESSES.	PASTORAL DISTRICT.	STATE.
SPRINGMOUNT YASS	A. McBean, Springmount, Yass	Yass	N.S.W.
S P ROSEDALE	W. Grambauer, Rosedale, Jericho	Aramac	Q.
S P SHADY DOWNS	Mrs. S. Peckett, Shady Downs, Tambo	Tambo ...	Q.
S R WEROCATA	S. S. Ralla, Werocata, Balaklava		S.A.
S S BOYANJA	A Sutherland, Boyanja, Millicent	Millicent ...	S.A.
S & S BURROWAY	R. & A. Scott, Burroway, Narramine...	Dubbo	N.S.W.
S & S FRASER'S CREEK NEW ENGLAND	J. Swan, Fraser's Creek, Ashford	Tenterfield	N.S.W.
S SUMMER HILL	H. Ensor, Summer Hill, Dalby	Dalby	Q.
S S S URALLA	J. Swales, Woodlands, Uralla	Armidale	N.S.W.
S T	S. S. Tully, Wickliffe	Wimmera	VIC.
STAUGHTON VALE	S. F. Staughton, Staughton Vale, Anakie	Western District....	VIC.
S & T C M	S. & T. Cozens, Yalpara, Ororoo	Ororoo	S.A.
ST. ENOCHS	Miss E. Bain, St. Enochs, Stockyard Hill		VIC.
S T GOONOO	Peel River N. & M. Co., Ltd., Goonoo Goonoo, Tamworth	Tamworth ...	N.S.W.
STONEFIELD	T. J. McDonald, Stonefield, Penshurst	Western District...	VIC.

WOOL MARKS.	WOOL GROWERS' NAMES AND ADDRESSES.	PASTORAL DISTRICT.	STATE.
STONEHENGE	J. Beaton (Manager), Stonehenge, Derrinallum	Western District	VIC.
STONE PARK	L. Renehan, Stone Park, Cootamundra	Young ...	N.S.W.
STOOL CLEAR VIEW	P. McGrath, Clear View, Burrowa	Young	N.S.W.
STRATH	J. S. Sands, Bowrgong, Gunning	Yass	N.S.W.
STRATHALBYN	G. Curry, jun., Strathalbyn, Dubbo	Dubbo ...	N.S.W.
STRATHDOWNIE W	H Watson, Wamboola, Strathdownie		VIC.
STRATHFILLAN W W	W. Watson, Strathfillan, Carapooee Railway Station	Kara Kara	VIC.
STRATHGARVE E R M	E. R. Morgan, Strathgarve, Warwick	Warwick	Q.
STRATHKELLA	R. A. Donald, Strathkeilar, Hamilton	Hamilton	VIC.
STRATHMORE	J. Moss (Manager), Strathmore, Kilmore	Kilmore	VIC.
STRATHVEAN	L. Bell (Manager), Strathvean, Cressy	Western District..	VIC.
STRONTIAN	A. McPherson, Strontian, Narrandera	Narrandera	N S.W.
STUART MILL (x)	E. Swanston Bros., Stuart Mill	Kara Kara	VIC.
STUDBROOK	J. & A. Armytage, Stud Brook, Birregurra	Western District ..	VIC.
SUNDOWN G C	G. M. & A. J. Campbell, Sundown, Moonan Brook	Armidale	N.S.W.

WOOL MARKS.	WOOL GROWERS' NAMES AND ADDRESSES.	PASTORAL DISTRICT.	STATE.
△ s v L	H. C. Stewart, Vine Lodge, Frogmore	Yonng ...	N.S.W.
SWANWATER	Biggs Bros., Swanwater, St. Arnaud ...	North-Western District	VIC.
S W CLIFFDALE	S. Wiseman (exors.), Cliffdale, Wingen	Murrurundi ...	N.S.W.
S W CUNGEGONG	S. Ward, Montefield, Cootamundra	Young ...	N.S.W.
S W GEROGERY	S. Watson, Gerogery West, Gerogery ...	Albury ...	N.S.W.
S. WILSON CORANGAMITE	T. Purcell, Corangamite, Pirron Yaloak	Western District...	VIC.
S WILSON ERCILDOUNE	Clarence and Wilson, Ercildoune, Burrumbeet...	Ararat ...	VIC.
S WILSON MARATHON	R. Wilson, Marathon, Anakie ...	...	VIC.
S WILSON URISINO	Wilson Bros., Urisino, Wanaaring	Wanaaring ...	N.S.W.
SWINTON	A. Gray and Co., Swinton, Glenorchy ...	Wimmera ...	VIC.
S W J SANDFORD	J. H. Jackson, Sandford, Sandford	Casterton	VIC.
S W M EULAMEET	S. & W. Mason, Eulameet, Cavendish ...	Western District...	VIC.
S W S & Co LAKE COWAL	S. Wilson, Son and Co., Lake Cowal, Marsden ..	Condobolin ...	N.S.W.
S W S WHITE CLARENDON	P. Byrne and Sons, Clarendon, Balranald	Balranald ...	N.S.W.
S X T NEW ENGLAND	D. Scholes, Danbury, Woolbrook ...	Armidale ...	N.S.W.

Š

WOOL MARKS.	WOOL GROWERS' NAMES AND ADDRESSES.	PASTORAL DISTRICT.	STATE.
S **< B** **NEWSTEAD**	Burbury Estate, Tonthill, Oatlands	Oatlands	T.AS.
S Y D **DRILDOOL**	S. Powell, Drildool, Wee Waa	Pilliga	N.S.W.
SYLVESTER BUTLER **MUNGINDI**	S. Butler, Glenroy, Mungindi, Moree	Moree	N.S.W.
SYLVIA VALE	J. Marsden, Sylvia Vale, Crookwell	Carcoar	N.S.W.
SYMONS BROS **FERNLEIGH**	Symons Bros., Fernleigh, Noradjuha ...	Horsham	VIC.

T

WOOL MARKS.	WOOL GROWERS' NAMES AND ADDRESSES.	PASTORAL DISTRICT.	STATE.
T ◇	J. Rutherford, Murrumbidgerie	Dubbo	N.S.W.
Ⓣ	A. C. Tom, Bartley's Creek, Parkes	Forbes ..	N.S.W.
T & A B LANDGROVE	T. & A. Bragg, Landgrove, Cullinga ...	Goondagai	N.S.W.
TABRATONG	Reid's Estate, Tabratong, Dandaloo	Canonbar	N.S.W.
T A & Co SUSSEX	Trust and Agency Co., Ltd., Sussex, Nyngan	Cobar	N.S.W.
⟨TA⟩ **KELLONGBUTTA**	Anderson Bros., Kellongbutta, Bathurst	Bathurst	N.S.W.
TALAWANTA	Dalgety and Co., Ltd., Talawanta, Bollon, Queensland	Brewarrina	N.S.W.
TALGAI WEST	Scottish-Australian Investment Co., Talgai West, Hendon	Allora	Q.
TAMAL	A. J. Ogilvie and Loyne, Shark's Bay, Caernarvon	Caernarvon	W.A.
TALMALMO	R. & C. Smithwick, Talmalmo, Wagra	Hume	N.S.W.
TAMBO	T. A. Hamilton, Tambo	Tambo	Q.
TAMBO XING	C. Davidson, Swift's Creek, Gippsland	Gippsland	VIC.
TAMBREY	Meares and Cusack, Tambrey, Roebourne	Roebourne	W.A.
TAMBUA W R	W. Rodier, Tambua, Cobar ...	Cobar ...	N.S.W.
TANDAWANNA	Chapman, Higgins and Co., Tandawanna, Goondiwindi	Goondiwindi	Q.

T

WOOL MARKS.	WOOL GROWERS' NAMES AND ADDRESSES.	PASTORAL DISTRICT.	STATE.
TAPIO	J. Ormond and Co., Tapio, Wentworth	Wentworth	N.S.W.
TARCOMBE	J. Chisholm (Manager), Tarcombe Station, Tarcombe		VIC.
TAREELARI	A. G. F. Munro, Tareelari, Moree	Moree ...	N.S.W.
TARENGO H	F. W. Hume, Tarengo, Burrowa	Young ...	N.S.W.
TATONG	F. McDonald, Tatong, Benalla	North-Eastern District	VIC.
T & A TOOLES CREEK	Thompson and Anderson, Toole's Creek, Wagga	Wagga ...	N.S.W.
T & B ARTESIAN DOWNS	Brabazon and Turner, Artesian Downs, Richmond	Hughenden	Q.
T B E	T. Brawlin, Enrongilly, Gundagai	Gundagai	N.S.W.
T B 7 U	T. Bowling, Toowoomba	Toowoomba	Q.
T B WILLOH	T. Bossley, Willoh, Brewarrina	Brewarrina	N.S.W.
T B Y	Torrumbarry Estate, Torrumbarry	Northern District	VIC.
⊢ C	W. & D. M. Cumming, Calabash Creek, Marengo	Young ...	N.S.W.
T C	T. Currey, Gridiron Farm, Lucky Corner	Coonamble	N.S.W.
TC AUBURN VALE	T. Cooper, Auburn Vale, Inverell	Glen Innes	N.S.W.
T C B BLINKBONNIE N E	T. C. Barnell, Blinkbonnie, Wollun ...	Armidale	N.S.W.

T

WOOL MARKS.	WOOL GROWERS' NAMES AND ADDRESSES.	PASTORAL DISTRICT.	STATE.
T C BOLOCO	T. Cogan, Boloco Creek, Boloco	Cooma	N.S.W.
T C DRILDOOL	S. Powell, Drildool, Wee Waa	Pilliga ...	N.S.W
T C G	T. Coleman, Glenrock, Gundaroo	Queanbeyan	N.S.W.
TCHELERY	A. M. & A. Co., Ltd., Tchelery, Booroorban	Moulamein	N.S.W.
T C KINYPANIEL	T. Cornish, Kinypaniel	North-Western District	VIC.
T CLIFTON	S. R. Turner, Clifton, Anakie	Geelong	VIC.
T CRAWFORD	J. Thompson, Crawford, Condah	Western District...	VIC.
T C RETRO	A Chirnside (exors.), Retro, Capella ...	Clermont	Q.
T C RISDON	T. Crane, Risdon, Silverwood	Muttaburra ...	Q.
T C S ⊢	T. C. Suttor, Triamble, Hargraves	Mudgee ...	N.S.W.
T C VINDEX	Chirnside, Riley and Co., Vindex, Longreach	Winton ...	Q.
T - C WOBURN	G. G. Wollaston, Lake Hamilton, Sheringa		S.A.
T D	J. F. Darcy, Birregurra	Western District...	VIC.
T D P YANNANY	T. DePledge, Yannany, Winning Pool	...	W.A.
T D R BLAKNEY	T. D. Roche, Blakney, Dalton	Yass ...	N.S.W.

WOOL MARKS.	WOOL GROWERS' NAMES AND ADDRESSES.	PASTORAL DISTRICT.	STATE.
T D **TARCOOLA**	A. M. L. & F. Co., Ltd., Tarcoola, Pooncarrie	Wentworth	N.S.W.
T E **BRINGAGEE**	T. L. Learmonth, Bringagee, Carrathool	Hay	N.S.W.
T E&CO **B**	T. Elliott and Co., Woolscourers, Sydney		N.S.W.
T E & Co **ROCKVIEW**	T. Edmondson and Co., Rockview, Wagga	Wagga	N.S.W.
T. EDOLS & Co LTD	T. Edols and Co., Ltd., Burrawang, Forbes	Forbes ...	N.S.W.
TEETULPA	Hamilton, Mills and Co., Teetulpa, Yunta	Yunta ...	S.A.
TELBA **CARROLL**	Simson Bros., Telba, Carroll, Gunnedah	Tamworth	N.S.W.
TELEMON	H. Collier, Telemon, Hughenden	Hughenden	Q.
TELFER **PORTANA**	J. Telfer, Portana, Way	Way	S.A.
TERELA	R. F. M. Eckford, Terela (T.P.O. No. 2), N.W. line	Moree	N.S.W.
TEREMBONE **F BROS**	J. Laycock, Terembone, Coonamble ...	Coonamble	N.S.W.
TERINALLUM **C C** **T**	Bailey and Wynne, Terinallum, Darlington	Camperdown	VIC.
TERLINGS **MOREE**	E. & L. M. Hill, Terlings, Moree	Moree	N.S.W.
TERRICKS	W. Carin, Terricks, Mitiamo	Bendigo	VIC.
T E W	Riley, Newman and Co., Circular Quay, Sydney		N.S.W.

T

WOOL MARKS.	WOOL GROWERS' NAMES AND ADDRESSES.	PASTORAL DISTRICT.	STATE.
T F **C**	T. Fitzpatrick, Carcoar	Carcoar	N.S.W.
T F & Co **GRACEDALE**	T. Foster and Co., Gracedale, Richmond	Hughenden	Q.
△ ▽ **T** **FELTON**	T. M. Greenaway, Felton, Cambooya ...	Toowoomba	Q.
T F **WHEEO**	W. Christie, Wheeo, Yass	Yass	N.S.W.
T G **CLIFTON**	S. Gall, Clifton, Moree	Moree ...	N.S.W.
T G **RICHAVON**	T. Gutherie (Manager), Richavon, Donald	Kara Kara	VIC.
T. G. WISEMAN **STIRLING**	T. G. Wiseman, Stirling, Attunga	Tamworth	N.S.W.
T H	Hore Bros., Horton	Northern District	VIC.
T H B **GRONG GRONG**	A. L. & F. Co., Ltd., Grong Grong, Narrandera	Narrandera	N.S.W.
THE GRANGE (in red)	P. Mitchell-Hill, The Grange, Moira	Deniliquin	N.S.W.
THE OVERFLOW	A. M. & A. Co., Ltd., The Overflow, Nymagee ...	Condobolin	N.S.W.
THE **PLAIN**	F. A. & W. R. Mack, The Plain, Bingara	Warialda	N.S.W.
② **THE PINES**	P. McGrath, The Pines, Grenfell	Forbes ...	N.S.W.
T H L **B C.**	T. H. Laidlow, Hamilton	Western District...	VIC.
T H **MUDGEE**	T. Heath, Glenvale, Crudine	Bathurst	N.S.W.

WOOL MARKS.	WOOL GROWERS' NAMES AND ADDRESSES.	PASTORAL DISTRICT.	STATE.
T. H. MURRAY MT BEEVOR	T. H. Murray, Mount Beevor, Nairne	Nairne ...	S.A.
T H M WOODSIDE	T. Hetherington, Woodside, Deniliquin	Deniliquin	N.S.W.
T H P MYLANDRA	W. Scott, Mylandra Creek, Goolagong	Forbes ...	N.S.W.
THORNLEIGH M P & Co	D. S. Paterson, Thornleigh, Blackall ..	Blackall ...	Q.
T H ROCKDELL	T. Hines, Rockdell, Lyndhurst	Carcoar	N.S.W.
T H R PANUARA	T. H. Richards, Panuara, Cadia, Orange	Bathurst	N.S.W.
T H S	T. H. Stephens, Pullstrong, Cadia	Carcoar	N.S.W.
THURULGOONA ◯	Squatting Investment Co., Thurulgoona, Cunnamulla ...	Cunnamulla	Q.
⊞ **WOOTOONA**	H. G. Thackery, Wootoona, Young	Young ...	N.S.W.
T H X ROSEGREEN	Heffernan Bros. and McCarthy, Rosegreen, Junee	Wagga ...	N.S.W.
TILLSBURY	R. A. Burcher, Tillsbury Hill, Oberon	Bathurst	N.S.W.
TILTAGOONA	W. H. Bannister, Tiltagoona, Cobar ...	Cobar ...	N.S.W.
TINENBURRA ▽T	J. Tyson (exors.), Tinenburra, Cunnamulla	Cunnamulla	Q.
TIPTREE	J. M. Black, Bibbenluke, Bombala	Bombala	N.S.W.
TITANGA	Mrs. H. Lang, Titanga, Lismore	Lismore	VIC.

T

WOOL MARKS.	WOOL GROWERS' NAMES AND ADDRESSES.	PASTORAL DISTRICT.	STATE.
T J F **BUNDELLA**	D. M. Irving. Bundella, Coonamble ...	Coonamble	N.S.W.
T J **MUDGEE**	T. Jackson, Slapdash, Gulgong	Mudgee	N.S.W.
T J O **PRETTY TOWER**	T. J. Oddie, Pretty Tower, Chepstowe	Western District...	VIC
T ⋈	T. Keefe, Wyangle, Tumut ...	Gundagai ...	N.S.W.
T K **DOODLE COOMA**	J. J. Keighran, Doodle Cooma, Henty	Albury	N.S.W.
T K **KAROOLA**	T. Knight, Karoola, Guyra ...	Armidale	N.S.W.
T K **WYANGLE**	T. Keefe, Wyangle, Tumut	Gundagai	N.S.W.
⟨TL⟩ **BRINGAGEE**	T. L. Learmonth, Bringagee, Carrathool	Hay	N.S.W.
T L **GORRINN**	J. & A. Richardson, Gorrinn, Dobie's Bridge		VIC.
T L I **COOLAH**	E. J. Scully, Coolah, Coonabarabran ...	Coonabarabran	N.S.W.
T M C **BUCKINBAH**	M. A. & H. F. McCulloch, Buckinbah, Yeoval...	Molong...	N S W.
T McD **NURRABIEL**	T. McDonald, Nurrabiel	...	VIC.
T McK **MACQUARIE**	T. McKibben, Macquarie Plains, Kelso	Bathurst	N.S.W.
T McM **AMAROO**	J. McMahon, Amaroo Station, Amaroo	Molong... ...	N.S.W.
T M C **MOORA**	T. McCormack, Moora Moora, Forbes	Forbes ..	N.S.W.

WOOL MARKS.	WOOL GROWERS' NAMES AND ADDRESSES.	PASTORAL DISTRICT.	STATE.
T MONIVALE	J. Thompson, Monivale, Hamilton	Western District ..	VIC.
YANDARLO	Tyrwhitt and Co., Yandarlo, Augathella	Augathella	Q.
T N ENGLAND	J. Stewart, Tangley, Guyra	Armidale	N.S.W.
T N N	Riley, Newman and Co., Circular Quay, Sydney		N.S.W.
T N URANA	T. Newton, Urana ...	Urana ...	N.S.W.
T 4 N WINDGIDGEON	T. Foran, Windgidgeon, Gilgandra	Coonabarabran	N.S.W.
T. OATES BELGRAVIA	T. H. Oates, Belgravia, Millthorpe	Bathurst	N.S.W.
TOLARNO W L R	Union Bank of Australia, Tolarno, Menindie	Menindie	N.S.W.
TOLTOL H C K	A. O. Creswick, Swan Hill ...	Mallee District	VIC.
TOM BOTUNDRA	T. O'Mara, Mount Pleasant, Dalgety	Cooma ...	N.S.W.
TONTO R A R	R. A. R. Robertson, Tonto, Normanville		S.A.
TOOLANG G T	G. Trangmar, Toolang, Coleraine	Western District...	VIC.
TOOMA	T. Robertson and Bros., Tooma	Hume	N.S.W.
TOORAK	Bayles Bros., Toorak, Richmond Downs	Cloncurry	Q.
TOPAR	J. A. Patterson, Topar, Broken Hill	Menindie	N.S.W.

T

WOOL MARKS.	WOOL GROWERS' NAMES AND ADDRESSES.	PASTORAL DISTRICT.	STATE.
TORRYBURN NEW ENGLAND	Burrow Bros., Torryburn, Uralla	Armidale	N.S.W.
T O T H	F. B. & E. A. Thomas, One Tree Hill		S.A.
TOTTINGTON ⟨R⟩	A. Anderson (exors.), Tottington, Winjallock		VIC.
TOULBY	Dalgety and Co., Ltd., Toulby, Brewarrina, N.S.W.; local headquarters, Bollon (Q.) ...	Brewarrina	N.S.W.
TOURABLE M & W	McKenzie and Wilson, Tourable, Gunnedah	Tamworth	N.S.W.
TOWRANG M & Co GOULBURN	W. H. Wheatley, Towrang, Goulburn	Goulburn	N.S.W.
T & P B BOGEWONG	Britton Brothers, Bogewong, Walgett	Walgett	N.S.W.
T. P. FAGAN NARRAWAY	T. P. Fagan, Narraway, Coonamble	Coonamble	N.S.W.
T P MANILLA S	T. Purcell, Manilla, Windorah	Windorah	Q.
T P W G	T. P. Wiseman, Gunnible, Gunnedah	Tamworth	N.S.W.
T R	Riley, Newman and Co., Circular Quay, Sydney		N.S.W.
T + R ÷	J. Martin, Bertery Bank, Delegate	Bombala	N.S.W.
T R CARWOOLA	T. Rutledge, Carwoola, Molonglo	Queanbeyan	N.S.W.
T R DOODLE COOMA	T. Keighan, Doodle Cooma, Henty	Albury ...	N.S.W.
TREFUSIS P B F	P. B. Fenwick, Trefusis, Kunopia	Moree ...	N.S.W.

T

WOOL MARKS.	WOOL GROWERS' NAMES AND ADDRESSES.	PASTORAL DISTRICT.	STATE.
T R E MURLINGBUNG	T. Reid, Murlingbung, Berridale	Cooma	N.S.W.
TRIDA	T. Williamson and Co., Trida, Mossgiel	Ivanhoe	N.S.W.
TRINKEY	W. D. Simpson, Trinkey, Quirindi	Tamworth	N.S.W.
T R NORTHWOOD	T. Ryan, Northwood, Cowra	Carcoar	N.S.W.
T R PRETTY TOWER STOCKYARD HILL	T. Rogers, Pretty Tower, Stockyard Hill	Beaufort	VIC.
T R SCONE	T. Ring, Woodlands, Scone	Murrurundi	N.S.W.
TRUNGLEY	Cuthbert Bros. and Shadworth, Trungley, Barmedman	Young ...	N.S.W.
T. RUSS D	T. Russ, Dandaloo, Dubbo	Dubbo ...	N.S.W.
T R W	T. Reid, Woolbrook, Armidale	Armidale	N.S.W.
⊢ R WATERFORD	T. Rice, Waterford, Peak Hill	Dubbo ...	N.S.W.
T S CLEVELAND	T. Scrivener, Cleveland, Mungindi	Moree	N.S.W.
T S FERNCLIFFE	T. Sparrow, Ferncliffe, Bungendore	Queanbeyan	N.S.W.
T S NARRALLEN	T. Stephenson, Narrallen, Burrowa	Young ...	N.S.W.
T S PADDYS PLAINS	T. Scott, Paddy's Plains, Dutton	Eyre	S.A.
T S PIBBON	T. Spicer, Pibbon, Mundooran	Coonabarabran	N.S.W.

T

WOOL MARKS.	WOOL GROWERS' NAMES AND ADDRESSES.	PASTORAL DISTRICT.	STATE.
T S & SON WARRAKOO	Smith and Son, Warrakoo, Tareena	Wentworth	N.S.W.
T (in shape) **TARATAP**	F. Tapefield, Taratap, Kingston	Port Caroline	S.A.
T T W	D. H. H. Atkinson, Prairie	Northern District	VIC.
TUPPAL	F. S. Falkner and Sons, Ltd., Tuppal, Tocumwal	Deniliquin ...	N.S.W.
TUREE	A. Hooke, jun., Turee, Cassilis	Merriwa ...	N.S.W.
TURKEITH	J. F. & G. Armytage, Turkeith, Winchelsea	Western District...	VIC.
TURN TURN	J. Aylward, Turn Turn, Eulo	Eulo ...	Q.
T W B	T. & W. Bond, Yarran, Lockhart	Urana	N.S.W.
T W C MUDGEE	T. W. Colley, Dan Dan, Hargraves	Mudgee	N S.W.
TWHC QUORN	T. W. H. Clarke, Quorn Hall, Campbelltown	Campbelltown	TAS.
T W R REEVESDALE	T. W. Reeves, Reevesdale, Wheeo	Yass	N.S.W.
T W WARBROOK	T. Whitehead, Warbrook, Grey Grey...	Hume	N.S.W.
T W WILLOW GLEN	C. Taylor, Willow Glen, Holt's Flat ...	Bombala	N.S.W.
T W W WOODLAWN	T. W. Wells, Woodlawn, Warialda ...	Warialda ...	N.S.W.
T (in triangle) **WYOBIE**	J. Tyson (exors.), Wyobie, Macalister	Toowoomba	Q.
TYRIE	W. J. Lyne, Tyrie, Dandaloo	Dubbo	N.S.W.
TYRRELL DOWNS	P. Howard (Manager), Tyrrell Downs, Sea Lake	...	VIC.

U

WOOL MARKS.	WOOL GROWERS' NAMES AND ADDRESSES.	PASTORAL DISTRICT.	STATE.
UABBA	G. L. Dickson, Uabba and Urandway, Hillston	Hillston	N.S.W.
UARDRY	C. Mills and Co., Uardry, Carrathool ...	Hay	N.S.W.
U CARUMBI	J. & W. McClintock, Carumbi, Cootamundra	Young	N.S.W
U C NEW ENG	J. B. Scholes, Puntulu, Stonehenge	Glen Innes	N.S.W.
5 U F	E. White, Martindale, Denman	Denman	N.S.W.
ULAMAMBRI	I. D. & J. E. Rogers, Ulamambri, Coonabarabran	Coonabarabran	N.S.W.
ULIMAN	J. Henderson, Uliman, Mullaley	Coonabarabran	N.S.W.
ULONGA	T. F. Patterson (exors.), Ulonga, Hay	Hay	N S.W.
ULOOLOO	J. Melrose, Ulooloo	Ulooloo	S.A.
UMBERCOLLIE	Trewecke and Sons, Umbercollie, Goondiwindi.	Goondiwindi	Q.
UMERELLA	J. Richmond, Umerella Siding, Cooma	Cooma ...	N.S.W.
U MURRAGULDRIE	A. Smith, Murraguldrie, Kyamba	Hume	N.S.W.
– U – N E	J. T. Mulligan, Booroolong, Armidale	Armidale	N S.W.
UPPER BUMBALDRY	J. Dwyer, Upper Bumbaldry, Cowra ..	Forbes	N.S.W.
URI PARK	Ross Bros., Uri Park, Darlington Point	Narrandera	N.S.W.

WOOL MARKS.	WOOL GROWERS' NAMES AND ADDRESSES.	PASTORAL DISTRICT.	STATE.
△ VALE	C. H. Barbour, Bellvale, Yass	Yass	N.S.W.
VALLEYFIELD T ◇ —	Menzies Bros., Valleyfield, Coolamon	Wagga ..	N.S.W.
VB BOYD	C. A. Haley, Boyd, Forbes	Forbes	N.S.W.
V B EUROKA	V. Burrett, Euroka, Bimbi	Forbes	N.S.W.
V C NARRANGULLEN	V. Cumming, Narrangullen, Yass	Yass	N.S.W.
VD MUDGEE	V. J. Dowling (exors.), Lue, Mudgee	Mudgee	N.S.W.
VERNON DOWNS	T. G. Millar and Co., Vernon Downs, Richmond	Hughenden	Q.
V G H OMEO	G. Hollands, Omeo	North-Eastern District	VIC.
V G NEW ENG	V. E. Green, Abbey Green, Llangollen	Armidale	N.S.W.
VICTO	A. A. Elliott, Victo, Cunnamulla	Cunnamulla	Q.
VI KINGS PLAINS	Vivers Bros., King's Plains, Inverell	Glen Innes	N.S.W.
VIRGINIA	Mrs. J. Donnelly, Virginia, Glen Innes	Glen Innes	N.S.W.
V JV	J. Vanters, Marghebolue		VIC.
V V HOWLONG	A. Macvean, Howlong, Albury	Albury ...	N.S.W.
V V NEW ENG	Mrs. C. M. Wright, Wollamimbi, Armidale	Armidale	N.S.W.
V V ROOKSDALE	A. McVean, Rooksdale, Little Billabong	Hume	N.S.W.
VYCHAN	T. Bray, Vychan, Forbes	Forbes	N.S.W.

W

WOOL MARKS.	WOOL GROWERS' NAMES AND ADDRESSES.	PASTORAL DISTRICT.	STATE.
(W)	R. C. Bull and Co., Warrambeen South, Shelford	Shelford	VIC.
(W heart)	O'Brien Bros., Yarrabundie, Trundle ...	Forbes	N.S.W.
W A C NORTH BRUNDAH	W. A. Clements, North Brundah, Grenfell	Forbes ...	N.S.W.
WAGINGOBEREMBEE J J RUDD	J. & F. Rudd, Wagingoberembee, Wagga	Wagga	N.S.W.
WAIHORA	H. B. Coward, Waihora, Cunnamulla...	Cunnamulla	Q.
W A K	W. A. Kelly, Mount View, Penshurst...	Warrnambool	VIC.
WALBUNDRIE	W. Kiddle, Walbundrie, Albury	Albury ...	N.S.W.
W A L G H	W. A. Lang, Carlinda, Cooma	Cooma ...	N.S.W.
WALLABADAH	J. M. L. McDonald, Wallabadah, Tamworth	Tamworth	N.S.W.
WALLAH TAPPEE (WJG) CAPERTEE	W. J. Gallagher, Wallah Tappee, Capertee	Mudgee	N.S.W.
WALLAROOBIE	Dalgety and Co., Wallaroobie, Coolamon	Wagga...	N.S.W.
WALL A T C NARRABRI	J. Wall, Appletree Clump, Narrabri	Narrabri	N.S.W.
WALLON	G. W. Ledingham, Wallon, Moree	Moree ...	N.S.W.
WALMA NAMOI	Moore Bros., Walma, Walgett	Walgett	N.S.W.
WAMBROOK COOMA	T. L. Learmouth, Wambrook, Cooma	Cooma ...	N.S.W.

W

WOOL MARKS.	WOOL GROWERS' NAMES AND ADDRESSES.	PASTORAL DISTRICT.	STATE.
W & A McC GOOMBURAH	W. & A McConnochie, Goomburah, Bollon	Bollon	Q.
W A M NEW ENG	J. Makin, Springfield, Gum Flat	Warialda	N.S.W.
WAMRAWAR T B B	T. B. Brown, Halfmoon Plains Canonbar	Canonbar	N.S.W.
WANAARING	Hebden Bros., Wanaaring Station, Wanaaring	Wanaaring	N.S.W.
WANDARY	W. H R. Stitt, Wandary, Forbes	Forbes ...	N.S.W.
WANDILLAH J E B	R. Reid, jun., Wandillah, Redruth	Redruth	S.A.
WANDILLAH R R	R. Reid, jun., Wandillah, Redruth	Redruth	S.A.
WANDO	Broughton Bros., Wando, Casterton	Western District	VIC.
WANDO DALE W M	National Bank, Wando Dale, Coleraine	Wannon ...	VIC.
WANDO VIEW T C	T. O. Connell, Wando View, Brimpaen	Western District...	VIC.
WANGAMANA J & L H	J. & L. Howatson, Wangamana, Bourke	Bourke... ...	N.S.W.
WANGAMONG ⟨S⟩	Saugar Bros., Wangamong, Corowa	Corowa ..	N.S.W.
WANGANELLA	A. Austin, Wanganella, Deniliquin	Deniliquin	N.S.W.
WANGRAWALLY COLLINGWOOD	S. T. Dent, Wangrawally, Walgett	Walgett ...	N.S.W.
WAOCK WIDGIEWA	J. S. Horsfall, Widgiewa, Urana	Urana	N S.W.

W

WOOL MARKS.	WOOL GROWERS' NAMES AND ADDRESSES.	PASTORAL DISTRICT.	STATE.
WARE	J. Ware (exors.), Yalla-y-Poora-Buangor, Ararat	Ararat	VIC.
WARGAM	R. H. Woodward, Wargam, Booroorban	Hay	N.S.W.
WARGUNDY E M B	Bowman Bros., Wargundy, Gulgong ...	Mudgee	N.S.W.
WARNAMBOOL DOWNS	Queensland Estates Co., Ltd., Warnambool Downs, Muttaburra	Longreach	Q.
WAROONGA	Scottish-Australian Investment Co., Ltd., Waroonga, Mitchell	Mitchell	Q.
WARRA D D DALBY	S. A. Taylor, Logic Plains, Warra	Dalby ...	Q.
WARRAKIMBO	C. L. Maslin (Manager), Worrakimbo, Marraehowrie		S.A.
WARRAMBEEN NORTH	Beggs Bros., Warrambeen North, Shelford	Western District...	VIC.
WARRENBRI WEE WAA	T. Knight, Warrenbri, Wee Waa	Narrabri	N.S.W.
WARRIE (T)	N. G. Thompson, Warrie, Bathurst	Bathurst	N.S.W.
WARROCK	G. R. Patterson, Warrock, Casterton ...	Glenelg...	VIC.
WARRONG S B	S. Baird, Warrong, Koroit ...	Western District..	VIC.
WARROO	C. S. McPhillamy, Warroo, Forbes	Forbes ...	N.S.W.
WARWARRICK	McArthur Bros., Warwarrick, Camperdown	Western District	VIC.
WARWILLAH	J. Palmer, Warwillah, Hawkesdale	Western District .	VIC.

14

W

WOOL MARKS.	WOOL GROWERS' NAMES AND ADDRESSES.	PASTORAL DISTRICT.	STATE.
W & A S **MT DESPOND**	W. & A. Shannon, Mount Despond, Moculta	Moculta	S.A.
WATCH HILL	C. E. Parsons, Watch Hill, Beeac	Western District...	VIC.
WATTLE **PARK** **JH**	J. H. Hartwick, Wattle Park, Hamilton	Hamilton	VIC.
WATUNGA	D. H. Shannon, Watunga, Kapunda ...	Kapunda	S.A.
W A **WHYENBAH**	Commercial Bank of Sydney, Whyenbah, St. George	St. George	Q.
WAYVILLE PARK	J. Phelan and Sons, Glenorchy, Wimmera	Wimmera	VIC.
W B	F. & C. F. Wood, Rupanyup, Wimmera	Wimmera	VIC.
W ω	J. J. Brown, jun., Yalberoi, Trangie ...	Dubbo ...	N.S.W.
W B **A** **NEW ENGLAND**	W. Burgess, Armidale	Armidale	N.S.W.
W B **BRIAR PARK**	A. J. Brownlow, Briar Park, Rockley...	Bathurst	N.S.W.
W B **F**	W. Bassett, Fairfield, Coonamble	Coonamble	N.S.W.
W B **FERNLEIGH**	W. Butler, jun., Fernleigh, Conmurra...	Conmurra	S.A.
W B **LITTLE CARAGABAL**	W. Burge, Little Caragabal, Grenfell. .	Forbes ...	N.S.W.
W B **NEWBRYGEN**	W. Brazier, Newbrygen, Euchareena...	Molong	N.S.W.
W B **NUBRYGYN**	Brazier Bros., Nubrygyn, Euchareena	Molong...	N.S.W.

W

WOOL MARKS.	WOOL GROWERS' NAMES AND ADDRESSES.	PASTORAL DISTRICT.	STATE.
W B P COMPTON	W. B. Perry, Compton, Narramine	Dubbo	N.S.W.
W. BROOKER DAVIES CK	W. Brooker, Davies Creek, Aberdeen	Murrurundi	N.S.W.
W BROS R I O	Walker Bros., Townsville ...	Townsville	Q.
W BROS SALTERN CREEK	Weinholt Estates Co., Saltern Creek, Saltern ...	Barcaldine	Q.
W B S & S MERRINGINA	W. & A. McConochie, Morringina, Brewarrina...	Browarrina	N.S.W.
W ⌐ TERANGAN	Bowens Estate, Terangan, Dandaloo ...	Canonbar ...	N.S.W.
⌐B THE BRAES	Sir W. Brown, The Braes, Dalblair, Klori	Tamworth	N.S.W.
⌐B TILBOROO	London Bank of Australia, Tilboroo, Charleville	Charleville	Q.
W B TRAWALLA	W. B. Bridges, Trawalla Estate, Trawalla ...	...	VIC.
W B / W	W. Bunyan, Woodlands, Germanton ...	Hume ..	N.S.W.
WB WILLANDRA	London Bank of Australia, Willandra, Booligal...	Hillston	N.S.W.
W B Y	F. D. McMaster, Dalkeith, Cassilis	Merriwa	N.S.W.
W. CALDWELL MOONBUCCA	W. Caldwell, Moonbucca, Morangorell	Young ...	N.S.W.
W C B DEROWIE	W. C. Bowman, Derowie and Goinbla, Cudal ...	Molong...	N.S.W.
W C BURWOOD	W. Clements, Burwood, Binda	Carcoar	N.S.W.

WOOL MARKS.	WOOL GROWERS' NAMES AND ADDRESSES.	PASTORAL DISTRICT.	STATE.
W C **JUGIONG**	J. Cooney, Reedy Creek, Jugiong	Young	N.S.W.
W C **KALUDAH**	W. Criep, Kaludah, Rock Flat	Cooma...	N.S.W.
⬥**WC** **LOWAN**	Mrs. J. Cranch, Lowan, Kalangadoo ...	Kalangadoo	S.A.
W C **LYNDHURST**	W. Coventry, Lyndhurst, Armidale	Armidale ...	N S.W.
W C **MOONBUCCA**	W. Caldwell, Moonbucca, Morangorell	Young ...	N.S.W.
W C M **SPRINGWOOD**	W. C. Messer (exors.), Springwood, Hamilton ...	Western District	VIC.
W C **NEWLANDS**	J. McQuillen, Newlands, Come-by-Chance	Walgett	N.S.W.
W. CONDON **TONGIO VALE**	W. Condon, Tongio Vale, Omeo	Gippsland	VIC.
W C & SON **BAARMUTHA**	W. Coade and Son, Baarmutha, Mitchell District	Longreach ...	Q.
W C **UNDERWOOD** **URALLA**	W. Crupp, Underwood, Uralla	Armidale	N.S.W.
W C W **MUDGEE**	W. C. Webb, Leaning Oak, Mudgee ...	Mudgee	N.S.W.
W D **D**	J. A. Duncan, Derrinal	Central District ...	VIC.
⬥**W D** **K**	W. Dearlove, Ketchowla		S.A.
W D **RED HILL**	W. Dingwall, Red Hill, Glenthompson	Western District	VIC.
W D **S C**	W. D. Stanford, Clydesdale, Scone	Murrurundi	N.S.W.

W

WOOL MARKS.	WOOL GROWERS' NAMES AND ADDRESSES.	PASTORAL DISTRICT.	STATE.
W D S **OMEO**	W. D. Smith, Omeo, Coonamble	Coonamble	N.S.W.
W D **T V**	W. Ditchfield, Tugger Vale, Lockhart	Urana ...	N.S.W.
W D **URALLA**	J. Wood, Carlowrie, Uralla ..	Armidale	N.S.W.
◇ **W** **E**	Mrs. A A Stevenson, Deniliquin	Deniliquin	N.S.W.
WEBB BROS **W**	Webb Bros., Wahroonga, Gunnedah ...	Tamworth	N.S.W.
WEEBOLLABOLLA	A. G. F. Munro, Weebollabolla, Moree	Moree	N.S.W.
W & E C	E. Crozier, Bimbowrie, *via* Olary	Olary	S.A.
W E & Co **OREEL**	J. W. C. Langhorne, Oreel, Bulyeroi ...	Walgett	N.S.W.
W E C **WINDERMERE**	W. E. Cunningham, Windermere, Marengo	Young	N.S.W.
WEERANGOURT **M N M** ↗	A Melville, Weerangourt, Macarthur...	Hamilton	VIC.
WEILMORINGLE J & K BROS	Jamieson and Keats Bros., Weilmoringle, Brewarrina	Brewarrina	N.S.W.
WEILMORINGLE **J & K BROS**	Jamieson and Keats Bros., Weilmoringle, Brewarrina	Brewarrina	N.S.W.
WEINTERIGA	G. & T. Riddoch, Weinteriga, Wilcannia	Wilcannia	N S.W.
WELAREGANG	T. Paton, Welaregang, Albury	Albury ...	N.S.W.
WELBON	N.S.W. M. L. & A. Co., Ltd., Welbon, Moree ...	Moree ...	N.S.W.

W

WOOL MARKS.	WOOL GROWERS' NAMES AND ADDRESSES.	PASTORAL DISTRICT.	STATE.
WELBON E	N.S.W. M. L. & A. Co., Ltd., Welbon, Moree ...	Moree	N.S.W.
WELLINGTON	A. McFarlane, Wellington Lodge, Wellington East	Wellington	S.A.
WELLTOWN DARLING DOWNS	Leonard and Sinclair, Welltown, Goondiwindi ...	Goondiwindi	Q.
WEMABUNG X	P. Kelly, Wemabung, Tenandra	Coonamble	N.S.W.
WERAI	McRae Bros., Werai, Deniliquin	Deniliquin	N.S.W.
WESTBOURNE	Western Queensland Meat Co. Proprietary, Ltd., Westbourne	Longreach	Q.
WESTBURY	M. & E. Crombie, Westbury, Longreach	Longreach	Q.
W E W THURRAGIE	W. E. Walmsley, Thurragie, St. George	St. George ...	Q.
W F	W. Faulks, Deniliquin ...	Deniliquin ...	N.S.W.
W F	The A. L. & F. Co. of Australia, Freemont, Kilfera	Balranald ...	N.S.W.
W FARRAR BRYMAIR RYLSTONE	W. Farrar, Brymair, Rylstone	Mudgee ...	N.S.W.
W. F. BUCHANAN KILLARNEY	W. F. Buchanan, Killarney, Narrabri	Narrabri ..	N.S.W.
W. F. BUCHANAN TARRIARO	W. F. Buchanan, Tarriaro, Narrabri	Narrabri ...	N.S.W.
W F FAIRFIELD	W. Ferguson, Fairfield, Trangie ...	Dubbo	N.S.W.
W GAMBOOLA	F. Jago Smith (trust a/c), Hawthorn, Bathurst; wool grown at Gamboola, Molong ...	Molong... ...	N.S.W.

W

WOOL MARKS.	WOOL GROWERS' NAMES AND ADDRESSES.	PASTORAL DISTRICT.	STATE.
W G **BOWEN VILLE**	W. Grant, Bowenville, Dalby	Dalby ...	Q.
W G **BURNBRAE**	W. Gubbins, Burnbrae, Penshurst	Western District	VIC.
W G **ELGIN**	W. Gagie, Elgin, Henty	Albury ...	N.S.W.
W G F **GERONGA**	W. G. Ferris, Geronga, Walgett	Walgett	N.S.W.
W G **7** **G I** **NEW ENG**	W. Gould, Rose Valley, Stonehenge	Glen Innes	N.S.W.
W G H **GLENAREN**	W. G. Haynes, Glenaren, Parkes	Forbes ...	N.S.W.
W **GILLENDOON**	T. Walker, Gillendoon, Warren	Coonamble	N.S.W.
W & G L **W**	W. C. M. Lane, Moulma, Coonamble ...	Coonamble	N.S.W.
W G M **BUDGERY**	W. G. Matchett, Budgery, Nyngan ...	Canonbar	N.S.W.
W G P **M**	W. G. Pryor, Mundallis, Port Augusta	Port Augusta	S.A.
W G **R**	W. Grambauer, Rosedale, Jericho	Aramac	Q.
W **GREEN CAMP**	Ward Bros., Green Camp, Nyngan	Canonbar	N.S.W.
W G **SCONE**	W. Gibson, Scone, Perth	Perth ...	TAS.
W G S **NAREEB NAREEB**	W. Simmons, Nareeb Nareeb, Chatsworth	Western District...	VIC.
W G **WERRIWA**	W. F. Gordon, Werriwa, Manar	Braidwood	N.S.W.

W

WOOL MARKS.	WOOL GROWERS' NAMES AND ADDRESSES.	PASTORAL DISTRICT.	STATE.
WHARPARILLA	W. W. Wragge (exors.), Wharparilla, Echuca...	Echuca...	VIC.
W H B TASMANIA	W. H. Bennett, Bloomfield, Ross	Ross	TAS.
W-O COLIBAN PARK	W. H. Davidson, Coliban Park, Elphinstone ...	Talbot ...	VIC.
WHEOGO	T. W. Chapman, Wheogo, Grenfell	Forbes ...	N.S.W.
W H FLAX VALE	W. Howard, Flax Vale, Carnsdale	Wagga...	N.S.W.
W H GURRANDAH	B. Heffernan, Gurrandah Park, Gurrandah	Goulburn ...	N.S.W.
W H HOLLIES	W. Herbert, The Hollies, Lockhart ...	Urana	N.S.W.
WHISSONSETT A L N	A. McDonald, Whissonsett, Timor	Murrurundi	N.S.W.
WHITES RIVER GOODE	W. E. Goode, White's River, Lincoln...	Lincoln... ..	S.A.
W H MARRAN	W. Hoskins, Marran, Mundooran	Coonabarabran ...	N.S.W.
W H M CLEVELANDS	J. B. Hammond (exors. of W. H. Moore), Clevelands, Walgett	Walgett ...	N.S.W.
W H O MILBURN CK	W. E. & H. M. Oliver, Milburn Creek, Woodstock	Carcoar ...	N.S.W.
W. H. P.	W. & H. A. Patrick, Eversleigh, Warren	Coonamble	N.S.W.
W H & P BOLARO	Patrick and Co., Bolaro, Cobborah ...	Dubbo	N.S.W.
W H P EVERSLEIGH	W. & H. A. Patrick, Eversleigh, Warren	Coonamble	N.S.W.

W

WOOL MARKS.	WOOL GROWERS' NAMES AND ADDRESSES.	PASTORAL DISTRICT.	STATE.
W H P L	W. Hunter, Prairie Lands, Forbes	Forbes ...	N.S.W.
W H PLAIN VIEW	W. Hoolahan, Plain View, Bugilbone...	Pilliga ...	N.S.W.
W H R A	W. H. Reid, Branxholm	Western District...	VIC.
W H S WHEAT HILL	Ellen Southern, Wheat Hill, Berridale	Cooma ...	N.S.W.
W H T LOCKWOOD	W. H. Traves, Lockwood, Canowindra	Molong	N.S.W.
W I W ALTON	W. U. Wheatley, Alton, Goulburn	Goulburn	N.S.W.
W H WOODSTOCK	W. Hall, Woodstock, Walgett	Walgett	N.S.W.
WHYTE PARK WIRRABARA	D. T. F. McKenzie, Whyte Park, Wirrabara		S.A.
WIDGIEWA	J. S. Horsfall, Widgiewa, Urana	Urana ...	N.S.W.
WILGA DOWNS	Goldsbrough, Mort and Co., Wilga Downs, Hermidale	Cobar	N.S.W.
WILGENA	A. W. Cocks, Wilgena	Wilgena	S.A.
WILLEROO	R. C. Cooper, Pylara, Tarago	Braidwood	N.S.W.
WILLEROON E. S. HALL	E. S. Hall, Willeroon, Coolabah	Canonbar	N.S.W.
WILLIAMBURY	M. C. R. Bunbury, Williambury, Carnarvon	Carnarvon	W.A.
WILLOW PARK P I	T. J. Plunkett, Willow Park, Bowna ...	Albury ...	N.S.W.

W

WOOL MARKS.	WOOL GROWERS' NAMES AND ADDRESSES.	PASTORAL DISTRICT.	STATE.
WILSON MT EMU	W. Wilson, Mount Emu, Snake Valley	...	VIC.
WILSON OLD BERRIGAN	A. & C. Wilson, Old Berrigan, Jerilderie	Jerilderie	N.S.W.
WILSON YARRABERB	J. H. Sargood (Manager), Yarraberb, Raywood	Bendigo	VIC.
WINBAR	Union Bank of Australia, Winbar, Bourke	Bourke ...	N.S.W.
WINDOURAN	L. McBean (exors.), Windouran, Moulamein	Moulamein	N.S.W.
WING C	W. Taylor, Cresline, Coonamble	Coonamble	N.S.W.
WINNICOT E W	E. White, Den Hills, Coleraine	Dundas	VIC.
WINTER BORAH	G. Winter, Borah, Manilla ...	Tamworth	N.S.W.
WINTONG	J. Murphy, Wintong, Balranald	Balranald	N.S.W.
WIRIDGIL	E. Manifold, Wiridgil, Camperdown ...	Western District...	VIC.
WIRLONG	Smith Bros., Wirlong, Cobar	Cobar	N.S.W.
WIRRAMINNA	G. Palmer (Manager), Wirraminna, Port Augusta	Port Augusta ...	S.A.
WIRRIALPA	— Paxton, Wirrialpa	Wirrialpa ...	S.A.
WITCHELINA	Ragless Bros., Witchelina, Tarina	Tarina ...	S.A.
WIT ROSEMOUNT	S. W. & C. F. Witts, Rosemount, Holt's Flat ...	Bombala ...	N.S.W.

W

WOOL MARKS.	WOOL GROWERS' NAMES AND ADDRESSES.	PASTORAL DISTRICT.	STATE.
W J	W. J. Magennis, Dookie	North-Eastern District	VIC.
W J B **B**	W. J. Broadribb, Germanton, Hume ...	Hume	N.S.W.
W & J B **DRYBURGH**	W. & J. Balgowan (exors.), Dryburgh, Reid's Flat	Young ...	N.S.W.
W J C **BOUNDARY VILLA**	W. J. Cartwright, Boundary Villa, Temora	Wagga ...	N.S.W.
W J **C F**	W. Jardine, Curry Flat, Nimitybelle ...	Cooma ...	N S.W.
W J C **TARRINGTON**	W. J. Carter, Tarrington, Hoch Kirch		VIC.
W J **GLENVALE**	W. Jackson, Glenvale, Moonan Flat ...	Murrurundi	N.S.W.
W J L **FAIRFIELD**	W. J. Lobb, Darrawent, Guim		VIC.
W J P **EULALIA**	Treweeke and Sons, Eulalia, Mogil	Walgett	N.S.W.
W J R **WARRANGONG**	W. J. Rice, Warrangong, Pleasant Hills	Urana ...	N.S.W.
W J S **NAREEB NAREEB**	W. Simmons, Nareeb Nareeb, Chatsworth	...	VIC.
W J S **WARRADERRY**	W. Jones, jun., Warraderry, Grenfell...	Forbes	N.S.W.
W J △ **TONGIO**	W. Johnston, Swift's Creek, Gippsland	Gippsland	VIC.
W J W **PANARAMITEE**	W. J. Wade, Panaramitee, Yunta	Yunta	S.A.
W K ◇	W. Kelly, Gould's Creek, One Tree Hill		S.A.

WOOL MARKS.	WOOL GROWERS' NAMES AND ADDRESSES.	PASTORAL DISTRICT.	STATE.
W K **ALLANVALE**	D. McKay (Manager), Allanvale, Great Western	Stawell...	VIC.
W K **D**	P. Kiley, Red Hill, Tumut	Gundagai	N.S.W.
W K **TICEHURST**	W. & E. Kennedy, Ticehurst, Ivanhoe	Ivanhoe	N.S.W.
W L	J. Lee, Kelso, Bathurst	Bathurst	N.S.W.
W L **ARDACHY**	A. G. Laidlow, Ardachy, Branxholme	Hamilton	VIC.
W L **CORINELLA**	W. Landers, Corinella, Coonamble	Coonamble	N.S.W.
W L **G B R L**	W. Laff, Gobarralong, Gundagai	Gundagai	N.S.W.
W L M **BURNSIDE**	D. Gooch (Manager), Burnside, Strathalbyn	Strathalbyn	S.A.
W L S **IRONBARK**	J. Skinner, Ironbark, Coonamble	Coonamble	N.S.W.
W L **STONELEIGH**	W. Lewis (exors.), Stoneleigh, Beaufort	Western District ..	VIC.
W L **WOMBEYAN**	W. Lang, c/o Bank of N.S.W., Sydney		N.S.W.
W M	W. A. Maynard, Yarravale, Trundle Road, Parkes	Forbes ...	N.S.W.
W M **-:-**	W. Mathews, Terang	Western District...	VIC.
W. MARINA **YOUNG**	W. Marina, Verana, Young ...	Young ...	N.S.W.
W M B **MASCOTTE**	G. H. Bloodworth, Mascotte, Coonamble	Coonamble	N.S.W

W

WOOL MARKS.	WOOL GROWERS' NAMES AND ADDRESSES.	PASTORAL DISTRICT.	STATE.
W M C **AVOCA**	W. M. Connell, Avoca Station, Gulargambone ...	Coonamble	N.S.W.
W M C **BURGOON**	W. M. Cahill, Burgoon, Molong	Molong ..	N.S.W.
W McC **WARBRECCAN**	Hon. W. McCullock, Warbreccan, Deniliquin ...	Deniliquin	N.S.W.
W McI **CLUNES**	W. McInnes, Clunes, Cowra...	Carcoar	N.S.W.
W McL **CLYDE**	W. McLanghlin, Clyde, Garah	Moree	N.S.W.
W McM **MANEROO**	Dalgety and Co., Ltd , Maneroo, Longreach	Longreach	Q.
W M **COOLAMON**	W. Macansh, Aunandale, Tenterfield ...	Tenterfield	N.S.W.
W M **COOMA**	W. Moore, Black Springs, Dry Plain ...	Cooma ...	N.S.W.
W McQ **TAHARA**	W. McQueen, Tahara Station, Coleraine	Dundas...	VIC.
W M **DOOBOOBETIC**	W. Merryless, Dooboobetic ...	North-Western District	VIC.
⊥ **W** **MERRENDEE**	Mrs. L. A. Webb, Merrendee, Mudgee	Mudgee	N.S.W.
W M **K A**	W. Macauley, Glenrowan	North-Eastern District	VIC.
W M **M C** **NEW ENG**	W. Misson, Main Camp, Murrurundi ...	Murrurundi	N.S.W.
W M **3** **ROSE HILL**	Mainwaring Bros., Rose Hill, Cootamundra	Gundagai	N.S.W.
W M **MTN VIEW**	W. Maxwell, Mountain View, Narrabri	Narrabri	N.S.W.

WOOL MARKS.	WOOL GROWERS' NAMES AND ADDRESSES.	PASTORAL DISTRICT.	STATE.
W. MOLONY **D B**	W. Molony, Dobies Bridge		VIC.
W. M. OMAN **LISMORE**	W. M. Oman, Lismore	Camperdown	VIC.
W M **ROCKDALE**	R. A. Miners, Rockdale, Nimitybelle	Bombala	N.S.W.
W **NARLGA**	T. G. Wragge, Narlga, Deniliquin	Deniliquin	N.S.W.
W O D **WOOD PARK**	W. Wood, per Bank of N.S.W., Moree	Moree ...	N.S.W.
WOGGONORA	R. Brown, Woggonora, Cunnamulla ...	Cunnamulla	Q.
W O **GRAVESEND**	W. Onus, Gravesend, Moree...	Moree ...	N.S.W.
WOMBIN	J. L. Whitmill, Wombin, Parkes	Molong...	N.S.W.
WOMBRAMURRA	F. Payne, Wombramurra, Nundle	Tamworth	N.S.W.
WONDOOBA	W. D. Simson, Wondooba, Gunnedah...	Tamworth	N.S.W.
WONGAJONG	W. L. Wilcox, Wongajong, Forbes	Forbes ...	N.S.W.
WONGLE **D DOWNS**	D. Ferrier, Wongle, Coomrith	Dalby	Q.
WOODBINE PARK **N W B WHEEO**	N. W. Burdekin, Woodbine, Wheeo ...	Yass ...	N.S.W.
WOODBROOK	Church, Gillam and Co., Woodbrook, Roebourne	Roebourne	W.A.
WOODHOUSE	A. & B. Ritchie, Woodhouse, Penshurst	Western District...	VIC.

WOOL MARKS.	WOOL GROWERS' NAMES AND ADDRESSES.	PASTORAL DISTRICT.	STATE.
WOODLANDS	Manager, Woodlands, Dandaloo ; head office, Goldsbrough, Mort & Co., Ltd., Melbourne	Dubbo ...	N.S.W.
WOODLANDS G X B	G. Bardwell, Woodlands, Wagga	Wagga...	N.S.W.
WOODLANDS T McL	T. McLennon, Little River, Geelong	Geelong	VIC.
WOODLANDS W McC	W. McCulloch, Woodlands, Crowlands	Wimmera	VIC.
WOODLAWN	T. W. Wells, Woodlawn, Warialda	Warialda	N.S.W.
WOODSIDE	P. Brennan, Woodside, via Sale	Gippsland	VIC.
WOODS POINT M	J. E. Gartner (Manager), Woods Point, Murray Bridge	Murray Bridge ...	S.A.
WOODTON	J. L. Suckling, Woodton, Quirindi	Tamworth	N.S.W.
WOOLACOOLA	P. H. Wheaton, Woolacoola, Red Hill	Red Hill	S.A.
WOOLLAHRA	H. Popplewell, Woollahra, Brewarrina	Brewarrina	N.S.W.
WOOLEEN	J. Sharp, Woolleen, via Yalgoo, Murchison	Murchison	W.A.
WOOLERINA	N. Z. Land Association, Woolerina, Mitchell	Mitchell	Q.
WOOLMIT	H. A. Morris, Woolmit, Kingston	Kingston	S.A.
WOOLONGOON W W	W. Weatherley, Woolongoon, Mortlake	Western District...	VIC.
WOOLTANA	McTaggart Lachlan, Blinman	Blinman	S.A.

W

WOOL MARKS.	WOOL GROWERS' NAMES AND ADDRESSES.	PASTORAL DISTRICT.	STATE.
WOOMARGAMA	H. Hedderick, Woomargama, Hume ...	Hume ...	N.S.W.
WONNAMINTA K Y	A. M. L. & F. Co., Ltd., Wonnaminta, Euriowie	Menindie	N.S.W.
WOONWARREN	H. J. Carbett, Woonwarren, Warrong	...	VIC.
WORMBETE	W. Hopkins, Wormbete, Winchelsea...	South-Western District	VIC.
WOWINGRAGONG G T FORBES	G. Thornton, Wowingragong, Forbes ..	Forbes ...	N.S.W.
W P PRINCE BARNES	W. Pearce, Prince Barnes, Stawell	Stawell...	VIC.
W P UMAGARLEE MUDGEE	W. R. Parkinson, Umagarlee, Mudgee	Mudgee	N.S.W.
W R BRAULIN	Mrs. W. Richards, Braulin, Forbes	Forbes ...	N.S.W.
W R FLAGGY MOUNT	W. Robson, Flaggy Mount, Woolbrook	Armidale	N.S.W.
W RINGWOOD	A. Wilson (exors.), Ringwood, Corowa	Corowa...	N.S.W.
W R M BOOMBAH	W. R. Munro, Boombah, St. George	St. George	Q.
W R MILLGALARR	S. Donaldson, Millgalarr, Warialda	Warialda ...	N.S.W.
W R M MOGILA	W. R. Moore, Mogila, Brewarrina	Brewarrina	N.S.W.
W R & S LAKE BATHURST	W. Reynolds and Son, Lake Bathurst	Goulburn	N.S.W.
W R S MOREE	W. R. Scott, Box Clump, Moree	Moree	N.S.W.

W

WOOL MARKS.	WOOL GROWERS' NAMES AND ADDRESSES.	PASTORAL DISTRICT.	STATE.
W R **W**	J. W. Barton, Wallerawang, Bathurst	Bathurst	N.S.W.
W. RYAN **S** **VALLEY**	J. Ryan, Germanton, Hume ...	Hume	N.S.W.
W S	W. Scott (exors.), Woodland, Kersbrook		S.A.
W S **BUNYIP**	W. Sanders, Bunyip, Sandsmere		VIC.
W. SEERS **GRASS VALLEY**	W. Seers, Grass Valley, Timberry Range	Cooma ...	N.S.W.
W **ⵏSⵏ** **CUCUMGILLIGA**	H. W. Shuttleworth, Cucumgilliga, Cowra	Young ...	N.S.W.
W S **LAKE VIEW**	W. Speers, Lake View, Watgania	Western District	VIC.
W S **ROSEDALE**	W. Smith, Rosedale, Trangie	Dubbo ...	N.S.W.
W T **CAROON**	W. Thompson, Caroon, West Wyalong	Condobolin	N.S.W.
W T E **BOMBALA**	W. T. Edwards, Oak Range, Mahratta	Bombala	N.S.W.
W T **FERNBANK**	W. Thompson, Fernbank, Jerilderie	Jerilderie	N.S.W.
W T H **A**	W. T. Hoare, Apsley	Western District	VIC.
W T H **PRAIRIE**	W. Thompson, Prairie, Green's Creek	Stawell ...	VIC.
W T **NEW ENGLAND**	W. Thorley (exors.), Salisbury Plains, Uralla ...	Armidale	N.S.W.
W **TOMBONG**	J. Ingram, Tombong, Delegate	Bombala	N.S.W.

W

WOOL MARKS.	WOOL GROWERS' NAMES AND ADDRESSES.	PASTORAL DISTRICT.	STATE.
W T SALISBURY. DS	W. Charters (exors.), Salisbury Downs, Wilcannia	Wilcannia	N.S.W.
W T T TERRIBLE VALE NEW ENGLAND	F. G. Taylor and Co., Terrible Vale, Kentucky	Armidale	N.S.W.
W TULLA	T. Wragge and Sons, Tulla, Deniliquin	Deniliquin	N.S.W.
W U W KANAKA	W. U. Wall, Kanaka, Tickera	Tickera ...	S.A.
W V H GOODBERRY HILLS	W. V. Holton, Goodberry Hills, Mitchell	Mitchell	Q.
W Ƶ	W. Wallace, Whitewood, Nyngan	Canonbar	N.S.W.
W W BELLTREES	H. E. A. & V. White, Belltrees, Scone	Murrurundi	N.S.W.
W W C B (blue)	W. Williams, Coonooer Bridge	St. Arnaud	VIC.
W W COLLEY CREEK	W. Weatherley, Colley Creek, Willow Tree	Tamworth	N.S.W.
W W K BULL PLAIN	W. W. Killen, Bull Plain, Corowa	Corowa ...	N.S.W.
W W MOSS VALE	W. Williams, Moss Vale, Moonan Flat	Murrurundi	N.S.W.
W W NORTON CREEK	W. Walsh, Norton Creek, Horsham	Horsham	VIC.
W W PASSES	Wall Bros., Seymour	Seymour	VIC.
W W Ƶ	W. Waddell, Bathurst	Bathurst	N.S.W.
W W W BELLTREES	H. E. A. & V. White, Belltrees, Scone	Murrurundi	N.S.W.

W

WOOL MARKS.	WOOL GROWERS' NAMES AND ADDRESSES.	PASTORAL DISTRICT.	STATE.
WYANAWAH	J. S. McPhillamy (exors.), Wyanawah, Cookardinia...	Hume	N.S.W.
WYORA	Killen Bros., Young and Co., Wyora, Winton	Winton...	Q.
WYUNA	Finlay Bros., Wyuna, St. Germains		VIC.
WYVERN	A. J. L. Learmouth, Wyvern, Carrathool	Hay	N.S.W
W Z **D**	W. Jacker, Darriman, Gippsland	Gippsland	VIC.

X

WOOL MARKS.	WOOL GROWERS' NAMES AND ADDRESSES.	PASTORAL DISTRICT.	STATE.
X E	Cox Bros., Rawden, Rylstone	Mudgee	N.S.W.
X 7 LILBURN	C. Bloxsome, Lilburn, Glen Innes	Glen Innes	N.S.W.
X L MOUTAJUP	G. Taylor (exors.), Montajup	Wannon	VIC.
X N G MUDGEE	P. Crossing, Enfield, Mudgee	Mudgee	N.S.W.
X STONEY PARK	W. Turner, Stoney Park, Jindera	Albury ...	N.S.W.
X X G	Mackay Bros., Gunyerwarildi, Warialda	Warialda	N.S.W.
X X ROSENEATH	C. Swinson (exors.), Roseneath, Casterton	Western District	VIC.

Y

WOOL MARKS.	WOOL GROWERS' NAMES AND ADDRESSES.	PASTORAL DISTRICT.	STATE.
Y	A. J. V. Cunningham, Tuggranong, Queanbeyan	Queanbeyan	N.S.W.
YAMBA	C. P. Hunter, Yamba, Brewarrina	Brewarrina	N.S.W.
YACKARA	W. L. Whyte, Yackara, Quorn	Quorn ...	S.A.
YAGOBIE	Mrs. S. Maidens, Yagobie, Moree	Moree ...	N.S.W.
YALCOWINNA	Mount Gipps P. & M. Co., Ltd., Yalcowinna, Broken Hill	Menindie	N.S.W.
YALGOGRIN	Goldsbrough, Mort and Co., Ltd., Yalgogrin, Narrandera ...	Narrandera	N.S.W.
YALLAROI J J B	J. J. Brown, Yallaroi, Trangie	Dubbo ...	N.S.W.
YAMBURGAN	F. H. Rutledge, Yamburgan, St. George	St. George	Q.
YANDA	A. M. L. & F. Co., Ltd., Yanda, Bourke	Bourke ...	N.S.W.
YANDIAH G M	Mahood Bros., Yandiah, Wirrabara	Wirrabara	S.A.
YANGA	E. S. & A. Bank, Ltd., Yanga, Balranald	Balranald	N.S.W.
YANTARA	McEdward and Robertson, Yantara, Milparinka	Milparinka	N.S.W.
YANYEAREDDY Y	W. & G. Lefroy, Yanyeareddy, Onslow	Carnarvon	W.A.
YARRABEE	S. McCaughey, Yarrabee Park, Narrandera	Narrandera	N.S.W.
YARRALUMLA	F. Campbell, Yarralumla, Queanbeyan	Queanbeyan	N.S.W.

Y

WOOL MARKS.	WOOL GROWERS' NAMES AND ADDRESSES.	PASTORAL DISTRICT.	STATE.
YARRAMAN	T. & W. Busby, Yarraman, Quirindi ...	Tamworth	N.S.W.
YARAROO	W. Fowler (exors.), Yararoo, Melton ...	Melton ...	S.A.
YARAWA	Bucknell Bros., Yarawa, Mungindi	Walgett	N.S.W.
YARDEA	A. Bailey (Manager), Yardea	Yardea ...	S.A.
YARMOUTH	A.J.S. Bank, Yarmouth, via Charleville	Cunnamulla	Q.
YARRARA	Goldsbrough, Mort and Co., Yarrara, Hume	Hume ...	N.S.W.
YARRAVILLE H M D	J. Hammond, Yarraville, Forbes	Forbes ...	N.S.W.
YARRAYNE	W. B. Shaw, Yarrayne, Bendigo	Bendigo	VIC.
YASS PLAINS YASS	H. C. Langtree, Yass Plains, Yass	Yass	N.S.W.
YATNAT	A. Sutherland (Manager), Yat Nat, Balmoral ...	Wannon	VIC.
YATTALUNGA	T. & H. E. Barritt, Yattalunga, Gawler	Gawler	S.A.
YAWONG SPRINGS	W. Hodson, Yawong Springs, Coonooer Bridge	St. Arnaud	VIC.
◄B INGLEWOOD	Burbury Bros., Inglewood, Andover ...		TAS.
◄B NEWSTEAD	Burbury Bros., Tonthill, Oatlands	Oatlands	TAS.
Y BURRAWONG	Burrawong Grazing Co., Burrawong, Cumnock...	Molong	N.S.W.

Y

WOOL MARKS.	WOOL GROWERS' NAMES AND ADDRESSES.	PASTORAL DISTRICT.	STATE.
Y **CANYANLEIGH**	B. H. Murray, Canyan Leigh, Berrima	Berrima	N.S.W.
Y & Co **MT TEMPLETON**	R. J. Young, Mount Templeton, Everard Central		S.A.
YEO **COLAC**	W. H. Bullivant (exors.), Yeo, Irrewarra		VIC.
YESTYLFERA	H. L. & A. E. Ayers, Yestylfera, Clare	Clare	S.A.
YOUNGARA	N. Z. L. & M. A. Co., Ltd., Youngara, Ungarie	Condobolin	N.S.W.
YUIN	W. & S. Burgess, Yuin, Mullewa	Mullewa	W.A.
YULONG	A. Scott, Yulong, Buninyong	Ballarat	VIC.
YULLUNDRY	R. Glasson, Yullundry, Cumnock	Molong...	N.S.W.
YUNDAH	McIntosh Bros., Yundah, Mountside, Dalveen ...	Dalveen	Q.
Y Y **M**	W. F. Youle, Kyabram	North-Eastern District	VIC.
Y Y **SPRING VALLEY**	J. Connell (exors.), Spring Valley, Jerilderie	Jerilderie	N.S.W.

Z

WOOL MARKS.	WOOL GROWERS' NAMES AND ADDRESSES.	PASTORAL DISTRICT.	STATE.
ZARA	W. Officer, Zara, Deniliquin...	Deniliquin	N.S.W.
Z HOBYDS	D. Larnach, Hobbys Yards, Caloola	Carcoar	N.S.W.
Z JEREMY	G. W. Hacking, Jeremy, Burraga	Carcoar	N.S W.
Z W MOGIL	J. R. Walker, Mogil Mogil, Walgett	Walgett	N.S.W.
— ① —	J. Bushby, Horsham, Wimmera	Wimmera	VIC.
ᙍᙍ	N. Brown, Guaki, Tocumwal	Corowa...	N.S.W.
○ +	J. E. Moore, Ellensville, Glenmore	Picton ...	N.S.W.

Addenda.

WOOL MARKS.	WOOL GROWERS' NAMES AND ADDRESSES.	PASTORAL DISTRICT.	STATE.
B G D	B. G. Dawson, Hilldale, Guyra	Armidale	N.S.W.
F & A G MOREE	F. & A. Glennie, Yarraman View, Moree	Moree	N.S.W.
GILL NEW ENGLAND	R. Gill, Rockvale, Armidale...	Armidale	N.S.W.
G P GLENCOE NEW ENG	G. Price, Belleview, Glencoe	Glen Innes	N.S.W.
H G COOLAH	H. Giffen, Pandoras Pass, Coolah	Coonabarabran	N.S.W.
H S G H	Sharp and Sons, Green Hills, Gundagai	Gundagai	N.S.W.
J M V MOOLOOMOON	J. Macvean, Mooloomoon, Moulamein	Moulamein	N.S.W.
J R TALLYGANG	Robertson Bros., Tallygang, Taralga ...	Goulburn	N.S.W.
NEW ENGLAND A H B	A. H. Belfield, Eversleigh, Dumaresq...	Armidale	N.S.W.
W CARBUCKY	G. Wilson, Carbucky, Boggabilla	Warialda	N.S.W.

SECTION II.

Comprises Wool Brands which the Compiler could not trace to the grower. Some are good station brands; but others include dealers' mixed lots, speculative lots, and scoured lots of unknown origin. - - - - - -

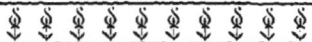

Wool sold at Sydney, N.S.W.

BRANDS.	BRANDS.	BRANDS.	BRANDS.
A B W	A O H NEW ENG	B J I C	C & A V M T
A Co A A	A P M	B J P N E	C B
A E F NEUREA	A P R S	B L ARMIDALE	CC
A E S	A R S K B	EL ROSLYN	C C R
A Ẹ MOLE	A S SCONE	BOLONG	C D D P
A J C	A S T NEW ENG	BOPZ	C D N S
A K	ATH B	B P	C GININDERA
AK	AVONDALE O D V LAKESIDE	B R	CH CHEVINAL LAKESIDE
◄ K MEADOW	A W A NEW ENG	B R ᵕ NEW ENG	C J M JUNEE
A M	A W C	B S	C J R
A McR	B B D NEW ENGLAND	B&S	C J S
A M E	B B X	B S A M C	C K
A M TUENA	B C HEMSBY	BURBENA	CLAREMOUNT
A M WALCHA NEW ENGLAND	B D D P ELTON	C	C L B
A N W	BIWONDAH D A P	CAR	C L LARONA

235

BRANDS.	BRANDS.	BRANDS.	BRANDS.
C L N	C S BARRABA	D L O B	EDGE HILL
7 C MEADOW FLAT	CUNNINGOROO A L	D M	E F
C & M F P	CUT B	D N	E G H
C NEW ENGLAND	C W N A	D N NEW ENG	E G H EDITHVILLE
Co A A B	D & B M M	DF AF (triangle)	EHL (diamond)
COBRAWRAGNY	D B MOREE	DF AF O (triangle)	E H M
Co Co	D C	DREELWARRINA	E L NORMAN STATION
Co JUGIONG	D (box)	D R G G	E M B N S W QUEENSLAND
COLLINGWOOD	D C C	D R G GUNNEDAH	E P LINWOOD
C O N S DALE	D. CLARK	D R G NEW ENGLAND N S W	ERSBY COLLINGWOOD
CORANGA PEAK LAKESIDE	D D D	D R M N S W	E S R V Y
CRANBROOK TASMANIA	D D P ELTON	D R W	EXTON COLLINGWOOD
CREEKSIDE	D E (diamond)	D R Y	E Y K
C R O CORRIEWARRIE	D F NEW ENGLAND	E C B GUNDOWRINGA	F A B
CRONIN	C (monogram) BRUNGLE	E C P WAGGA	F B NEBO

BRANDS.	BRANDS.	BRANDS.	BRANDS.
F F M ARMIDALE	C|M %	GUMBANK	H — H
FFRENCH	G GAYLES LAKESIDE	GUNNINGRAH	H H NEW ENG
F S	G H N E	G W D	H H V
G & A S N E	G J B	G W P BUNABA	H J S AVIEMORE
G B ƎD	G J & W. R.	G YASS	⚓ H K NEW ENGLAND
G B & S THE GLEN	GLENDON	H B	H M B ROSEVALE
G & Co ALONG	G M E C	H B HAY	
G D ASHFORD	G N LYANGA	H B NEW ENGLAND	◇H MUDGEE
G O B O T	◇ G R G NEW ENGLAND	H C H	◇ H R OURIMBA
GEM MUDGEE	G S C	H C X	H S
G E NEW ENG	G S K B K	HERO	H S T
G E P	G S M	H E SNOWY RIVER	⬤
G G	G S X	H F NEW ENGLAND	H T 2
G H C	G T F	H G L	H T COOMA
G H A G	G T RHODESIA	H H	H Z OAKLEIGH
	G U		I D D P ELTON

237

BRANDS.	BRANDS.	BRANDS.	BRANDS.
I F	J (in circle) BONA FIDE	J B COOLAC	J M 2
I — G	J Br MITCHELL'S CREEK	J B S	J M B G
I L ASHBROOK	J B ROSENEATH	J H WALLENDBEAN	J M BINDA
ILLION	Ⓒ	J J M	J M BUNDARRA
IPSWICH	J C M	J J McN	J M L
I X M	J C NARRABRI	J J M NEW ENG	J M R JUNEE
J (in box)	J C NEW MEXICO	J K	⌐ M ROBROY
J A N	J C S D	J K (in triangle)	J M SPRINGVALE
J A T	J ≏	J K ELSMORE	J M THURROWA
J A W Q Q	J E BOKHARA	J K GOLSPIE	J M ULOOLA
J B B D	J ⌐ (in circle)	J L (in diamond)	JN BELLEVUE
J B G	J F H RIDGE	J L A	J N E
J B L	J F S	J L CASTLE ROCK	J N G
B M ≈	J G	J L O NEW ENG	J N LANDERS
J B MUDGEE	J H C	J L S EUCHAREENA	J O B TYRONE

BRANDS.	BRANDS.	BRANDS.	BRANDS.
J O C	J S	J T R	K Y D
J O WAGGA	J S A	◁J T Y▷ (in triangle)	LADOONA
◇ J P ◇	J S B L	◇ J & V ◇	LAKESIDE
J P MATONG	J S B TIMOR	J & V	L B H S
J P MUDGEE	J S C T	◇ J V ◇ J	L. BROS Y
J P W NEW ENG	J S F BOGAN	J W	L B SUGARLOAF
J P WOODLANDS	J S GLENWOOD	[K] (in square)	L D
J Q MERINGO	J S H	KALUDAH	L F S MT PLEASANT
J Q N	J S SCONE	KELVIN GROVE S M NEW ENGLAND	◇ T H ◇ B
R̃	J S T	K E N	L H NEW ENG
J R ≡	J S W N E	KIEWA	L K
J R L PIKES CREEK	J T	ЖM	J L
J R M A	J T A	◇ K ◇ RIVERVIEW	LLANILLO
J R NEW ENG	J T AVONDALE	K & S WELAMURRA	L L L
R̃ S	J T N N	K T MUDGEE	L R

BRANDS.	BRANDS.	BRANDS.	BRANDS.
L R NANANGROVE	M B Y	M L Y	MURRAY DOWNS
L T	M C D & A YASS	M M	M W D
L T WOODLAND	M C K B	M M K WOOLBROOK	MYALLA
LYNTON	McKECHNIE	M M S	MYALL N O
LYNTON GULGONG COLLINGWOOD	M C K IVOR JUNEE	M MULYAN	NANANGROE
◇ M	MEIN NARRAN	MOORONG	NARLEENE
M & A	M F	MOUNT VIEW W M S	NEW ENDEN NEW ENG
M A C	M GALVIN BUTE	M P BOLOKO	N L S
MANGO	M G KALORA	M R	N N
MAYALA	M H C	M R S	N O W
M B	MICABIL	M & R S	N♢S W
M B C	M J SNOWY RIVER	M S ♢M	O C
M BERRIGAN	M K	L P	O C T
M B GLENAVON	M K S	MUGAN	O & D N S W
M B NEPEAN	M L C	MULGAH MUN	O G U

BRANDS.	BRANDS.	BRANDS.	BRANDS.
O L B COOMA	q D ROCHFORD	A McM	R L BUNGAMBIL
O L V R	P G JUGIONG	R A Y MUDGEE	R LUCKNOW
O M MT PLEASANT	P H	R B C	R M
O NEW ENDEN	P J B	R B G	ROSEWOOD E B E
O O O D DOWNS Q'LAND	P L A	R D BUNGAN BOGGABRI	R O W MUDGEE
O R R I	P L ARMIDALE	R D FAIRFIELD	⬦ B P
O SPRINGMOUNT NEW ENGLAND	P L BOORAMIE	R D G	R R MUDGEE
O ✝ WOODBURN	P L N E	R G	R R R
O X D	P L W	R G B N	R R W V
PADDINGTON LAKESIDE	P M COOLAC	R G H W O LAKESIDE	R S B G COOMA
PARKVALE P B	P O TATE	R G J	R S P N E
P B	PRINGLE	⬦ R H	R T B
(P B R)	P V	R H B WARNE	R T GLEN N E
P C	Q E D	FH NORTHERN	Я W
P CURY CLOVER HILL	RALEIGH HOL BROS	R K D BURROWA	RYANS VILLA BURROWA

241

16

BRANDS.	BRANDS.	BRANDS.	BRANDS.
R Z S (in diamond)	S J S C (in diamond)	T F EMU	T S H NEW ENG
S A M	SL (in diamond)	T F ENMORE	T T
S B (in chevron)	S M F P	T F M AVONDALE	T W PAYTON
S B M R NEW ENG	S (over heart)	T F P (in inverted triangle)	T W WOOLWAY
S (in diamond) COLLINGWOOD	MOUNTAIN VIEW SOMERSET	T & G B	ULYA
S E	S S	Ħ	U T
S E P	S S F E B	T H C	V A E
SHAW	S S M	T I N K	V F COOMA
SHEHARD	S T U	T M BUNDARRA NEW ENG	V H
S H (in circle)	S WOODLANDS	T NEW ENG	V J S BREWARRINA
S H L C P	T (in heart)	T NEW ENG	V NEW ENG
S H S (in circle)	T A	T O D JUNEE	V 2 V WOLLAMUMBI
S J S	TARA	T P W T	W A JERILDERIE
S J S B (in diamond)	T 5	T R E	WALDAIRA
	T C T HOLTS FLAT	T R L	WARRUMNGA
		T S	

Wool sold at Sydney, N.S.W. *–continued.*

BRANDS.	BRANDS.	BRANDS.	BRANDS.
WATERLOO	W H MARYVALE	W M R	W W
W B B	W H NEW ENG	W NEW ENG	W W B COOTHA
W B COWRA	W H S	w NEW ENG	W W SPRING CREEK
W B URANA	W H S ROCKY GLEN	W N G B LAKESIDE	W X
W C	WILGA	W C	W Y SCONE
W C	W I L MUDGEE	WOODBURN	X
W C BANGADANG	W J C	W O P WARINDI	X NEW ENG
W C C	W J S WANDONG	WORRABUNDIE	X O X
W C G	W J TARLO	W P BATHURST	YAMMA
W D	W K	W P S A	YANILLA
W D W LAKESIDE	W L B	W R L MARYS VALE	Y B D MUDGEE
W G A	W M CARGO	W TARLO	Y C H LAKESIDE
W H	W M D	W T F	Z R Z
	W M F		

Wool sold at Melbourne, Victoria.

BRANDS.	BRANDS.	BRANDS.	BRANDS.
A C H	G R	JONES BROS HARROW	S PINES
A H NEWCASTLE	GRANARD PARK P M	J P MIRAMPIRAM	S S
ARKELL BROS	GREENMOUNT	J R H THE ROCKS	S S Co
BRANTWOOD	G S AVON	J T W	S S PARADISE
S BRILLANT	G SEARLE	LALBERT O X	T
C F OVERTON PARK	H	L B	T C
CHERRY MOUNT	H E H CRAIGIEBURY	M C V	T T COROWA
CREEK	H H B	N AVONDALE	T W
C S AVON	H H ELWOOD HAY	NYHAN	W
D D E	HILL PARK	P P F ALAMBUR	
D M TATYOON	J A DUNEDIN	POWERS COURT	W
D & P I	J C	R & Co TALLEYRAND	W. HENDRY B
E D		R L BRYNGOLA	W H ONAGH ARARAT
EDINA	J D COOMAIDAI	R M VELLORE	
E T N	J O M	ROKEBY	W SEFTON
F D BRANCEPETN	J M ALTON VALE	R S B	Z B S H
GILLAP	J M C	S MERRINGAL	◇ ◇

244

Wool sold at Adelaide, S.A.

BRANDS.	BRANDS.	BRANDS.	BRANDS.
	BROOK BROS	C SEWELL	GLENLOSSIE
A M L	BROWN BOOWILLIA	D BROS GULNARE	G P NANTABRA
A P T L Y	BUNBURY	D C Y	GRIEVE
ARDUNE S E	BUNDALEAR SPRINGS	D McC M	G U H
A R T	B W P V	D M C MOERLONG	GUNYAH
A S THSLPARK		DODD LAKE	G W S S
A W W W	C	DODD MUNDO	
BAAROOKA	CAMPSIE	E H L	H B H BOOYOOLEE
BALCA	C B MEADOWS	G A	H. CARTER ROEONNOC
B B B F	C CRYSTAL BROOK	G A R P	H C & Co KINCHGAP
B B C H	CHOWILLA	G B ERIN	H DAVIES YONGALA
B B GILLAP	C H P		
B E	CORDILLO	G D M	MEAFORD
B M	C P L	G D M H C	
BP	CROFTON	G H POLDA	MURRAY VIEW

245

Wool sold at Adelaide, S.A.—*continued.*

BRANDS.	BRANDS.	BRANDS.	BRANDS.
HILES	◿ ᴶᶜ • M	J T B	M D NORINGA
H K A	J C P V	K B B H	M L & Co
H L BULLISLAND	J C S	KEILIRA	MORAMBRO
H M	J C S WICKHAM PARK	KOOP	MORTLOCK YALLUNA
H M Y	J H A HILL RIVER	KULNINE	MORTLOCK Y U D
H S BRAEFOOT	J H A H R	L DALE	MOUNT I V E
HUGHES BOOYOOLEE	J H A NETLEY	L. DE GARIS NARRACOORTE	NABRANCA
H & W B	J. KEAMY	L G B	NAUTABRA J C
H H A C	J K S CAMBUSDOON	L O K NARRACOORTE	NED'S CORNER
JAMES MELROSE	J K SPRINGS	LORETTO L McC	O C S T H AVENUE
J. BASCOMBE TINLINE	J M SEAVIEW	L W N E	PANDURRA
J. BLIGHT	J P M G	MANOR FARM J J P W	PEARCE GUMS
J B P	J P R H	MANUNDA	PETRA
J C	J S M	M C MILLICENT	P M N
J C LANDAZER	J S ROCKY	M C T S & Co NOUNING	PREAMIMMEA M C D

246

Wool sold at Adelaide, S.A. *continued.*

BRANDS.	BRANDS.	BRANDS.	BRANDS.
P R R	PLEASANT PK	W A F	WITCHELINA C
(R)	SUFFOCK	WARNES	W. M. DONALD N
R A R AVON	TALIA	(W)	W P & S
R BAKER'S RANGE	T C LORRAINE	BELLEVUE W B S	[W S] LOSSIE
R C J	TENNANT H . M T G E	LOWAN	X H
RICHMOND	TIVER	W C S	YAKILO
R R NEAR GOLDEN GROVE	T Mc **MF**	W E C SUFFOLK	YARROCK C
SOUTH GAP	VALENCIA HECTOR	[W F] GOWAN BRAE	Y JARRAWA
SPILSBY I S	(W)	W G F MINBURRA	Y J BOOLCOOMATTA
			Y P A M

www.ingramcontent.com/pod-product-compliance
Lightning Source LLC
Chambersburg PA
CBHW030732280326
41926CB00086B/1193